Comprehensive Autism Planning System

Implementing Evidence-Based Practices Throughout The Day

Shawn Henry & Brenda Smith Myles, PhD

CAPS: Comprehensive Autism Planning System
Implementing Evidence-Based Practices Throughout The Day

All marketing and publishing rights guaranteed to and reserved by:

FUTURE HORIZONS

(817) 277-0727

(817) 277-2270 (fax)

E-mail: info@fhautism.com

www.fhautism.com

ISBN: 978-1-957984-95-7

Contents

CHAPTER 1

Beginning With the End in Mind

As members of the individual education program (IEP) team, including parents, strive to develop the most meaningful educational opportunities for their autistic students, they would do well to begin with the end in mind. That is, the ultimate goal of the team is to create a comprehensive daily schedule for the student that embeds all of the supports needed to be successful. In addition, the schedule should include the continual development of skills and measurement of those skills with a vision of how this will affect the student now and in the future.

When working with autistic students, the team must pay special attention to addressing students' social, communication, and sensory needs. This is exactly where the Comprehensive Autism Planning System (CAPS) comes in.

Benefits of CAPS

The CAPS was developed for several reasons. First and foremost, it was created to ensure that students' needs are met across the school day. In addition, it was founded on the recognition that autistic students have complex strengths and needs in multiple areas, including structure/modifications, reinforcement, sensory/regulation, and communication/social skills. All must be addressed in order for the student to reach their limitless potential.[1]

1. Thanks to Lee Stickle for sharing this important phrase with us!

CAPS

Figure 1.1. Comprehensive Autism Planning System (CAPS)

Child/Student: _____   Date: _____

SS = state standards

Time	Activity	Skills to Teach	Structure/ Modifications	Reinforcement	Sensory/ Regulation	Communication/ Social Skills	Data Collection	Generalization to Community

Further, the CAPS is individualized and comprehensive. Each student has their own CAPS, planned by the IEP team that understands the student's unique needs. CAPS is built on the foundation of inclusionary practice, embedding supports in the most natural way that is the best match for student success in any environment. Its structure takes into account all the activities in which the student participates and ensures that supports are integrated throughout the day in a smooth, systematic manner.

CAPS also fosters independence in students by providing a roadmap of embedded supports that includes the information necessary to support individual achievement without the constant physical presence of an adult. After a CAPS is developed and implemented in the classroom and the student is experienced using the system, the student can begin to jointly plan with members of the educational team.

Independence

Brenda Smith Myles, PhD, and Amy Bixler Coffin, MA

noun in·de·pen·dence \in-de-pen-den(t)s\: freedom from outside control and support

Few qualities are more important than independence. Universally, nations and their citizens strive for independence. Teenagers seek independence from their parents. Small children tell their parents, "I do it." Research tells us that independence is fundamental for success, boosts confidence, reduces over-reliance on others, promotes happiness, increases s sense of accomplishment, and promotes better decision-making. Independence is important to function effectively in the world.

As those who support, care for, and love autistic individuals, we are often mired in day-to-day issues without enough time. But we want to be helpful.

- Jon has to be on the bus in one minute and he hasn't gotten dressed yet;
- Yulia hasn't packed her lunch for her day at the beach with her provider, and a friend who is going with them is already parked in the driveway;
- Marco can't find his favorite red shirt, and if someone does not react quickly, he will meltdown.

What do we typically do? We often "do for" the autistic individual because of (a) time constraints, (b) the autistic person's lack of skills, (c) our own lack of skills necessary to teach the student, and (d) to keep everyone calm. And ... the autistic individual and we survive the moment.

Is this the right thing to do? In the short run, absolutely! Action is needed quickly. In the long run if this becomes a pattern, perhaps not.

It all starts with a belief system.

- We need to believe that autistic individuals can be independent. Our actions, expectations, and assumptions all need to communicate this to the person on the spectrum.
- We also must believe that independence is a basic human right. Everyone, including autistics, should have the ability to make choices and have a voice in everything they do.
- We need to believe our goal is to be expendable. We want to work ourselves out of a job. We are seeking to develop and foster the "I can do it by myself" skills and attitude on the part of the person with ASD.
- We also need to believe that the skills that autistic individuals use daily are the important ones to address. We need to target skills that foster the individual's ability to act on her own. Skills such as getting dressed, getting to work, asking a peer to play, or following a schedule to complete a task are essential.

We need to have the appropriate system of action. We don't "do for" the autistics, we teach and support, as necessary. We ask ourselves, "How can I work myself out of the activity?" "What supports need to be in place to foster independence?" "What is the long-term goal?" The ultimate goal is an empowered autistic who knows what they need and want, and have the ability (with supports, as necessary) to achieve this.

In short, it's our "job" to foster the "I can do it" attitude for the autistic individual. This is what independence looks like.

CAPS

But enabling the student to demonstrate their independence by implementing CAPS is just the beginning. CAPS can be used beyond the school-age years. For example, the student may need a CAPS to help structure their college program or to succeed at work.

Finally, CAPS is universal. That is, it can be used with students from preschool to higher education to employment. It can be used in developing programs for students with a range of support needs across various instructional settings. And it can be used at home, at school, and in the community. Thus, the structured flexibility of CAPS encourages the use of supports and methodologies that match the student's needs. In fact, CAPS permits a variety of methodologies or just one methodology to be present throughout the student's day—this decision is made by the educational team.

CAPS was originally used to address student transition as illustrated in the following.

Sally's team worked with her extensively during fifth grade to ensure that she was successful. A variety of supports were put in place during her school day, which resulted in increased time spent in general education, fewer meltdowns, and a Circle of Friends who joined her at lunch, recess, and field trips. Sally appeared happy, as did her parents and the rest of her educational team. When Sally moved to sixth grade, her resource room teacher met with the sixth-grade educational team (none of whom had been on Sally's previous team) to describe the supports that had helped her be successful the previous year.

The team felt well prepared. However, Sally's early days in sixth grade did not go well. It appeared that Sally did not know how to use the supports that were put in place, and her behavior revealed that she was anxious and unhappy. The team was puzzled and contacted the resource room teacher to explain the challenges they and Sally were experiencing. The resource room teacher, Mr. Henry, often described as a packrat, prepared for the meeting by going through all his old files and writing out Sally's fifth-grade daily schedule, including the photographs he had taken of all of Sally's supports the previous year. When he met with the new team, he presented Sally's fifth-grade schedule activity by activity, including photographs of the supports and structures that were in place throughout the day.

By the Time There Is a "Problem Behavior," It's Too Late: How We Are Failing Autistic Students

Ruth Aspy, PhD, and Barry G. Grossman, PhD

The approach used in our schools to address the needs of autistic students has proven to be a dismal failure, leaving the true challenges of the majority of students unrecognized or unaddressed. As a result, for most autistic students—regardless of ability level—the outcomes after graduation are grim even with the efforts of extraordinary professionals.

What are the outcomes?

- Only about one third attend postsecondary education/training of any kind.
- Four in every 10 never hold a paying job, and those who do find employment tend to work in low-wage part-time jobs.
- Finally, only 19% of young adults with ASD have ever lived away from their family without supervision (Roux, 2015).

How did we get here?

Failure to Focus on Autism Characteristics

Schools tend to focus on two concerns: academic progress and "behavior problems." But the underlying characteristics of autism (Aspy & Grossman, 2022) that create tremendous challenges throughout life—isolation, unemployment, and difficulty gaining independence—often do not result in academic failure or disruptive "problem behaviors" and, therefore, do not receive adequate attention. Most behavior intervention plans are created only *after* a "behavior problem" occurs. If a student is making passing grades, doing well on state achievement tests, and not disrupting the school day, the odds of that student getting meaningful support to address needs related to autism, as outlined below, are almost zero.

Common Underlying ASD Characteristics

- Difficulty understanding what others may be thinking
- Needing routines and predictability for daily activities
- Difficulty knowing if someone is flirting with them
- Standing too close to others
- Taking things too literally
- Easily taken advantage of
- Finding it hard to start or join a conversation
- Interests that differ from most peers
- Difficulty using and interpreting facial expressions and gestures
- Difficulty knowing when others are teasing or why others find things funny
- Fear or anxiety about trying new things
- Difficulty distinguishing important from unimportant
- Difficulty participating in social activities or feeling overly shy
- Difficulty talking about others' interests
- Noticing the details but having difficulty getting the big picture
- Difficulty filtering comments—do not know when not to say what they are thinking
- Hesitating to ask for information because it may be something they are expected to know
- Difficulty understanding the connection between behavior and consequences

Note: Items are from Aspy, R., & Grossman, B. G. (2022), *The Underlying Characteristics Checklist—Adult Self-Report.* Dallas: Ziggurat Group. Used with permission.

Most autistic people are not aggressive or disruptive; therefore, it is not these "problem behaviors" that prevent them from holding a job. Rather, the subtler communication and social differences such as those described above interfere with successful employment. Almost always, it is not "problem behaviors" that prevent autistics from living independently or having community connections. Instead, it is the impact of these underlying characteristics that have not been addressed during the school years that leaves them socially isolated.

"Problem Behavior" vs. Underlying Needs

The framework for addressing behavioral differences used in the majority of schools is built around "problem" or disruptive behaviors and related concepts such as replacement behaviors, function of behavior, antecedents, and setting events. Most behavior intervention plans are dictated by this terminology, but this approach is not a good match for addressing the critical needs of autistic individuals beyond any "problem behaviors" that may emerge.

After years of frustration and discouragement caused by a lack of help in addressing their underlying needs, some autistic students do develop "problem behaviors." At this point, these students, who have struggled to fit into a world built for people with a different neurology from their own, may finally have a team gather to address their "problem behavior." Yet, often the school team still does not recognize the true underlying needs related to autism. Other students (disadvantaged by their "failure" to produce "problem behaviors") graduate, never receiving any specific strategies or supports. Either way, for most autistic students school supports and services are "Too little. Too late!"

> Is the student having "problem behavior" because they need routines and predictability for daily activities and none are provided? In this instance, providing routines and schedules and teaching the student how to use them will support the student in moving more easily around the classroom without anxiety.

The horrific post-high school outcomes for autistic students confirm that their underlying needs are not being met by the existing curriculum and behavioral strategies. Schools must stop waiting for a "problem behavior" to emerge before changing the curriculum or designing a behavior plan. Proactive strategies that address underlying characteristics before "problem behaviors" emerge have the potential to change the life trajectory of autistic individuals. It's not too late.

Bibliography

Aspy, R., & Grossman, B. G. (2022) *The Underlying Characteristics Checklist—Adult Self-Report*. Dallas, TX: Ziggurat.

Roux, A. M., Shattuck, P. T., Rast, J. E., Rava, J. A., and Anderson, K. A. (2015). *National autism indicators report: Transition into young adulthood*. Philadelphia, PA: Drexel University, Life Course Outcomes Research Program, A. J. Drexel Autism Institute.

Once the sixth-grade educational team saw this structure, they realized the complexity of Sally's needs and understood better what supports she needed. At the team's request, Mr. Henry walked them through Sally's day, identifying supports and structures needed. Thus, CAPS was created.

CAPS can facilitate the transition of students from one grade to the next, as illustrated in more detail in Chapter 15: Case Studies. A clearly developed plan with pictures of the supports used throughout the student's day can help a receiving team develop a plan for the upcoming year. A notation on the CAPS that a student needs a visual support, outlining each activity and accompanying pictures of the support, for example, helps the new team create a structure that is meaningful and consistent for the student. In addition, the process saves time. That is, once the teacher has a digital picture or other visual image of the support or modification used by the child, they are ready for further replication or modification of the student's program.

Professional Development

In addition to supporting student success in school, CAPS also fosters targeted professional development. Because CAPS identifies the supports needed for each of the student's daily activities, it is possible for those working with the student to readily identify the methods, supports, and structures in which they, the adults, need training. For example, if a student's schedule indicates that priming is needed prior to math class, it is essential that the math teacher understand the concept of priming and how to implement it. This educator's professional development plan, then, structured directly from the CAPS, will include training on priming.

By its very focus, CAPS facilitates professional development. Team members working together to develop the student's CAPS who have expertise in a given area become the instructors who describe, model, and support adult application of new skills.

Outcomes of Autistic Individuals

An analysis of the outcomes of autistic individuals provides valuable information about how effective we have been in providing a meaningful education to our students. What are the outcomes for autistics and related disabilities under a compliance-driven system?

- **Unemployment and underemployment.** The majority of autistic adults are unemployed (Bouck & Park, 2018). Besides, those who do work are underemployed—working few hours and/or placed in jobs for which they are overly qualified (cf. Shattuck et al., 2012; Solomon, 2020). Young autistic adults have been identified as graduating from "school to couch"—a tragic commentary for individuals who are capable of and want to be contributing members of society.

- **Lack of independence.** The majority of adults on the spectrum live with family members (Bouck & Park, 2018). This is often not by choice but is dictated by a lack of means to afford independent living options and a dearth of independent living skills (cf. Ghanouniu et al., 2021; Marsack-Topolewski et al., 2021). The latter should not be mistaken for an inability to learn these skills but represents a lack of instruction.

- **An absence of friendships.** Despite wanting meaningful relationships, most autistics do not have close friends and have limited social networks (Jackson et al., 2018). Furthermore, most do not engage in leisure or recreational activities outside the confines of family (Black et al., 2022; Henninger & Taylor, 2013). As a result, spare time is often spent alone, as autistics are not generally invited to "hang out with peers" or go to the movies with friends.

In summary, fewer than 45% of autistic students spend the majority of their day in a general education setting (cf. Bolourian et al., 2021), and it appears that lack of inclusion in school leads directly to lack of community inclusion. Autistic adults struggle with achieving independent living and employment, maintaining friendships, and managing co-occurring mental health conditions (Howlin, 2021; Roux, 2015). Indeed, most young adults rely on their families as sources of shelter, activities, and relationships (Lord et al., 2022; Mason et al., 2021).

Higher Expectations—Embedding Evidence-Based Practices

Even as the field of special education has identified evidence-based practices (EBP) that improve the outcomes for students with disabilities (Cook et al., 2014), there is still a need to implement and embed these practices. The Council for Exceptional Children (CEC) and the Collaboration for Effective Educator, Development, Accountability and Reform (CEEDAR) Center have identified twenty-two high-leverage practices (Rogers, 2019) for working with students with disabilities (see Chapter 4: A Brief Review of Evidence-Based Practices in Autism, for a discussion.)

These high-leverage practices (HLP) are critical to student learning across academic as well as social/emotional development (The Regents of the University of Michigan, 2024). The HLP are organized around four general topics (CEC, 2023): (a) collaboration, (b) assessment, (c) social/emotional/behavioral, and (d) instruction (Council of Chief School Officers, 2017). CAPS is consistent and compatible with all four.

Collaboration

Collaboration among parents/caregivers, general and special educators, paraprofessionals, and support staff is necessary to ensure that the complex needs and strengths of autistic students are addressed. Collaboration ensures that all adults understand the student and know how to best support their learning. Collaboration also reduces redundancy. This is important because it seems that there are never enough resources—and likely never will be.

CAPS is built on a collaborative model. All stakeholders participate in the development and implementation of CAPS, ensuring that essential supports and instruction are identified and placed into the student's daily schedule. CAPS is the document of efficiency.

Very simply, CAPS is one document that provides (a) the student's daily schedule; (b) skills on which the student is working—Common Core, IEP goals and benchmarks, and other socially valid skills, such as problem solving, self-regulation, social interactions, and the hidden curriculum; (c) supports necessary to facilitate access to the general education curriculum, including structure/modifications, sensory, social/

communication accommodations for each activity on the learner's schedule; (d) continuous progress monitoring that specifies data that must be collected for each activity; and (e) information on how and when to generalize supports and skills across environments, activities, and individuals.

Assessment

Assessment is foundational to an effective special education program. Through assessment, educational professionals and parents/caregivers identify student strengths, interests, and needs—elements that are essential to developing a strong program. Ongoing data collection helps professionals to continually hone their student's program for maximum success.

CAPS supports assessments that are designed to increase student achievement. Built into CAPS are targeted skills to teach as well as a data collection component. Skills include IEP goals as well as the Common Core. As a result, data are collected throughout the student's day across all settings.

Social/Emotional/Behavioral

CEEDER and CEC state that educational professionals should "explicitly teach" interpersonal skills, including communication, self-management, and classroom and schoolwide expectations, to students. Students should have adequate instruction and practice opportunities until mastery is achieved (Rogers, 2019).

CAPS recognizes that social/emotional/behavioral issues impact every aspect of the student's day. In fact, the CAPS requires that the IEP team, including parents/caregivers, identify social/emotional/behavioral and communication support needed for each class, each transition between classes, and before and after school.

Instruction

Well-designed instruction should focus on (a) student acquisition of learning goals, including those that lead to independence in home, school, and community; (b) adapting curriculum to match the student's learning goals and skill level; (c) using various systematically designed modes of instruction; (d) teaching students to generalize new learning across their many environments; and (e) providing instruction in self-regulation skills.

It's as Necessary as Breathing: A Key to Success for Autistic Individuals ... and Everyone Else

Brenda Smith Myles, PhD

We need to think differently about what is important in life. What skills and qualities allow us to be successful? While everyone defines success differently, there are common elements. Whether you are a plumber, owner of a comic-book store, president of a Fortune 500 company, there are certain things that you need to be able to do. One of them is self-regulation—being able to control how you act.

In other words, how do you react when ...

- You have to do something you don't necessarily want to?
- You have to compromise but dread it?
- Your schedule changes unexpectedly?
- Someone says or does something that you don't want them to and that person is *in charge*?
- You feel yourself spinning out of control—from agitation to meltdown?
- You need to stay alert but you are not feeling that way?
- You really just *need to say something* but this isn't the right time?

If you have ever thought the following about yourself or someone else, you are talking about self-regulation. In other words, if you have ever said to your significant other, "You need to settle down," you are talking about self-regulation. Other phrases related to self-regulation include (a) control your temper, (b) calm down, (c) pay attention, (d) hang in there, (e) chill, (f) don't say what you are thinking, (g) keep your mouth shut or you will get fired, and (h) you are going to get in trouble if you keep doing that. And there are many more.

Problems with self-regulation are common in autistic children and youth. Many have difficulty detecting how they are feeling, matching their emotions to events, and calming after they become upset or overwhelmed.

Self-regulation challenges often happen when people face challenging social situations with limited social awareness, social understanding, and social problem-solving skills, a sense of loss of control, difficulty in predicting outcomes, an inherent emotional vulnerability, misperception of social events, and a concrete sense of right and wrong. These scenarios are inherent in autism.

In the light of present-day events, we must be mindful that problems with self-regulation are not related to violence. Autistic individuals are not inherently violent, and self-regulation challenges should not in any way be linked to planned violence.

Again, how important are self-regulation skills? There is not an hour in our lives when we don't practice self-regulation. Those without these skills can find themselves without friends, jobs, or the opportunity to be included in the community.

We must provide instruction and supports to foster the development and use of self-regulation skills. Thus, it is important that those who live and/or work with autistic individuals understand the interventions and supports that promote self-calming, self-management, and self-awareness as a means of preventing or decreasing self-regulation challenges.

Self-regulation is more important than science, history, literature, etc. Self-regulation is the foundation for all of these and more. For example, you will not get and/or keep job (even if you are very smart) unless you can regulate your behavior. The same applies to friendships, intimate relationships, living with others, and other things that we value and/or need to do to function every day.

Remember: It's never too late to learn, but learning early is best. And time is limited. If you have to choose between teaching the names of the generals who were most important during World War I or self-regulation, what should you choose?

Autistic individuals have limitless potential. Support that potential to develop.

CAPS supports meaningful instruction and generalization by identifying the goals and supports the student needs for each activity. The concept of evidence is inherent in CAPS. Evidence-based instructional strategies are embedded within the student's daily schedule to ensure progress throughout the day (Alkhawaldeh et al., 2023; Garrad et al., 2022). That is, each activity is seen as a learning opportunity that occurs by implementing EBP. This approach gives the educator a clear understanding of where and when to embed these strategies (Hume et al., 2021; Jimenez & Kamei, 2015). Philosophically, CAPS charges that this instruction be provided in the student's least restrictive environment (LRE). That is, we start with the assumption of LRE—we begin with the end in mind. Our goal is to help ensure that the student is meaningfully included with their peers to the greatest extent possible.

CAPS ...

- Supports full student engagement and membership in the most inclusive setting that is best for each student
- Promotes collaboration among parents/caregivers, qualified school staff, and the community
- Ensures the student's strengths are recognized and needs are met throughout the school day using evidence-based practices
- Recognizes that the complex strengths and needs of autistic students are individualized
- Is comprehensive
- Is structured, yet flexible
- Facilitates transition from one grade to the next
- Facilitates professional development for staff members
- Includes the goals and benchmarks, the Common Core, and other targets as identified by the school team
- Ensures that high-leverage instructional and behavioral supports are provided throughout the day
- Monitors student progress continuously using meaningful data
- Encourages decisions by a collaborative team of school staff and parent/caregiver who review student progress
- Includes interventions that address the individual student's strengths and challenges at the needed level of intensity

Who Can Use the Comprehensive Autism Planning System (CAPS)?

The CAPS process is designed to be used by an educational team consisting of parents, general educators, special educators, paraprofessionals, administrators, speech-language pathologists, occupational therapists, physical therapists, administrators, psychologists, consultants, siblings, the individual themselves, and others who are stakeholders in the student's education. In addition, adults on the spectrum can plan their own CAPS for activities that occur at home, work, or in the community.

Overview of the Book

This book introduces CAPS—a method of planning a student's daily schedule that ensures that all supports are in place to facilitate academic, social, and behavioral success. The book begins with an overview of CAPS, with succeeding chapters describing the components that make up this unique tool. The first three columns of the plan, Time, Activity, and Targeted Skills to Teach, are described in one chapter. In addition, a special chapter outlines how the CAPS may be used for technical assistance/consultation. The book concludes with case studies that describe the wide range of situations where CAPS can be used—within preschool, elementary, and middle/high school, as well as at home.

CAPS is about outcomes—it helps ensure that the autistic learner (from toddlerhood through adulthood) has supports tailored to each activity throughout their day. In addition, it ensures that each activity is tied to instruction, learning, and evidence that learning has occurred. We hope that you enjoy this edition of CAPS.

The original CAPS has been updated to address current trends in special education instruction and research. In this edition, emphasis is placed on inclusion; HLP that support learning for autistic students; updated EBP; and case studies that show the application of CAPS. Through CAPS, autistic individuals have access to meaningful instruction that will allow them to reach their limitless potential.

Summary

Consistent with current mandates and trends in education, CAPS is a unique method of developing and implementing a meaningful program for an autistic student. Its structure fosters consistent use of supports to ensure student success as well as data collection to measure that success. Finally, among its many benefits—CAPS is simple and easy to use.

Bibliography

Alkhawaldeh, Mohammad Abedrabbu, Mohamad Ahmad Saleem Khasawneh, Elham Mustafa Alqsaireen, Mohammad Nayef Ayasrah, Firas Ahmad Saleem Al Taqatqa, and Mohammed Omar Abu Al Rub. "Evidence-Based Interventions in Developing Communication Skills Among Students with Autism Spectrum Disorder (ASD)." *Journal of Southwest Jiaotong University* 58, no. 4 (2023).

Black, M.H., Kuzminski, R., Wang, J. et al. "Experiences of Friendships for Individuals on the Autism Spectrum: A Scoping Review." *Journal of Autism and Developmental Disorders* (2022).

Bolourian, Yasamin, Ainsley Losh, Narmene Hamsho, Abby Eisenhower, and Jan Blacher. "General Education Teachers' Perceptions of Autism, Inclusive Practices, and Relationship Building Strategies." *Journal of Autism and Developmental Disorders* 52 (2022) 3977–3990.

Bouck, Emily C., and Jiyoon Park. "Exploring Post-School Outcomes Across Time Out of School for Students With Autism Spectrum Disorder." *Education and Training in Autism and Developmental Disabilities* 53, no. 3 (2018): 253-263.

Cook, Bryan, Virginia Buysse, Janette Klingner, Tim Landrum, Robin McWilliam, Melody Tankersley, and Dave Test. *Council for Exceptional Children: Standards for Evidence-Based Practices In Special Education Teaching Exceptional Children* 46, no. 6 (2014): 206.

Council of Chief School Officers. CCSO Principles of Effective School Improvement Systems. Author, 2017.

Council for Exceptional Children. "High Leverage Practices." (2023). Accessed 1/19/24 from https://highleveragepractices. org.

Garrad, Traci-Ann, Samantha Vlcek, and Angela Page. "The Importance of the Promotion of Evidence-Based Practice as a Reasonable Adjustment in Mainstream Education Settings for Students With Autism Spectrum Disorder." *Australasian Journal of Special and Inclusive Education* 46, no. 1 (2022): 101-112.

Ghanouni, Parisa, Stephanie Quirke, Jennifer Blok, and Amanda Casey. "Independent Living in Adults with Autism Spectrum Disorder: Stakeholders' Perspectives and Experiences." *Research in Developmental Disabilities* 119 (2021): 104085.

Henninger, Natalie A., and Julie Lounds Taylor. "Outcomes in Adults with Autism Spectrum Disorders: A Historical Perspective." *Autism* 17, no. 1 (2013): 103-116.

Howlin, Patricia. "Adults With Autism: Changes in Understanding Since DSM-III." *Journal of Autism and Developmental Disorders* 51 (2021) 4291–4308.

Hume, Kara, Jessica R. Steinbrenner, Samuel L. Odom, Kristi L. Morin, Sallie W. Nowell, Brianne Tomaszewski, Susan Szendrey, Nancy S. McIntyre, Serife Yücesoy-Özkan, and Melissa N. Savage. "Evidence-Based Practices for Children, Youth, and Young Adults With Autism: Third Generation Review." *Journal of Autism and Developmental Disorders* (2021): 1-20.

Jackson, Scott LJ, Logan Hart, Jane Thierfeld Brown, and Fred R. Volkmar. "Brief Report: Self-Reported Academic, Social, and Mental Health Experiences of Post-Secondary Students With Autism Spectrum Disorder." *Journal of Autism and Developmental Disorders* 48 (2018): 643-650.

Jimenez, B. A., & Kamei, A. (2015). Embedded instruction: An evaluation of evidence to inform inclusive practice. *Inclusion*, 3(3), 132-144.

Lord, Catherine, James B. McCauley, Lauren A. Pepa, Marisela Huerta, and Andrew Pickles. "Work, Living, and the Pursuit of Happiness: Vocational and Psychosocial Outcomes for Young Adults with Autism." *Autism: The international Journal of Research and Practice* 24,7 (2020): 1691-1703.

Marsack-Topolewski, Christina N., Preethy Sarah Samuel, and Wassim Tarraf. "Empirical Evaluation of the Association Between Daily Living Skills of Adults With Autism and Parental Caregiver Burden." *Plos one* 16, no. 1 (2021): e0244844.

CAPS

Mason, David, Simone J. Capp, Gavin R. Stewart, Matthew J. Kempton, Karen Glaser, Patricia Howlin, and Francesca Happé. "A Meta-Analysis of Outcome Studies of Autistic Adults: Quantifying Effect Size, Quality, and Meta-Regression." *Journal of Autism and Developmental Disorders* 51 (2021) 3165–3179.

Regents of the University of Michigan. *High-Leverage Practices*. Teachingworks, 2024.

Rogers, Brendan G. *The Use of High-leverage Practices for Special Education*. Immaculata University, 2019.

Roux, Anne M. *National Autism Indicators Report: Transition Into Young Adulthood*. AJ Drexel Autism Institute, 2015.

Shattuck, Paul T., Sarah Carter Narendorf, Benjamin Cooper, Paul R. Sterzing, Mary Wagner, and Julie Lounds Taylor. "Postsecondary Education and Employment Among Youth with an Autism Spectrum Disorder." *Pediatrics* 129, no. 6 (2012): 1042-1049.

Solomon, Calvin. "Autism and Employment: Implications for Employers and Adults With ASD." *Journal of Autism and Developmental Disorders* 50, no. 11 (2020): 4209-4217.

CHAPTER 2

Autism Characteristics

Kathleen A. Quill, EdD, BCBA-D

As we focus our attention on the complex challenges in autism and the precise strategies required to support their learning, we can also "nurture their individual strengths, and celebrate the diversity of thought they bring to our lives."

— Russell, 2023, retrieved from https://www.theyarethefuture.co.uk/autism-strengths.

t's difficult to synthesize the complexities of autism[1]—to put into words the essence of a person. When we talk about characteristics it is often done so impersonally and overlooks the many strengths and talents of autistics. Why do we use deficit-driven language? Very simply, due to governmental regulations, you must show a significant need to receive the specialized instruction and support autistics need—from early childhood through adulthood—to meet their limitless potential.

It is past time that we present a more balanced view of autism—its strengths, challenges, and limitless potential. In this chapter, we seek to do just that by describing the many facets of autism. Included in the discussion are the voices of autistic people—who better to help us understand this very human condition?

---

1. Although DSM-5 uses the term "autism spectrum disorders," we have chosen to use the term "autism" throughout because, as autistic advocate Dena Gassner says, "No one wants to be described as 'disordered.'"

While it is difficult to say with certainty given [my son] Noah's manner of communication, I believe he would say his greatest strength is his upbeat temperament, and his challenges are being internally and externally distractible and impulsive. When his teachers offered him a list from which to choose words to describe himself, he chose Noisy-Outgoing-Awesome-Happy. It couldn't be more accurate!

— Shared by Abby, mom to a 22-year-old son

Autism isn't something a person has, or a "shell" that a person is trapped inside. There's no normal child hidden behind the autism. Autism is a way of being. It is pervasive; it colors every experience, every sensation, perception, thought, emotion, and encounter, every aspect of existence. It is not possible to separate the autism from the person—and if it were possible, the person you'd have left would not be the same person you started with ...

— Jim Sinclair (1993). *Don't Mourn for Us.*

Definition of Autism

Autism spectrum disorders (ASD, autism) is defined in Diagnostic and Statistical Manual [DSM-5], as a complex set of lifelong neurodevelopment conditions that significantly impact social interaction and communication, and restricted, repetitive behavior, interests, or actions (American Psychiatric Association [APA], 2013). These characteristics vary significantly across individuals with the diagnosis.

Since autism was first identified, our understanding has increased, but the underlying causes remain unknown. Given the complexity of the spectrum and how characteristics vary, it is unlikely that autism results from a single root cause. Rather, many biological and environmental causes, and related subgroups within autism, are emerging (Nordahl, 2022).

Prevalence of Autism

Autism affects all racial, ethnic, and socioeconomic groups. Males are four times more likely to be diagnosed autistic than females, a fact that has prompted concerns about possible under-identification of girls (Lockwood et al., 2021; McCrossin, 2022). The U.S. Centers for Disease Control (CDC) and Prevention reported that prevalence of autism grew from 1 in 150 children to 1 in 36 children in the 20-year period between 2000 and 2020 (Shaw et al., 2023). Some foresee a further increase in the number of individuals diagnosed with autism. Zahorodny and colleagues (2023) recently reported that approximately 25% of autistic adolescents remain undiagnosed.

While the reasons for this rapid rise are complex and not clear, possible explanations include (a) a broader definition of autism, (b) better diagnostic procedures, (c) greater awareness, and (d) realization that autism can co-occur with other disabilities. Regardless of the explanation, there has been a measurable increase in the number of children diagnosed with autism. At the same time, Black and Hispanic children are less likely to be diagnosed autistic, but this disparity is slowly decreasing (Shaw et al., 2023).

The significant increase in prevalence has focused research efforts to determine which evidence-based practices (EBP) meet the needs of this diverse group. Most professionals agree that intervention requires a multidisciplinary team of medical, educational, and mental health providers.

Diagnosis

A medical diagnosis of autism is given when a child meets the standards outlined in the DSM-5 (APA, 2013) as determined by a developmental pediatrician or neurologist, who systematically observes the child's behavior and obtains information about their developmental

Figure 2.1. Autism Spectrum Disorders: DSM-5 Criteria.

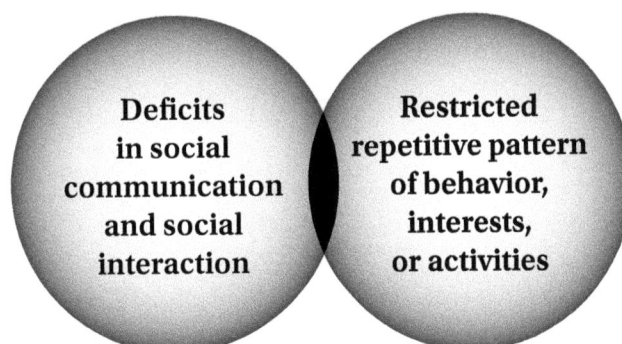

skills with specific attention to persistent concerns in two areas: (a) social communication and social interaction, and (b) restricted, repetitive patterns of behavior, interests, or activities.

A medical diagnosis does not necessarily mean that a child is eligible for special education services under the educational category of autism. The school district's multidisciplinary evaluation must consider this and other medical factors when conducting an assessment. While similar in some respects to the medical criteria, the educational identification criteria specifically requires that the child's educational performance is impacted in order for them to receive services. The definition of autism under the Individuals with Disabilities Education Act (IDEA)—the law that mandates a free appropriate public education for eligible children with disabilities through special education and related services—appears below.

Educational Definition of Autism

i. Autism means a developmental disability significantly affecting verbal and nonverbal communication and social interaction, generally evident before age three, that adversely affects a child's educational performance. Other characteristics often associated with autism are engagement in repetitive activities and stereotyped movements, resistance to environmental change or change in daily routines, and unusual responses to sensory experiences.

ii. Autism does not apply if a child's educational performance is adversely affected primarily because the child has an emotional disturbance.

iii. A child who manifests the characteristics of autism after age three could be identified as having autism if the criteria in paragraph (i) of this section are satisfied.

From IDEA: https://sites.ed.gov/idea/regs/b/a/300.8/c/1.

A closer look at the major characteristics included in the educational definition follows.

Prediction and the Brain

With gratitude and apologies to Peter Vermeulen

Imagine not being able to predict what is going to happen next. What would do you do?

Most likely you would:

- Cling to the activities and events that are familiar
- Unwilling to try new ventures
- Experience anxiety and/or behavior challenges at *merely being introduced to the possibility* of participating in new events or activities
- Protest, refuse, or melt down when forced to engage in a new activity or event
- Feel overwhelmed by the possibility of the actuality of a change (Myles, 2023).

How important is prediction in daily life? Research suggests that even **before** activities and events occur, people know or can largely estimate what is likely to happen. This is known as "external chance." People an also estimate their chance of success even before they attempt an activity or event—this is called "internal chance." The ability to predict guides us toward tasks and problems we are likely to solve and steers us way from those that might be too difficult.

Peter Vermeulen (2022), in his book, *Autism and the Predictive Brain: Absolute Thinking in a Relative World*, shares that prediction is neurologically based. He explains that the way people experience the world comes from within. Neuromajority brains sense, in advance, what they will see, hear, touch, smell, taste and feel. In fact, the brain actually creates a model of what is expected. But the autistic neurology does not know how to predict.

Autistic people experience challenges in knowing what will happen next: they cannot anticipate how they are to react and they do not have a sense of whether they will be successful or not. Indeed, they anticipate the opposite—confusion and failure.

Sinha et al. (2014) shares this quote about prediction, equating it to magic:

An essential component of a magical phenomenon is the lack of a discernible cause: An event that we are unable to predict happens "as if by magic." Given how well-honed our predictive abilities are, magicians have to resort to clever contrivances to achieve their mystifying effects. However, if our predictive abilities were somehow to be compromised, then even mundane occurrences in the environment might appear magical. Although a brief magical performance is enjoyable, unrelenting immersion in it can be overwhelming. A magical world suggests lack of control and impairs one's ability to take preparatory actions.

Indeed, their inability to predict means that the autistic individual cannot prepare for upcoming events and activities and feels as if they have no control over their environment. In the above quote, substitute the word "terror" for "magical," and we might begin to understand why autistic people cling to sameness, do not like change, and consider surprises as negative.

Social Communication and Social Interaction

Autism symptoms appear across children with vastly different cognitive strengths and challenges and can co-occur at all levels of intelligence (Jin, 2023; Thurm et al., 2019). What differentiates children with an intellectual disability from an autistic child with an intellectual disability are challenges in social communication that are significantly more impacted than delays observed in the child's other developmental domains. That is, autism is defined by social communication challenges that are uniquely impacted.

Social communication and social interaction include features such as (a) unique use of eye contact, gestures, and facial expressions to engage in social interaction; (b) difficulty maintaining back-and-forth conversation; and (c) struggles to understand and maintain relationships and friendships without direct instruction and practice opportunities.

Language skills vary widely in autism, from absence of spoken language to unique language acquisition (Quill, 2017). Some autistic children remain nonspeaking for their lifetime. Some children may start speaking as toddlers but later lose or regress in spoken language (Pearson et al., 2018; Pickles et al., 2022; Werner & Dawson, 2005). Others have intact language while demonstrating impaired conversational skills (Abbot-Smith, 2023).

> I cannot speak. Many people might believe that I cannot think, but despite their thinking I can. What's more is that I listen.
>
> — Neal Katz, nd, https://livingautism.com/24-quotes-autistic-individuals/

But even with these challenges, many autistics want to interact with others and put forth tremendous effort to develop connections, which is often evidenced when they seek to discuss their special interests—a common autistic characteristic.

> My son forms long and lasting relationships with those that make him "feel safe." For example, Matt does not want us to say the phrase "very, very." We realized that this started after Matt's grandfather died 10 years ago. At that time, we explained to Matt that Papa was "very, very sick." Since then, Matt becomes quite agitated if someone

says, "we are very, very happy to see you" or "I'm very, very hungry." Matt felt the loss of his grandfather deeply and continues to express it in his own way.

— Shared by Ernie, father of a 44-year-old son

It's not that I lack the social skills others have, it's just that I had to learn them actively and have to keep them in the conscious part of my head whereas others can do this subconsciously. It's why my mind is easily overwhelmed in social situations and it's not easy to keep a train of thought going when your train of thought consists of what, for most people, flies under the radar completely.

— GryphonGuitar, 2015, https://www.reddit.com/r/AskReddit/comments/3hl04l/comment/cu89y39/

Restricted, Repetitive Behaviors or Interests

Restricted, repetitive behaviors or interests includes features such as (a) engaging in repetitive activities and stereotyped motor movements; (b) distress in response to environmental change or changes in daily routines; (c) marked interests with a high level of intensity; and (d) unusual responses to sensory experiences such as sight, sound, smell, taste, touch/pain (Gal & Yirmiya, 2021; Santore et al., 2020).

Summary

Not every child displays all of the characteristics, and each feature of autism's impact can be variable and exist at various degrees of severity and, therefore, require different levels of support. The DSM-5 criteria require that professionals report on the severity of a child's social communication and behavioral challenges by choosing one of four levels of supports.

Table 2.1. DSM-5 Autism Spectrum Disorders Descriptors.

	Level 0	Level 1	Level 2	Level 3
SOCIAL COMMUNICATION	None	**Mild Requiring Support** (i.e., Without supports in place, deficits in social communication cause noticeable impairments. Has difficulty initiating social interactions and demonstrates clear examples of atypical or unsuccessful responses to social overtures of others. May appear to have decreased interest in social interactions.)	**Moderate Requiring SUBSTANTIAL Support** (i.e., Marked deficits in verbal and nonverbal social communication skills; social impairments apparent even with supports in place; limited initiation of social interactions and reduced or abnormal response to social overtures from others.)	**Severe Requiring VERY SUBSTANTIAL Support** (i.e., Severe deficits in verbal and nonverbal social communication skills cause severe impairments in functioning; very limited initiation of social interactions and minimal response to social overtures from others.)
RESTRICTED INTERESTS AND REPETITIVE BEHAVIORS	None	**Mild Requiring Support** (i.e., Rituals and repetitive behaviors [RRB] cause significant interference with functioning in one or more contexts. Resists attempts by others to interrupt RRB or to be redirected from fixated interest.)	**Moderate Requiring SUBSTANTIAL support** (i.e., RRB and/or preoccupation and/or fixated interests appear frequently enough to be obvious to the casual observer and interfere with functioning and interfere with function in a variety of contexts. Distress or frustration is apparent when RRB are interrupted; difficult to redirect from fixated interest.)	**Severe Requiring VERY SUBSTANTIAL support** (i.e., Preoccupations, fixed rituals and/or repetitive behaviors markedly interfere with functioning in all spheres. Marked distress with rituals or routines are interrupted; very difficult to redirect from fixated interest or returns to it quickly.)

Comorbidity

When two or more diagnoses are identified in one child, this is referred to as co-occurring or comorbidity. Autistic children may experience a range of developmental delays or differences in cognitive, language, and motor areas. Autism can also occur in association with other developmental disabilities (aphasia, apraxia), mental health disorders, and medical conditions (Casanova et al., 2020; Jin, 2023). Some autistic students are considered twice-exceptional—gifted and autistic (Reis et al., 2023).

Cognitive, Language, and Motor Differences

Approximately 44% of autistic individuals have average to above-average IQ; 25% have borderline levels of intelligence, and 30% have an intellectual disability (Maenner, 2020). Approximately 0.7-2% are gifted (Silvertant, 2023; Wolff, 2022). Other cognitive strengths found in autism include (a) a strong rote memory; (b) problem-solving skills that can be used to generate novel creative ideas; and (c) the ability to focus intensively on a subject, topic, or task (Gelbar, 2022; Silvertant, 2023).

Challenges in receptive and expressive language vary widely within autism, from language delay to absent spoken language, along with unique language acquisition. Some children may start speaking as toddlers but later lose or regress in spoken language. Some autistic individuals remain nonspeaking for their lifetime. Others have well-developed, very precise language skills, sometimes prompting the term "little professors" to describe their advanced communication. Further, differences in vocabulary and conversational skills are common (Quill, 2017).

> I have a very uneven profile of strengths and weaknesses, where often my strengths mask my very real difficulties.
>
> — Ros Blackburn, nd, https://livingautism.com/24-quotes-autistic-individuals/

Motor challenges in autism can range from mild to severe (Hannant, 2016). Defined as a skill that helps us remember and use body movements to perform tasks, motor planning challenges manifest in a variety of ways, including (a) using labored and often indecipherable handwriting, (b) appearing uncoordinated, (c) having inconsistent performance, and (d) struggling to identify steps and their sequence in activities.

Mental Health Conditions

At least 78% of autistic children have one mental health condition, and nearly one half have two or more (Kerns et al., 2021). These include hyperactivity/attention deficit (50-70%), anxiety (94%), depression (10-50%), and bipolar (5%). In addition, autistic children and adolescents demonstrate a complex interplay between impaired emotional regulation, difficulty with change, lack of predictability, anxiety, and depression (Cai et al., 2018). Suicide ideation and attempts are significant, at 34% and 24%, respectively (Newell et al., 2023).

> Ben always wants to come home to a package of cookies on top of the refrigerator; he wants to make sure that no-one touches his card collection; he needs to know that the "Y Wednesday" bus arrives on time; and that his father will take him to get donut holes and see the "green truck" (Waste Management truck) on Saturday. Ben can become anxious and repetitious when there are changes to his expected routine, so we need to respect his preferences and make sure we prepare him ahead of time for changes.
>
> — Shared anonymously by a mom of a 32-year-old son

> The anxiety can be insane and overpowering. There are days where I refuse to leave my house because the idea of interacting with people is just too overwhelming. As autistic people, we are constantly having to think about every little thing we do and say, which can be absolutely draining.
>
> — Obliviouskiss, 2015, https://www.reddit.com/r/AskReddit/comments/ 3hl04l/serious_redditors_on_the_autistic_spectrum_whats/

Medical Conditions

Certain medical conditions are also common, such as genetic disorders (40-80%), seizure disorders (10-50%), autoimmune conditions (1%), and gastrointestinal conditions (47%) (Casanova et al., 2020; Hours et al., 2022; Oakley et al., 2021; Stefanski et al., 2021). Eating disorders (i.e., anorexia, bulimia, 70%) and/or eating restrictions (i.e., limited food preferences) and sleep disorders (25-80%) are also prevalent (Whelan et al., 2022).

Summary

It remains unclear how the full range of diagnostic characteristics and related co-oc-curring conditions is impacted by gender. Furthermore, the exact impact of puberty on autistic individuals has not yet been well explored.

Because autism affects each person differently, one intervention approach does not benefit all autistic children equally. To develop effective intervention strategies, an understanding of each child's complex developmental, mental health, and medical profile is necessary.

Autism Strengths

While autism strengths are mentioned throughout this chapter, we believe it is important to highlight them again as autistics' wide range of strengths and positive traits are often not included in program planning and instruction. Intense interests, attention to detail, logical thinking, strong visual skills, and memory for details can contribute to strengths in areas such as math, science, and technology. Repetitive qualities can be viewed through the lens of perseverance and, therefore, be a strength. And a different way of understanding social relationships adds value such as honesty, integrity, and creativity to school, community, and work environments.

Visual Skills

Many autistic children are visual learners and excel in tasks that require visual and spatial reasoning, such as drawing, building, and navigating. As a result, they may rely more heavily on their visual-perceptual skills than verbal strategies to understand and navigate new information. In her personal account of living with autism, Temple Grandin, PhD, an autistic and a professor in animal science, and one of *TIME* magazine's 100 Most Influential People, termed this trait "visual thinking" and emphasized her need to rely on visual images for understanding (Grandin, 2022).

Figure 2.2. Autism Strengths.

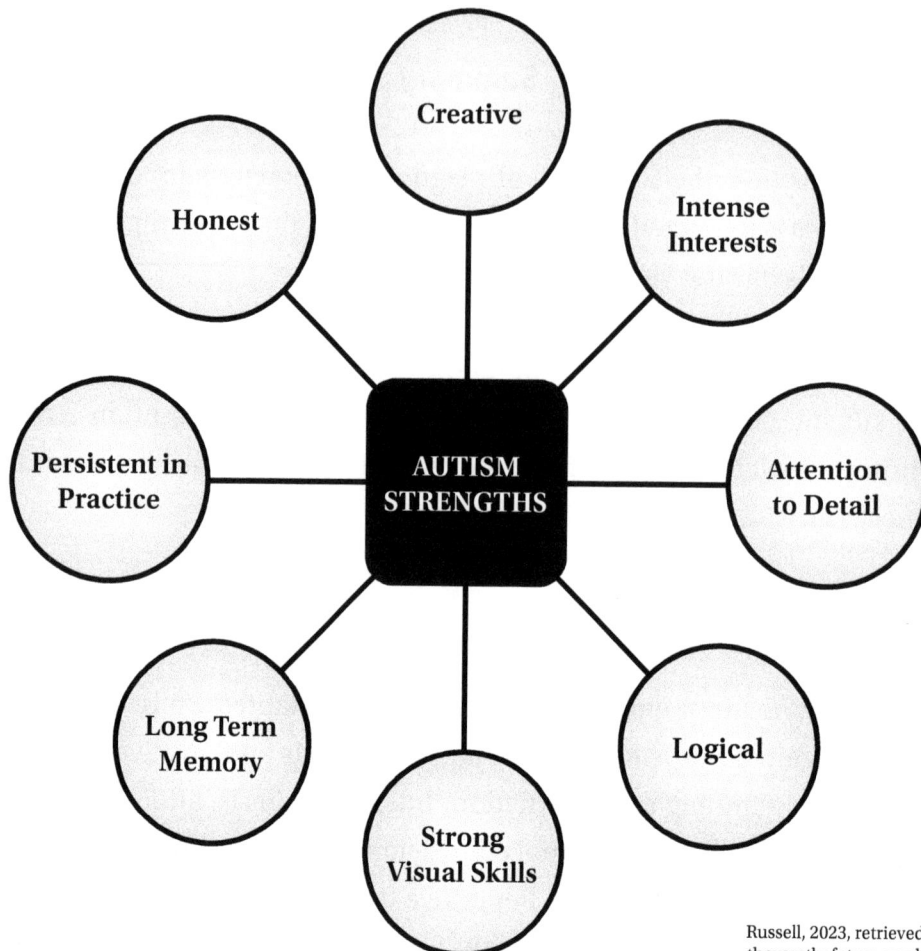

Russell, 2023, retrieved from https://www.
theyarethefuture.co.uk/autism-strengths)

Intense Interests

The ability to focus on specific tasks or intense interests often allows autistic individuals to develop expertise in their areas of interest, which can lead to meaningful hobbies, great career opportunities, or perhaps even an important worldwide movement. For example, Greta Thunberg, the young Swedish activist, has taken an uncompromising stance to climate conservation, traveling around the world using eco-friendly transportation, to help others understand that preserving the earth is important. Her persistence has been seen at United Nations Climate Change Conferences and other symposia. She firmly stated, "I have promised myself that I'm going to do everything I can for as long as I can" (Harvey, 2023).

Context and the Brain

With gratitude and apologies to Peter Vermeulen

According to dictionary.com, *context* is the conditions and circumstances that are relevant to an event, fact, etc. How we interpret the world around us depends on context. For example, context helps us quickly recognize and identify situations and things in our environment and helps us to understand what is relevant. Context also provides predictability: It tells us what to expect.

In his review of neurological research and context for autistic individuals, Vermeulen (2012) pointed out that everything is sensitive to context. "Nothing in the world has an absolute meaning. A bag of garbage is not always a bag of garbage. Sometimes it is art". How we interpret our boss' message depends on the situation; how we understand our mother's facial expression depends on the situation. Everything is based on context—emotion recognition, the perceptions of others, our statements and questions, and overall behavior.

For most people, context "just is." Neuromajority individuals automatically interpret context—usually within 200 milliseconds. In contrast, autistic individuals often must assemble situations and contexts in order to make sense of them (Vermeulen, 2012)—they are "context blind."

In the documentary film *Autimatically*, Michelle tells how she recognizes her living room. Contrary to people without autism, Michelle does not recognize her living room in the blink of an eye. She first sees totally separate things: a flower, a VCR, a TV, a figurine on the mantle, the CD rack, and so on. Only when she makes a conscious effort does she succeed in assembling all of these impressions into a living room. Michelle also immediately notices when something has changed in her living room, even if it is only a slight detail (Vermeulen, 2012).

According to Vermeulen (2012), autistic people "have a keen eye for details, but not for all details. They excel in details for which context does not play a role". This means that they must expend considerable energy on first identifying objects, situations, people, and so forth, in their environment in a rote manner, and then, *if they have been taught how to understand context*, attempt to make the information meaningful. For autistics, this is a deliberate process. For those without autism, this is a split-second automatic task. How exhausting this must be for an autistic person!

It is easy to see how interpretation without context can lead to misunderstandings, error, and frustration. Context blindness can lead to heightened stress and anxiety because of the likely occurrence of mistakes in understanding social interactions or to an overreliance on predictability. Once an autistic individual has interpreted one situation correctly, they tend to rely on that interpretation in other events even if the context is different.

Attention to Detail

The ability to methodically attend to details is an advantage in fields such as science, engineering, mathematics, and other areas where precision is crucial. For example, small details make a significant difference in graphic art, film editing, and technology.

Logical Thinking and Long-Term Memory

Similarly, logical thinking and an exceptional memory for details can lead to unique problem-solving skills, academic strengths in science, technology, engineering, and math (STEM), and opportunities for success in a wide range of careers.

> To access spoken information that I have heard in the past, I replay a video of the person talking to me. To retrieve facts, I read them off a visualized page of a book or replay the video of some previous event. This method of thinking is slow ... it takes time to play the videotape in my imagination.
>
> — Temple Grandin, 2009. *Thinking in Pictures.*

Persistence in Practice

Repetitive behaviors or routines can also have a range of benefits, including reducing anxiety, increasing focus and attention, and providing a sense of comfort and predictability in everyday life. Repetitive practice also contributes to mastery in particular areas of interest—in academics, the arts, and sports. And adherence to structured daily routines and the ability to follow precise schedules are also strong organizational skills.

> So, often ... someone will say something to me or I will hear something and I will repeat it back. Most of the time, I will repeat it back with the same rhythm and tonality that I heard this in ... So, it can be a spoken word or two; it can be a whole sentence; it can be a sound that I like sometimes. ... The problem sometimes is people think I'm mocking them. ... I'm not mocking anyone and I don't think anyone is trying to

mock anyone else when they do this. The first reason a lot of times—and this is more when I'm relaxed—is because I like the sound I've just heard or the way someone has said a word. It just struck me in a way that was pleasurable and I wanna hear it again because when I am repeating something back, it's replaying it in my mind like a tape recorder. ... So, ... if I am not doing this because I need more time to process information or if I'm not doing this to try and make sense of something I've just heard, I'm likely doing this for the pleasure of it. It's often that I really love the way someone said something or I really liked that sound. So, it should be flattering. It's not mocking ... if that makes sense."

— Lyric Rivera, n.d., neurodivergentrebel.com

Creativity

The unique sensory experiences of many children with autism can create striking and original art (Chan, 2024; Park, 2002) and contribute to advances in technology. Whether it's a painting or a digital creation, the ability to create an unusual perspective can lead to awe-inspiring beauty and meaningful innovations.

Honesty

Finally, in the social realm, autistic children tend to have a strong sense of right and wrong. This black-and-white thinking contributes to a sense of social justice and adherence to clear rules. They tend to be honest, dependable, and trustworthy.

Summary

While traditionally often overlooked, autistic individuals demonstrate countless areas of strength that with the proper support and encouragement can not only allow them to show their limitless potential but also benefit society.

Rituals and Related Behaviors

Engagement in restricted, repetitive patterns of behavior, interests, or activities is another primary characteristic of autism, defined as (a) stereotyped and repetitive movements; (b) intensely focused or special interests; (c) rigid desire for sameness; (d) insistence on routines and rituals; (e) inflexible adherence to specific, nonfunctional rituals; and/or (e) unique responses to sensory input (APA, 2013).

> I don't need to apologize for Reid [my son] as much as interpret his behavior for the uninitiated. His actions aren't immoral or wrong; they just get misconstrued or misinterpreted.
>
> — Andrea Moriarity, March 20, 2022, https://the-art-of-autism.com/favorite-quotes-about-autism-and-aspergers/

Autism severity is determined by the degree to which these restricted, repetitive behaviors interfere with functioning in a variety of contexts and cause distress to the individual (APA, 2013). According to Uljarević et al. (2022), higher severity of repetitive movements and intense interests are experienced by more autistic males than females. Males also exhibit less severe compulsions and self-injurious behaviors than females. On the other hand, no gender differences exist in desire for sameness; likewise for both males and females, severity of social and communication predicts the severity of restricted, repetitive behaviors.

Challenged to understand how to interact with others in conventional ways, autistic children use a range of restricted, repetitive, and unique behaviors to connect and communicate their needs and feelings. These behaviors are both positive (i.e., social-communication efforts) and challenging (i.e., interfere with the flow of social interactions). The challenge for others is to figure out what the autistic child is attempting to convey through these patterns of behavior.

Table 2.2. Examples of Social and Communication Rituals.

Social		Communication	
Engages in self-stimulatory behaviors that involve the body	Spins body, flaps hands, blinks eyes	Immediate echolalia	Repeats what is said immediately after it is said
Perseverates and/or repetitively engages in restricted, behaviors that involve using objects (i.e., lining up cars)	Repeatedly twirls string, spins wheels of toy car	Perseverates/fixates on a topic or question	Consistently talks about a topic, such as weather, medieval dress, or albino bats
Preoccupies self with one activity intensely	Excessively looks at car catalogs; excessively uses one Internet website	Delayed echolalia	Repeats and says words/phrases/monologue from a song, book, TV/media
Displays negative reaction to change in routines	Upset by changes in daily schedule, changes in meal routines, different school bus driver	Asks the same question or talks about the same topic without concern for the context	
Experiences phobias and/or intense fears that restrict social interaction	Weather conditions, fire drills, germs	Engages in restricted and repetitive vocal or motor movement while communicating	Repetitively squeals, taps a person's shoulder at every approach prior to talking

Stereotyped Behavior

Stereotyped behavior or stereotypies are semi-voluntary body movements, vocalizations, and verbalizations. Movement rituals are varied and include rocking, jumping in place, flapping arms, or staring at fingers in specific positions. Vocal rituals may include unusual sounds or nonsense words or repetition of words and/or phrases.

Stereotypies can have many functions and play an important role in environments where autistics are overwhelmed by sensory stimuli. They can be self-stimulatory, self-regulating, and/or a response to sensory aspects of the environment (McCarty & Brumback, 2021), helping with feelings of anxiety, nervousness, or feeling "wound up," serving as a self-regulation mechanism, according to autistics (Myles, 2024; Santore et al., 2020). Similarly, they can be helpful in organizing thoughts, attending, or reducing excess energy (Santore et al., 2020).

> When I did stims such as dribbling sand through my fingers, it calmed me down. When I stimmed, sounds that hurt my ears stopped. Most kids with autism do these repetitive behaviors because it feels good in some way. It may counteract an overwhelming sensory environment ...
>
> — Temple Grandin, 2011, https://the-art-of-autism.com/favorite-quotes-about-autism-and-aspergers/

Special Interests

Almost all autistic children have at least one special interest (Grove et al., 2018; Nowell et al., 2021). Special interests may range from television (71%) to collections (53%) to transportation (45%) (Nowell et al., 2021). An intense interest in one toy, object or movie can result in a ritualized play pattern that does not vary overtime. A strong interest in items, such as bus or train schedules or historical dates, is common. Personal collections, that may contain an unlimited supply of the same restaurant menu or movie schedule, may be organized incessantly and touched by no one but the autistic. The tendency to hyperfocus on one or more intense interests and may be an attempt to create order in a confusing social environment.

> When I'm going through stress or life changes, I literally need my special interests to stay functional.
>
> — Haas, 2023, https://themighty.com/topic/autism-spectrum-disorder/special-interests-autism-spectrum/

Communication patterns can also be dominated by singular interests and rituals. Some children only respond when social cues are precisely the same. Sometimes, they repeat the same words or phrases, asking the same questions over and over again, needing a specific answer. Some children associate one specific topic with one person and insist on having the same conversation during all interactions with that person.

Desire for Sameness

Most autistic children have a strong preference for routines. Routines provide order, structure, and predictability, and help manage feelings of anxiety amid perceived social chaos. Some autistics follow strict daily schedules, have limited food preferences, feel more comfortable wearing specific clothing, or need personal possessions to be organized in a very specific manner. To these individuals it can be very distressing when changes occur and/or a routine is disrupted (Stock & Lucyshyn, 2023).

Unique Responses to Sensory Input

Autistic children's reactions to their sensory environment are often unexpected to these around them; for example,

- 94% experience sensory hyperreactivity
- 29% have hypo-reactivity
- 41% describe sensory- seeking behaviors
- 49% experience two types of sensory challenges (i.e., hyperactivity/sensory-seeking, hypo-reactivity, sensory-seeking)
- 25% experience all three.

Only 4% reported no sensory challenges (MacLennon et al., 2022).

While sensory challenges have been linked to anxiety, distress, and distraction as well as disrupted learning (Jones et al., 2020), sensory differences can lead to (a) increased attention to detail, (b) seeing color with greater intensity, (c) superior auditory discrimination, and (d) heightened pitch detection in music (Woods & Estes, 2023).

Regulation can be challenging for autistics, with up to 50% experiencing meltdowns (Mazefsky et al., 2013). Autistics report that meltdowns occur when they (a) feel overwhelmed; (b) need to release extreme emotions; (c) feel out of touch with themselves and want to regain self-control; and (d) feel as if they are losing logic, thinking, or memory (Lewis & Stevens, 2023). Approximately 85% have difficulty identifying and understanding their emotions making it extremely difficult to detect how they are feeling early on and initiate self-calming strategies (Mahler et al., 2022).

I feel trapped. I have a weird tension in my head or my arms; I want to get out. Everything around me suddenly feels extremely real, like I've just come out of the water. I feel all sorts of emotions all at once and I want to run away from them all. I lose sight of what is socially appropriate and start to say things I either don't mean or something I've wanted to say deep down. Whenever that happens, I end up hurting someone or confusing everyone.

— Chi, n.d., https://livingautism.com/24-quotes-autistic-individuals/

Our experiences are all unique. Regardless, I do believe that it is important to find the beautiful. Recognize that there is bad, there is ugly, there is disrespect, there is ignorance and there are meltdowns. Those things are inevitable. But there is also good.

— Erin McKinney, October 5, 2015; https://kerrymagro.com/10-inspiring-quotes-from-people-with-autism/

Understanding Why Ritualistic Behavior Occurs

Although RRB vary from person to person, there seem to be four general schools of thought regarding ritualistic behavior. Firsthand accounts given by autistic adults provide valuable insights.

1. **Rituals are a means of regulation.** Rituals manifested as repetitive motor patterns may be an attempt to seek sensory input (e.g., rocking may be a way to stimulate the vestibular system; lining up objects may provide visual stimulation) (Santore et al., 2022). Rituals can be calming or self-regulating—an attempt to reduce input that is overwhelming and uncomfortable (e.g., focusing on one select sound to tune out multiple distressing sounds). The behavior provides comfort across the sensory systems.

2. **Rituals are an expression of emotion.** Rituals may reflect an emotional state—an expression of enjoyment, and/or fear or anxiety (Russell et al., 2019). Anxiety-provoking activities, such as a transition between activities, can trigger the onset of repetitive behavior. For some, the stress of major events like holidays or birthdays create unexpected changes and increase the likelihood that intense ritualistic behavior will occur. Difficulty understanding social information can result in children experiencing the world as chaotic and frightening, thus contributing to anxiety (Jefferson et al., 2023;

Catatonia and the Brain

Catatonia is a brain-based disorder of posture/movement, speech, mood, and behavior (Ghaziud-din et al., 2021). The latest edition of the *Diagnostic and Statistical Manual of Mental Disorders* (5th ed., DSM-5; American Psychiatric Association, 2013) includes catatonia as a specifier for autism. Indeed, approximately 10-20% of young autistic people demonstrate some symptoms of catatonia (Vaquer-izo-Serrano et al., 2022).

Catatonia has many complex (and frankly confusing) presentations. Some of them overlap with the underlying characteristics of autism. Indicators of catatonia include:

- Increased slowness
- Increased repetitive movements and hesitations
- Difficulty crossing thresholds, such as doorways
- Marked reduction in speech or complete mutism
- Engaging in a behavior when verbalizations indicate the opposite intent.
- Becoming locked in a posture or freezing during actions
- Difficulty in starting or stopping a motion or action, such as eating, drinking, or picking up a pencil

Burns et al. (2021) described this high school youth with catatonia:

[The student] ... slept 1–2 h per night and was rarely at rest. He displayed purposeless and bizarre stereotypical movements, including repetitive knocking on walls and flapping his arms. He perseverated on activities such as opening and closing his door. At times he muttered or was mute. Staff attributed these behaviors to autism though he had never exhibited such behaviors previously. Disinhibited behavior included episodes of maniacal laughter. He jumped impulsively ... and wandered into others' rooms, taking belongings. He flooded bathrooms, gleefully running through the water or urine, yelling "Poseidon!" He impulsively stabbed a social worker with a plastic fork.

Quilliam et al. (2020) presented a case study of a 6-year-old boy:

[The child] had become nonverbal for a few weeks and used his iPad to point to pictures. The student stopped attending school because of this mutism, it was clear that he had experienced a sudden behavioral change. Six months after the mutism occurred, he was found lying on the floor unresponsive. Further episodes occurred, each lasting a few minutes and two hours. During these episodes he would not speak, move, or respond to sound or touch. These episodes would end as abruptly as they started. The episodes became more frequent and prolonged, lasting between ten and 48 hours. Because his weight dropped significantly, he was provided with a feeding tube for nutrition and fluids.

At this time, interventions are limited largely to medical treatments. Wing and Shah (2006) describe their approach to catatonia, which includes a comprehensive medical assessment and the following interventions:

- Reducing and eliminating stress factors
- Providing verbal and physical prompts to overcome movement difficulties
- Maintaining and increasing activities that the person enjoys or has previously enjoyed
- Providing motivation to keep the person engaged and responsive
- Increasing structure and predictability

The educational and medical communities are just beginning to understand catatonia in autism. An increased awareness of catatonia-like deterioration in autistic individuals helps ensure appropriate assessment and treatment. Left untreated or improperly treated, catatonia can become chronic or develop into its most severe presentation (Downey & McDonald, 2019). Until we learn more about this debilitating condition, individuals with ASD with catatonia will likely remain "hidden in plain sight" (Aspy & Grossman, 2015-16).

Williams et al., 2021). Fears can, in fact, become ritualized. Children can make negative associations between a fearful event and an unrelated person or object and develop ritualized panic reactions. Even self-injurious behavior can begin as a fear response and gradually become a ritualistic behavior. Reliance on routines can increase during times of change, stress, or illness, and the routines may become more intense or elaborate at these times. The repetitive pattern of routines may provide structure, order, and predictability, helping autistic children cope with the uncertainties of daily life (cf., Myles, 2024).

3. **Rituals are related to cognitive functioning.** Ritualized patterns of behavior may be the by-product of difficulties in attention and executive function. The difficulty in shifting focus and generating novel patterns of behavior can also result in the child becoming locked in a routinized pattern of thinking and behavior. For example, when Fej's teacher suddenly announced a change from math to an assembly, Fej began to pace because she didn't know what would happen during the assembly and predictability was very important to her. Her mounting anxiety meant that she was unable to find the words to ask her teacher.

4. **Rituals signal social and communication frustrations.** Without instruction and multiple practice opportunities on how to communicate and interact in conventional ways, autistic individuals often communicate in routine, predictable ways. For example, a student may want you to say a specific script in specific situations, and/or they say the same thing in specific situations. Many derive comfort from such routine ways of interacting. Clearly, this poses difficulty in a world that is constantly changing. That is, few conversations are routine, except for the beginning of a telephone conversation or a greeting. Most conversations require us to be flexible moment to moment. The ability to communicate in a flexible way is challenging for autistic individuals. They need to know what you will say next and derive comfort from the familiar routine (Quill, 2017).

Although autism is identified by ritualistic patterns of behavior, this characteristic continues to be the least understood and least studied. As a result, we do not fully understand the source of ritualistic behaviors and the relationship between ritualistic behavior in autism and related anxiety disorders, obsessive-compulsive disorders, and other neurological disorders (Spackman et al., 2023; Turner-Brown & Frisch, 2020).

Summary

Autistic children experience the world and develop differently from others, specifically in the areas of communication, social interaction, and socioemotional development. As a result of viewing the social world from a unique perspective, they struggle to understand messages, comprehend social perspectives, interpret emotions—their own and those of others—and integrate information meaningfully.

Autistics also have difficulty deciphering the complexity of social relationships, making reciprocal social and communication interactions challenging. Challenges in interpreting the social behaviors and emotions of others can contribute to social isolation and frustration. To cope with the "social chaos," autistic children may become intensely preoccupied with small details and seek a high level of predictability in the physical world. These coping mechanisms may be externalized as RRB that, at times, bring meaning and comfort, and at other times, express uncertainty and anxiety.

Each autistic child uses a somewhat different compensatory strategy—some isolate themselves, some are passive observers, some pick up patterns that they hear frequently in the environment to communicate with others (especially words heard most often spoken by adults, and in TV, radio, movies), some learn a few fundamental social rules and use them continuously, and most learn the best means to get their personal needs met.

The behavior patterns observed in autistic children are their best effort to communicate their needs and interact with others. Remembering these fundamental, yet critical characteristics of autism enhances our ability to understand the strengths and challenges of autism and helps us interact and teach autistic children more successfully.

Although there have been significant gains in understanding the nature of autism, there still is no singular explanation for this exceptionality. New theories continue to emerge regarding etiology and intervention. Investigations into the development of shared attention, theory of mind, and socioemotional reciprocity provide insights into autism, but questions remain about how these aspects of development interface with other characteristics, such as RRB, sensory sensitivities, and anxiety. The notion of "a theory of autism"—a singular explanation for the multitude of learning and behavior challenges associated with the disorder—is highly unlikely (Ure et al., 2018). Instead, it is more likely that each proposed theory contributes to an evolving understanding of the uniqueness of the full spectrum of autism without providing a clear understanding of their interdependence.

Professionals and parents need to understand the autistic's strengths and challenges in communication, social perspectives, socioemotional, sensory and regulation, and thinking patterns to guide selection of effective interventions. Awareness, understanding, and compassion regarding the complexity of the strengths and challenges experienced by the autistic should guide intervention planning as a means of supporting students in meeting their limitless potential.

Bibliography

Abbot-Smith, Kirsten, Julie Dockrell, Alexandra Sturrock, Danielle Matthews, and Charlotte Wilson. "Topic Maintenance in Social Conversation: What Children Need to Learn and Evidence This Can Be Taught." *First Language* 43, no. 6 (2023): 614-642.

American Psychiatric Association. *Diagnostic and Statistical Manual of Mental Disorders* (5th ed.) Author. (2013).

Aspy, R., & Barry G. Grossman. Catatonia and ASD: Hidden in plain sight. (2015-2016). Accessed January 28, 2024 from: https://www.cde.state.co.us/cdesped/catatonia_part01_ppt_2016-02-10.

Burns, Nora Kathleen, Kathleen Grissett, Marc Macaluso, Mohsin Raza, and Barbara Gracious. "Excited Catatonia in Autism Spectrum Disorder: A Case Series." *Frontiers in Psychiatry* 12 (2021): 674335.

Cai, Ru Ying, Amanda L. Richdale, Mirko Uljarević, Cheryl Dissanayake, and Andrea C. Samson. "Emotion Regulation in Autism Spectrum Disorder: Where We Are and Where We Need To Go." *Autism Research* 11, no. 7 (2018): 962-978.

Casanova, Manuel F., Richard E. Frye, Christopher Gillberg, and Emily L. Casanova. "Comorbidity and Autism Spectrum Disorder." *Frontiers in Psychiatry* 11 (2020): 1273.

Centers for Disease Control and Prevention. "Racial and Ethnic Differences in Children Identified with ASD." Centers for Disease Control and Prevention (April 26, 2018). Accessed October 20, 2023 from www.cdc.gov/ncbddd/autism/addm-community-report/differences-in-children.html#:~:text=Black%20and%20Hispanic%20children%20continued.

Chan, Alison. 13 Amazing Artists With Autism You Need to Check out. *The Mighty*. (January 16, 2024). Accessed January 14, 2024 from https://themighty.com/topic/autism-spectrum-disorder/artists-autism-spectrum/.

Downey, Jan. M., & Mary E. McDonald. Clinical Corner: Catatonia in Autism Spectrum Disorder. *Science in Autism Treatment* 16, no. 3 (2019).

Gal, Eynat, and Nurit Yirmiya. "Introduction: Repetitive and Restricted Behaviors and Interests in Autism Spectrum Disorders." *Repetitive and Restricted Behaviors and Interests in Autism Spectrum Disorders: From Neurobiology to Behavior* (2021): 1-11.

Gelbar, Nicholas W., Alexandra A. Cascio, Joseph W. Madaus, and Sally M. Reis. "A Systematic Review of the Research on Gifted Individuals with Autism Spectrum Disorder." *Gifted Child Quarterly* 66, no. 4 (2022): 266-276.

Ghaziuddin, Mohammad. "Catatonia: A Common Cause of Late Regression n Autism." *Frontiers in Psychiatry* 12 (2021): 674009.

Grandin, Temple. *Visual Thinking: The Hidden Gifts of People Who Think in Pictures, Patterns, and Abstractions*. Penguin (2022).

Hannant, Penelope, Teresa Tavassoli, and Sarah Cassidy. "The Role of Sensorimotor Difficulties in Autism Spectrum Conditions." *Frontiers in Neurology* 7 (2016): 124.

Harvey, Brandon. "32 Greta Thunberg Quotes to Inspire Climate Action." *Goodnewspaper*, (May 25, 2023). Accessed December 28, 2023 from https://www.theyarethefuture.co.uk/autism-strengths.

Hours, Camille, Christophe Recasens, and Jean-Marie Baleyte "ASD and ADHD Comorbidity: What Are We Talking About?" *Frontiers in Psychiatry* 13 (February 8, 2022).

Jefferson, Sean G., and Lauren S. Erp. "Relation between Restricted and Repetitive Behaviors and Anxiety in Autism Spectrum Disorder: A Meta-Analysis." *Child & Family Behavior Therapy* 45(1) (2023): 1-22.

Jin, Wen-Yuan, Ling-Ling Wu, Li-Fei Hu, Wen-Hao Li, Chao Song, Yan-Yan Wang, Xiao-Lin Liu, and Zhi-Wei Zhu. "Intelligence Profiles and Adaptive Behaviors of High-Functioning Autism Spectrum Disorder and Developmental Speech and Language Disorders." *Frontiers in Pediatrics* 10 (2023): 972643.

Jones, Elizabeth K., Mary Hanley, and Deborah M. Riby. "Distraction, Distress and Diversity: Exploring the Impact of Sensory Processing Differences on Learning and School Life for Pupils with Autism Spectrum Disorders." *Research in Autism Spectrum Disorders* 72 (2020): 101515.

Kerns, Connor M., Jessica E. Rast, and Paul T. Shattuck. "Prevalence and Correlates of Caregiver-Reported Mental Health Conditions in Youth With Autism Spectrum Disorder in the United States." *The Journal of Clinical Psychiatry* 82, no. 1 (2020): 11637.

Lewis, Laura Foran, and Kailey Stevens. "The Lived Experience of Meltdowns for Autistic Adults." *Autism* (2023): 13623613221145783.

Lockwood Estrin, Georgia, Victoria Milner, Debbie Spain, Francesca Happé, and Emma Colvert. "Barriers to Autism Spectrum Disorder Diagnosis for Young Women and Girls: A Systematic Review." *Review Journal of Autism and Developmental Disorders* 8, no. 4 (2021): 454-470.

MacLennan, Keren, Sarah O'Brien, and Teresa Tavassoli. "In Our Own words: The Complex Sensory Experiences of Autistic Adults." *Journal of Autism and Developmental Disorders* (2022): 1-15.

Mahler, Kelly, Kerri Hample, Claudia Jones, Joseph Sensenig, Phoebe Thomasco, and Claudia Hilton. "Impact of an Interoception-Based Program on Emotion Regulation in Autistic Children." *Occupational Therapy International* (2022): 1–7.

Mazefsky, Carla A., John Herrington, Matthew Siegel, Angela Scarpa, Brenna B. Maddox, Lawrence Scahill, and Susan W. White. "The Role of Emotion Regulation in Autism Spectrum Disorder." *Journal of the American Academy of Child & Adolescent Psychiatry* 52, no. 7 (2013): 679-688.

McCarty, Meredith J., and Audrey C. Brumback. "Rethinking Stereotypies in Autism." In *Seminars in Pediatric Neurology*, vol. 38, p. 100897. WB Saunders (2021).

McCrossin, Robert. "Finding the True Number of Females with Autistic Spectrum Disorder by Estimating the Biases in Initial Recognition and Clinical Diagnosis." *Children* 9, no. 2 (2022): 272.

Maenner, Matthew J., Zachary Warren, Ashley Robinson Williams, Esther Amoakohene, Amanda V. Bakian, Deborah A. Bilder, Maureen S. Durkin et al. "Prevalence and Characteristics of Autism Spectrum Disorder Among Children Aged 8 Years—Autism and Developmental Disabilities Monitoring Network, 11 sites, United States, 2020." *MMWR Surveillance Summaries* 72, no. 2 (2023): 1.

Myles, Brenda Smith. *Autism and Difficult Moments, Revised Edition: Practical Solutions for Reducing Meltdowns.* Future Horizons (2024).

Myles, Brenda Smith. *Prediction and the Autistic Brain.* pp. 26-29. (August-October, 2023).

Newell, Victoria, Lucy Phillips, Chris Jones, Ellen Townsend, Caroline Richards, and Sarah Cassidy. "A Systematic Review and Meta-Analysis of Suicidality in Autistic and Possibly Autistic People Without Co-occurring Intellectual Disability." *Molecular Autism* 14, no. 1 (2023): 1-37.

Nordahl, Christine Wu, Derek Sayre Andrews, Patrick Dwyer, Einat Waizbard-Bartov, Bibiana Restrepo, Joshua K. Lee, Brianna Heath et al. "The Autism Phenome Project: Toward Identifying Clinically Meaningful Subgroups of Autism." *Frontiers in Neuroscience* 15 (2022): 786220.

Nowell, Kerri P., Courtney J. Bernardin, Cynthia Brown, and Stephen Kanne. "Characterization of Special Interests in Autism Spectrum Disorder: A Brief Review and Pilot Study Using the Special Interests Survey." *Journal of Autism and Developmental Disorders* 51 (2021): 2711-2724.

Oakley, Bethany, Eva Loth, and Declan G. Murphy. "Autism and Mood Disorders." *International Review of Psychiatry* 33, no. 3 (2021): 280-299.

Park, Clara Claiborne. *Exiting Nirvana: A Daughter's Life with Autism.* Hachette+ ORM (2009).

Pearson, Niamh, Tony Charman, Francesca Happé, Patrick F. Bolton, and Fiona S. McEwen. "Regression in Autism Spectrum Disorder: Reconciling Findings From Retrospective and Prospective Research." *Autism Research* 11, no. 12 (2018): 1602-1620.

Pickles, Andrew, Nicola Wright, Rachael Bedford, Mandy Steiman, Eric Duku, Teresa Bennett, Stelios Georgiades et al. "Predictors of Language Regression and its Association with Subsequent Communication Development in Children with Autism." *Journal of Child Psychology and Psychiatry* 63, no. 11 (2022): 1243-1251.

Quill, Kathleen. Selecting Evidence-Based Practices to Enhance Social and Communication Skills. In K. Quill, K. & L. Stansberry Brusnahan. *Do-Watch-Listen-Say: Social and Communication Intervention for Autism Spectrum Disorder*. 2nd edition. Paul H. Brookes (2017).

Quilliam, Robin, Samantha Quilliam, Morag Turnbull, Shelagh Parkinson, and Godwin Oligbu. "Catatonia as a Presentation of Autism in a Child: A Case Report." *AIMS Neuroscience* 7, no. 3 (2020): 327.

Reis, Sally, Nicholas Gelbar, and Joseph Madaus. "Pathways to Academic Success: Specific Strength-Based Teaching and Support Strategies for Twice Exceptional High School Students with Autism Spectrum Disorder." *Gifted Education International* 39, no. 3 (2023): 378-400.

Russell, Kaylin M., Kyle M. Frost, and Brooke Ingersoll. "The Relationship Between Subtypes of Repetitive Behaviors and Anxiety in Children with Autism Spectrum Disorder." *Research in Autism Spectrum Disorders* 62 (2019): 48-54.

Russell, L. The Power of Neurodiversity: Celebrating Autism Strengths. (2023). Accessed January 4, 2024 from https://www.theyarethefuture.co.uk/autism-strengths.

Santore, Lee A., Alan Gerber, Ayla N. Gioia, Rebecca Bianchi, Fanny Talledo, Tara S. Peris, and Matthew D. Lerner. "Felt But Not Seen: Observed Restricted Repetitive Behaviors are Associated With Self-Report—But Not Parent-Report—Obsessive-Compulsive Disorder Symptoms in Youth with Autism Spectrum Disorder." *Autism* 24, no. 4 (2020): 983-994.

Shaw, Kelly A., Matthew J. Maenner, Amanda V. Bakian, Deborah A. Bilder, Maureen S. Durkin, Sarah M. Furnier, Michelle M. Hughes et al. "Early Identification of Autism Spectrum Disorder Among Children Aged 4 years—Autism and Developmental Disabilities Monitoring Network, 11 Sites, United States, 2018." *MMWR Surveillance Summaries* 70, no. 10 (2021): 1.

Silvertant, Martin. Autism and Giftedness. (2023). Accessed February 1, 2024 from https://embrace-autism.com/autism-and-giftedness/#:~:text=Estimated%20rates%20of%20intellectual%20giftedness,1%25%20in%20the%20general%20public.

Sinha, Pawan, Margaret M. Kjelgaard, Tapan K. Gandhi, Kleovoulos Tsourides, Annie L. Cardinaux, Dimitrios Pantazis, Sidney P. Diamond, and Richard M. Held. "Autism as a Disorder of Prediction." *Proceedings of the National Academy of Sciences* 111, no. 42 (2014): 15220-15225.

Spackman, Emily, Luke D. Smillie, Thomas W. Frazier, Antonio Y. Hardan, and Mirko Uljarević. "Characterizing Subdomains of Insistence on Sameness in Autistic Youth." *Autism Research* 16, no. 12 (2023): 2326-2335.

Stefanski, Arthur, Yamile Calle-López, Costin Leu, Eduardo Pérez-Palma, Elia Pestana-Knight, and Dennis Lal. "Clinical Sequencing Yield in Epilepsy, Autism Spectrum Disorder, and Intellectual Disability: A Systematic Review and Meta-Analysis." *Epilepsia* 62, no. 1 (2021): 143-151.

Stock, Richard, and Joseph Lucyshyn. "Insistence on Sameness in Autistic Children: a Stimulus Control Analysis with Implications for Assessment and Support." *Advances in Neurodevelopmental Disorders* (2023): 1-14.

Thurm, A., Farmer, C., Salzman, E., Lord, C. and Bishop, S., State of the Field: Differentiating Intellectual Disability from Autism Spectrum Disorder. *Frontiers in Psychiatry*, (2019): 10, p.526.

Turner-Brown, Lauren, and MaryKate Frisch. "Understanding and Addressing Restricted and Repetitive Behaviors in Children with Autism." *Clinical Guide to Early Interventions for Children With Autism* (2020): 61-77.

Uljarević, Mirko, Thomas W. Frazier, Booil Jo, Wesley D. Billingham, Matthew N. Cooper, Eric A. Youngstrom, Lawrence Scahill, and Antonio Y. Hardan. "Big Data Approach to Characterize Restricted and Repetitive Behaviors in Autism." *Journal of the American Academy of Child & Adolescent Psychiatry* 61, no. 3 (2022): 446-457.

Ure, A., Veronica Rose, Charmaine Bernie, and Katrina Williams. "Autism: One or Many Spectrums?" *Journal of Paediatrics and Child Health*, 54 (2018), pp. 1068-1072.

Vaquerizo-Serrano, J., G. Salazar De Pablo, J. Singh, and P. Santosh. "Catatonia in Autism Spectrum Disorders: A Systematic Review and Meta-Analysis." *European Psychiatry* 65, no. 1 (2022): e4.

Vermeulen, Peter. *Autism as Context Blindness*. Future Horizons, 2012.

Vermeulen, Peter. *Autism and the Predictive Brain: Absolute Thinking in a Relative World*. England: Routledge 2022.

Vermeulen, Peter. "Context Blindness in Autism Spectrum Disorder: Not Using the Forest to See the Trees as Trees." *Focus On Autism And Other Developmental Disabilities* 30, no. 3 (2015): 182-192.

Werner, Emily, and Geraldine Dawson. "Validation of the Phenomenon of Autistic Regression Using Home Videotapes." *Archives of General Psychiatry* 62, no. 8 (2005): 889-895.

Whelan, Sally, Arlene Mannion, Azeem Madden, Fine Berger, Rachel Costello, Saeid Ghadiri, and Geraldine Leader. "Examining the Relationship Between Sleep Quality, Social Functioning, and Behavior Problems in Children With Autism Spectrum Disorder: A Systematic Review." *Nature and Science of Sleep* (2022): 675-695.

Williams, Kathryn L., Emily Campi, and Grace T. Baranek. "Associations Among Sensory Hyperresponsiveness, Restricted and Repetitive Behaviors, and Anxiety in Autism: An Integrated Systematic Review." *Research in Autism Spectrum Disorders* 83 (2021): 101763.

Wing, Lorna, and Amitta Shah. "A Systematic Examination of Catatonia-Like Clinical Pictures in Autism Spectrum Disorders." *International Review of Neurobiology* 72 (2006): 21-39.

Wolff, Nicole, Sanna Stroth, Inge Kamp-Becker, Stefan Roepke, and Viet. Roessner. "Autism Spectrum Disorder and IQ—A Complex Interplay" *Frontiers in Psychiatry* 13 (2022).

Woods, Sara Eileen O'Neil, and Annette Estes. "Toward a More Comprehensive Autism Assessment: The Survey of Autistic Strengths, Skills, and Interests." *Frontiers in Psychiatry* 14 (2023): 1264516.

Zahorodny, Walter, Josephine Shenouda, Kate Sidwell, Michael G. Verile, Cindy Cruz Alvarez, Arline Fusco, Audrey Mars et al. "Prevalence and Characteristics of Adolescents with Autism Spectrum Disorder in the New York-New Jersey Metropolitan Area." *Journal of Autism and Developmental Disorders*. (2023): 1-7.

CHAPTER 3

The Comprehensive Autism Planning System

Two major challenges plague the educational planning and implementation process for autistic children and youth. The first relates to the individualized education program (IEP). The other relates to the process of transitioning from year to year.

The IEP

Multidisciplinary teams, including parents, spend a significant amount of time on a student's IEP, identifying present levels of performance as well as goals and benchmarks that will help the student be successful in school. However, even though student outcomes are delineated in the IEP, it is often difficult to fully transfer them to a student's daily program (Aspy & Grossman, 2022).

For example, a student's IEP may indicate that she needs sensory input; yet, educators, in particular general educators and paraprofessionals, often do not know what types of support should be provided—a therapy ball, a break, or a koosh ball?—and when they should be provided. Further, if the sensory support is a break, how long is the break? How is the child prompted to take a break—with a break card or a teacher prompt? If a break card is used, what color is it, what font is used, and what size is it? And when should the break be used—in physical education (PE), during reading, at lunch?

The child may need a choice board or a visual schedule to enhance performance. Such accommodations may not be listed on the IEP even though they are integral to the child's success, leading to frustration for both the teacher and the child, limitations in access to the general education curriculum, and/or severe behavior challenges.

In addition, where is the child's IEP kept? Generally, it is stored in a locked file cabinet outside of the learner's classroom—a place that is not easily accessible by front-line staff who often has limited planning or release time during the school day.

Transitioning From Year to Year

In addition to transitioning from year to year, many autistic students transition from system to system. That is, they move from the 0-3 system (often known as Part C of the Individuals With Disabilities Education Act [IDEA]) to the 3-5 system (referred to as Part B of IDEA or preschool), and to the public school system, where they transition from elementary to middle and, eventually, high school. Indeed, a student may have transitioned across at least 3 systems, up to 5 physical buildings, and across up to 18 school teams by the time they turn 18 years old!

This would not be so bad if communication was efficient and effective between and across educational teams when students transition. Unfortunately, in general, the various educational teams do not meet with one another to discuss the transitioning child, and while the IEP may be considered as the transitional document, as mentioned earlier, it does not provide specific information for programming.

As illustrated below, each year the child's transition to a new grade begins with a discovery process. And sometimes a box—a box of supports used during the previous year without any information on how and when these supports are to be used.

As a result, educational professionals, without the benefit of collaboration with the previous year's team, begin the school year with assessment or trial and error. They implement a variety of supports for the student and assess their effectiveness—a process that often takes up to three months. Ideally, at the end of the three months, the new teacher has a solid program

Figure 3.1. The Transition Box.

in place—supports and accommodations have been identified and are being implemented during the classes and activities in which they are needed.

In reality, three months is not a long time to determine the strengths, needs, accommodations, and supports of a learner with complex needs. However, this process happens annually! This means that for the learner who begins their education at age 2, this occurs 19 times! Multiply 19 x 3 months, and the result is 57 months or 6.33 school years. That is, we spend over six school years reinventing the wheel—attempting to identify supports and their nuances (size, shape, color, when to use, where they should be placed, etc.).

Figure 3.2. The School Year.

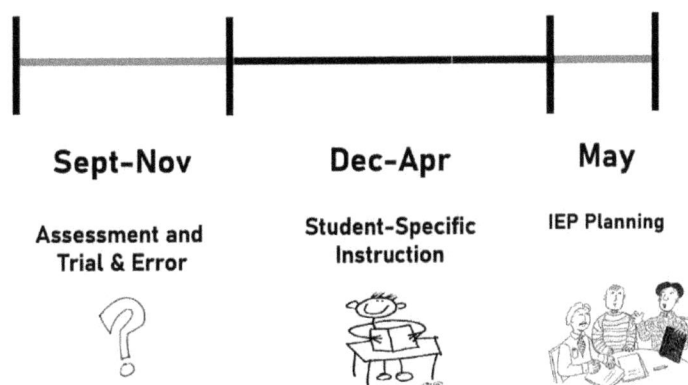

Sept–Nov	**Dec–Apr**	**May**
Assessment and Trial & Error	Student-Specific Instruction	IEP Planning

Given the above, it could be argued that those who are in the greatest need receive the least education because they spend 6.33 years in a process of trial and error. And during this process, what is the learner's state of mind? Autistic learners who generally manifest a high level of anxiety, particularly in unpredictable settings, are likely to experience heightened anxiety as educators struggle to identify supports. This further has a negative impact on instructional time—when anxiety is high, the ability to learn is low.

Figure 3.3. Inverse Relationship Between Anxiety and Learning.

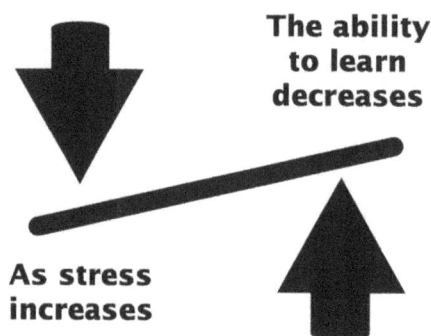

Clearly, this system is not effective, efficient, or fair to autistic learners—nor is it fair to those who teach and support them. This is where the Comprehensive Autism Planning System (CAPS) comes in.

Using the Comprehensive Autism Planning System

The Comprehensive Autism Planning System (CAPS) provides an overview of a student's daily schedule by time and activity as well as the supports the student needs during each period.

Following the development of the student's IEP, all educational professionals who work with the student develop the CAPS. Thus, the CAPS allows professionals and parents to answer the all-important question for students with an ASD: *What supports does the student* need for each activity?

The CAPS consists of a list of a student's daily tasks and activities, the times they occur, along with a thorough delineation of the supports needed to support success. In addition, it includes space for making notations about data collection and how skills are to be generalized to other settings:

1. **Time.** This section indicates the clock time when each activity that the student engages in throughout the day takes place.
2. **Activity.** This includes all tasks and activities throughout the day in which the student requires support. Academic periods (e.g., reading, math), nonacademic times (e.g., recess, lunch), and transitions between classes would all be considered activities.
3. **Skills to Teach.** This may include IEP goals, Common Core, and/or general skills that lead to school success. These skills can serve as the basis for measuring response to intervention (RTI) or annual yearly progress (AYP).
4. **Structure/Modifications.** This can encompass a wide variety of supports, including placement in the classroom, visual supports (e.g., choice boards, visual schedules), peer supports (e.g., Circle of Friends, peer buddies), and instructional strategies (e.g., priming, self-monitoring).
5. **Reinforcement.** Student access to specific types of reinforcement as well as reinforcement schedules is listed under this section.
6. **Sensory/Regulation.** Sensory supports and strategies, including those that address regulation needs, as identified by an occupational therapist are listed in this area.
7. **Communication/Social Skills.** Specific communication goals or activities as well as supports are delineated here. Goals or activities may include (a) requesting help, (b) taking turns in conversation, or (c) protesting appropriately. Supports, which are also diverse, may encompass (a) language boards; (b) PECS (Picture Exchange Communication System; Frost & Bondy, 2002); or (c) other augmentative communication systems.
8. **Data Collection.** This includes gathering information on behavior(s) to be documented during a specific activity. Typically, this section relates directly to the student's IEP goals and objectives, behavioral issues, and state standards.
9. **Generalization to Community.** Because individuals with ASD often have problems generalizing information across settings, this section of the CAPS was developed to ensure that generalization of skills is built into the child's program.

Figure 3.4. The Comprehensive Autism Planning System.

Child/Student: _____   Date: _____

SS = state standards

Time	Activity	Skills to Teach	Structure/ Modifications	Reinforcement	Sensory/ Regulation	Communication/ Social Skills	Data Collection	Generalization to Community

As mentioned, CAPS answers the following essential question for school professionals and parents: *What supports does the student/child need* for each activity? As a "living" document, it is likely that new supports will be needed after the CAPS has been developed. To ensure that supports are available when needed, the CAPS Development Form is completed at the time the CAPS is developed. It is important to designate not only what supports need to be developed and/or selected, but also (a) who will develop them, (b) who will teach the use of the support, and (c) how and when the effectiveness of the support will be evaluated.

It is essential that data collection forms be included on the CAPS Support Development Form. Often the individual who is responsible for taking data is not the one who develops the form. The latter may not be a classroom teacher, but may be a special educator, school psychologist, speech-language pathologist, or an occupational therapist.

Figure 3.5. Sample CAPS Support Development Form.

Student Name: _____   Date: _____

Support	Who Will Develop Support	Date Supported Needed	Who Will Teach Support Use	When to Evaluate Effectiveness	How to Evaluate Effectiveness

The CAPS model may be used alone or in combination with another model—the Ziggurat Model (Aspy & Grossman, 2022). Each of these models is strong on its own, but together they are even stronger. The Ziggurat Model is designed to address a student's true needs or underlying deficits that result in social, emotional, and behavioral concerns. The centerpiece of the Ziggurat Model is the Intervention Ziggurat, which contains five levels in a hierarchical structure. Starting with the foundation level—Sensory Differences and Biological Needs—each level represents an area that must be addressed in order for an intervention plan to be comprehensive for a given student. Further, each level contributes to the effectiveness of the others.

Figure 3.6. Levels of the Ziggurat Model.

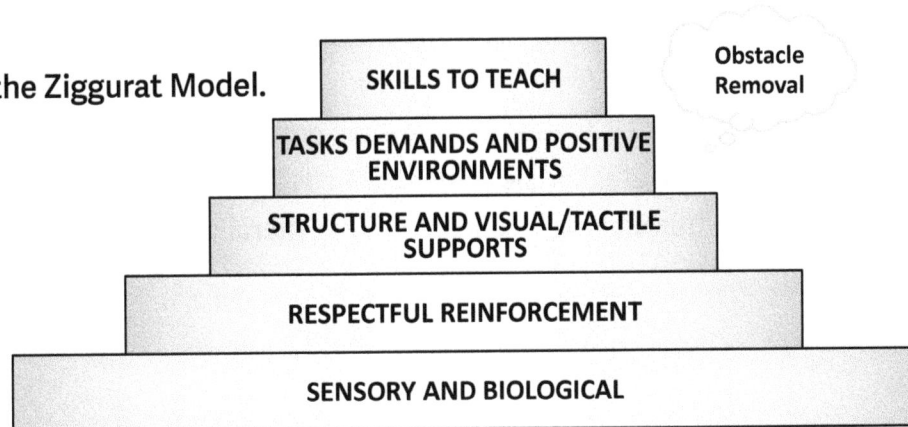

SKILLS TO TEACH

Obstacle Removal

TASKS DEMANDS AND POSITIVE ENVIRONMENTS

STRUCTURE AND VISUAL/TACTILE SUPPORTS

RESPECTFUL REINFORCEMENT

SENSORY AND BIOLOGICAL

Underlying needs and characteristics related to autism must be addressed—this is a key premise of the Ziggurat Model. To that end, the Ziggurat Model includes six versions of the Underlying Characteristics Checklist (UCC): (a) HF (high-functioning), (b) CL (classic), (c) EI (early intervention), (d) Self Report Child, (e) Self-Report Adolescent, and (f) Self-Report Adult. The UCC provides a snapshot of how autism is expressed for an individual.

Figure 3.7. Cover Page of UCCs.

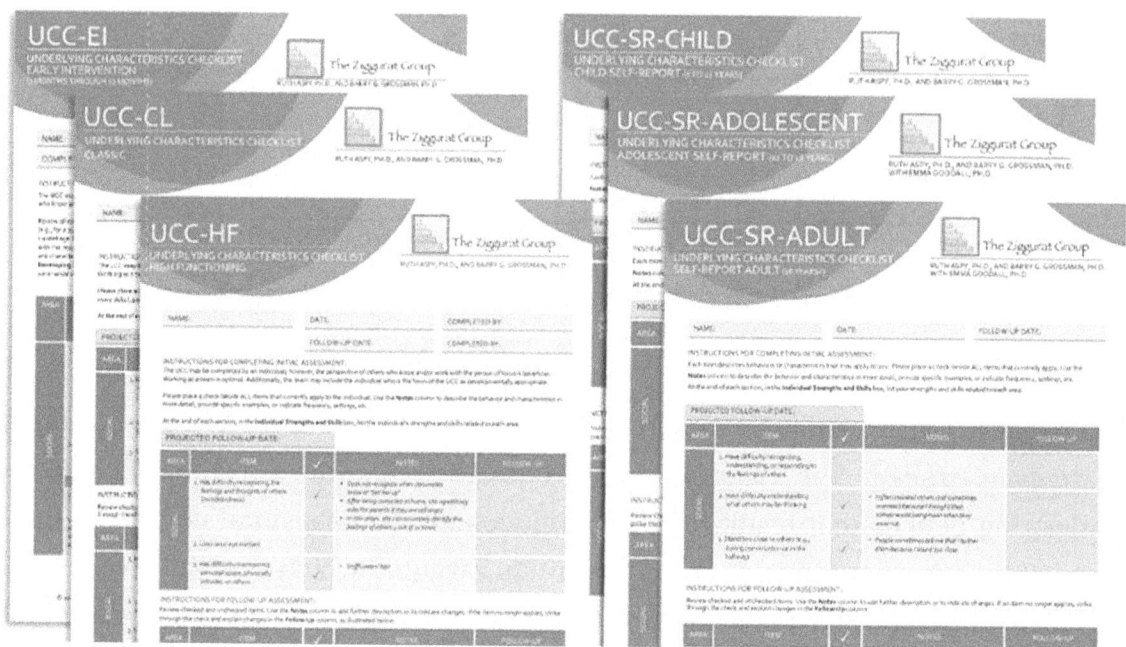

When using the Ziggurat and CAPS together, the process begins with completion of the UCC and ISSI to identify the child's autism and their strengths and skills. Then interventions are identified in each of the five Ziggurat levels, starting with Sensory Differences and Biological, to ensure that all the UCC and ISSI items are covered. This information is then incorporated into the CAPS to ensure that the student's needs and interventions are addressed throughout their daily schedule with data collection and generalization built in.

Ginny's CAPS

The following brief case study shows how CAPS was implemented for an 8-year-old autistic student, Ginny. Ginny is in the second grade and tested in the below-average range on a test of cognitive ability. Ginny uses PECS (Frost & Bondy, 2002) to communicate, but shows limited generalization to school staff and none among peers. She receives her education in a kindergarten/first-grade resource room and is included during "specials" and early-morning calendar group.

Ginny is very social and would like opportunities and skills to interact with her fellow students. She has been demonstrating some behavioral issues related to transitions, attention to task, and interacting appropriately with peers. Observations in Ginny's classrooms confirmed behavioral issues and revealed an inconsistent use of supports. Ginny's team met to create a CAPS to match Ginny's daily schedule (see partial view of Ginny's CAPS in Figure 3.8).

Similar to most students, Ginny's day begins before her first academic class. She starts with breakfast at school. As shown on the CAPS, Ginny will be learning three skills during this time: (a) making choices, (b) using a language board, and (c) following a schedule. Use of choice and language boards and the reinforcement is natural—eating the food she chooses from the breakfast menu. While Ginny does not need sensory supports for this activity, she does require communication and social interventions. Therefore, she has a list of social questions on her language board and a visual support that illustrates table manners. Data collected include (a) frequency of making choices and (b) the number of times she used her language board.

Between 8:05 and 8:20, Ginny completes independent morning work. The CAPS details the supports she needs for this task. For example, for morning work, Ginny is to complete five math problems that will result in her earning a break. A visual support is used to break down the task into its component parts, and sensory supports include a box that masks problems on the worksheet and a slant board that aids in writing. Data are collected by (a) Ginny through self-monitoring of following class rules posted in the room and (b) her teacher on Ginny's completion of the five math problems. Self-monitoring was chosen for generalization, and Ginny has asked to monitor her behavior at different times throughout the day.

Figure 3.8. Ginny's CAPS.

Comprehensive Autism Planning System (CAPS)			
Child/Student: *Ginny*			(ss = state standards)
Time	Activity	Skills to Teach	Structure/ Modifications
7:30-7:55	Breakfast	• Choose breakfast using breakfast board • Use language board • Work on table manners	• Choice board of breakfast items • Interactive language board • Visual schedule
8:05-8:20	Independent morning work Lunch count prep	• Independent work on mastered math problems with self-monitor • Review menu for lunch choices • Chart lunch count • Collect and organize data (ss) • Follow 2- and 3-step verbal directions (ss)	• Visuals to break down task (1-5, raise hand, finished) • Visual focusing aid • Visual schedule • Prime for lunch count • Trained peer buddy

Figure 3.8 (continued)

Reinforcement	Sensory/ Regulation	Communication/ Social Skills	Data Collection	Generalization to Community
Choice of food items		• Have additional social language on board (greetings, questions)	• Choice: I/P, #, daily • Language board: I/P, opportunities vs. use, daily; (+ if she uses board, * if she uses board & verbalizes) • Utensils: I/P, daily	Use language board during lunch or dinner at home
• Complete 5 problems; get a break of choice • Social reinforcement from peers	• Black construction paper box around problem to write in box • Slant board with textured paper underneath for more feedback • Sticky string for lunch graphing sheet	• Follow general education classroom rules • Review lunch choices • Ginny will ask peers if they have one of the lunch choices by holding the choice up and saying the name (i.e. hamburger, home, lunch) • Interpersonal skills (proximity to peer)	• Self-monitor: I/P, % correct, daily • Lunch choice: I/P, #, daily • Chart: I/P #; daily • Data: Chart I/P, daily • Directions: I/P, W/TR	• Use self-monitoring in other subjects • Use peers' names throughout the school day

Figure 3.8 (continued)

Time	Activity	Skills to Teach	Structure/ Modifications
8:20-9:00	1. Atten-dance 2. Lunch count 3. Morning Work 4. Calendar	• Collect and organize data (ss) • Names of classmates • Reciprocal interaction with peers • Self-monitor • Use language board for calendar skills • Measure calendar time (ss) • List days and months in order (ss) • Verbally/ nonverbally responds to message • Intentionally direct a message • Engage in back-and-forth conversation on a topic (3+ exchanges)	• Systematic prompting (least-most) for use of language board • Task analysis of morning work using pictures (she will put in finished slot when completed) • Visual Schedule
9:00-9:30	SPECIALS M: Computer T: Library TR: Video	• Use language board to increase MLU • Follow 2- and 3-step oral directions (ss) • Independent use of schedule for transitions • Verbally/ nonverbally respond to message • Intentionally direct a message • Engage in back-and-forth conversation on a topic (3+ exchanges)	• Trained peer buddies • Modified rules to game to increase communication • Visual schedule • Mini-schedule (task analysis)
9:35-10:00	Whole group Reading Spelling Writing	• Print legibly (ss) • Use active listening strategies (ss) • Establish purpose for reading (ss) • Verbally/ nonverbally respond to message • Intentionally direct a message • Engage in back-and-forth conversation on a topic (3+ exchanges)	• Visual schedule • Visuals accompanied by text • General visual support from common items needed in class • Games to go along with text

Figure 3.8 (continued)

Reinforcement	Sensory/ Regulation	Communication/ Social Skills	Data Collection	Generalization to Community
• Social reinforcement from peers	• Sensory items available (lotion, koosh ball) • Change positions if laying on desk • Slant board	• PECS book • Language board for lunch count • Language board for calendar activities • Interpersonal skills (proximity to peer)	• Data: Chart I/P, daily • Names: I/P, daily • Self-monitor: I/P, % correct, daily • Language board use: + if she uses board, * if she uses board • Language board: respond/directs a message: TR, #, compared to a peer • Transitions: I/P, daily • Calendar, days, months: grade-book • Exchanges: F, #	Use classmates' names in hall, playground, lunch, etc.
• Game playing • Movement • Social reinforcement from peers	Smaller and controlled setting	• Reciprocal interaction with peers • Increasing MLU through use of • language board • Turn taking • Cooperative learning groups	• Language board: (+ if she uses board, * if she uses board & verbalizes), MLU, T, # • Directions: I/P, W/TR • Transitions: I/P, daily • Language board: respond/direct a message: TR, #, compared to a peer • Exchanges: F, #	Use language board during lunch and dinner at home
• Game playing • Movement	Build in physical activity (i.e., fishing game)	Reading or game with peer	• Print: Y/N, daily • Orient to listener: I/P, W/TR • Reading: grade-book • Language board: respond/directs a message: TR, #, compared to a peer • Exchanges: F, #	Use visual schedule at home

Ginny's CAPS and the materials that help her complete her daily tasks follow. This figure represents a mini-portfolio of Ginny's day and serves multiple purposes:

1. It links the task to needed supports.
2. It provides a visual model for substitute teachers, paraeducators, and others who may work with Ginny throughout the day.
3. It can help Ginny's future teachers understand the supports that Ginny needs in each environment and, therefore, ease the transition phase.

In this way, the CAPS, with supporting visual representations, ensures current and future success for Ginny at school.

Figure 3.9. Ginny's CAPS Showing Support Materials Used.

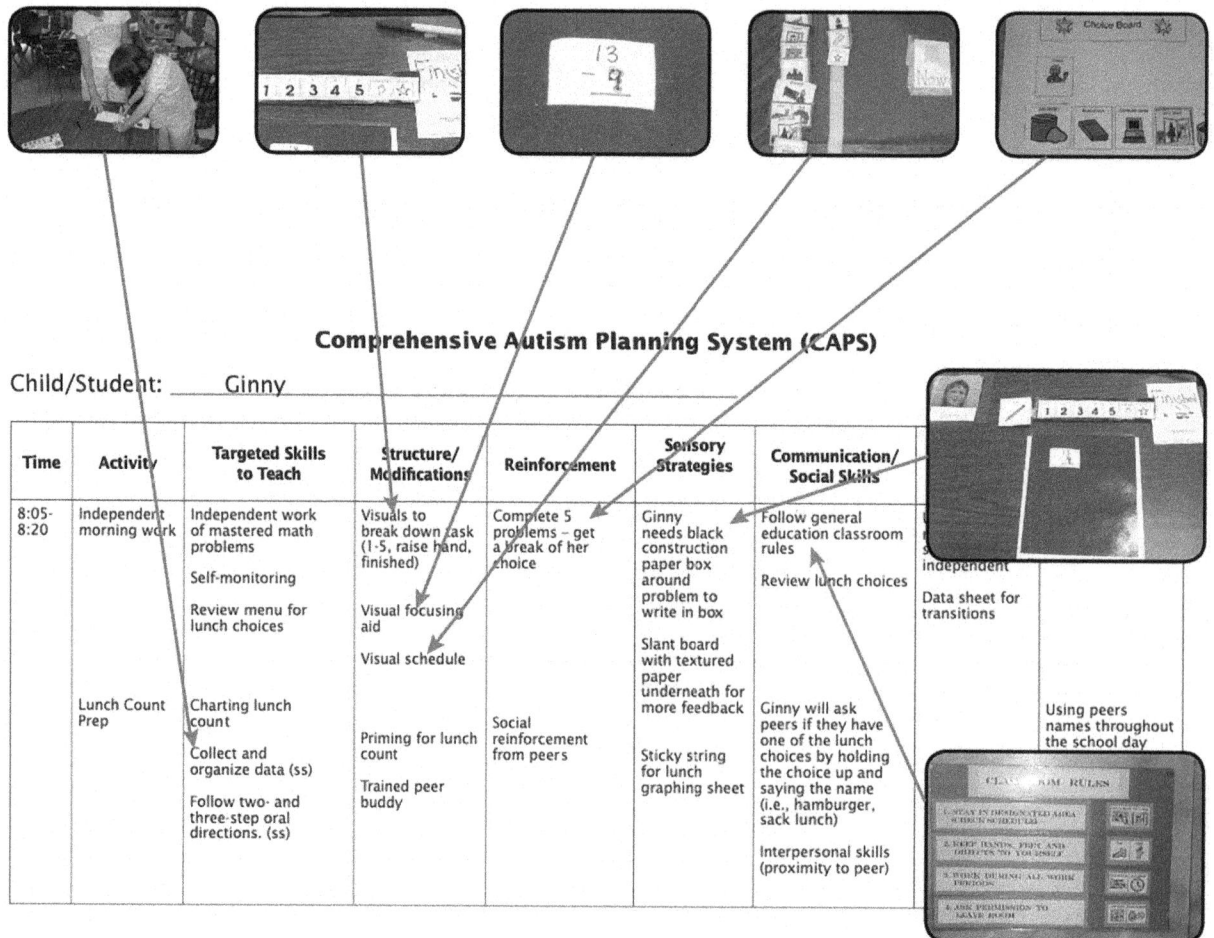

Comprehensive Autism Planning System (CAPS)

Child/Student: _____ Ginny _____

Time	Activity	Targeted Skills to Teach	Structure/ Modifications	Reinforcement	Sensory Strategies	Communication/ Social Skills	
8:05-8:20	Independent morning work	Independent work of mastered math problems Self-monitoring Review menu for lunch choices	Visuals to break down task (1-5, raise hand, finished) Visual focusing aid Visual schedule	Complete 5 problems – get a break of her choice	Ginny needs black construction paper box around problem to write in box Slant board with textured paper underneath for more feedback	Follow general education classroom rules Review lunch choices	independent Data sheet for transitions
	Lunch Count Prep	Charting lunch count Collect and organize data (ss) Follow two- and three-step oral directions. (ss)	Priming for lunch count Trained peer buddy	Social reinforcement from peers	Sticky string for lunch graphing sheet	Ginny will ask peers if they have one of the lunch choices by holding the choice up and saying the name (i.e., hamburger, sack lunch) Interpersonal skills (proximity to peer)	Using peers names throughout the school day

Summary

The CAPS is a multifaceted system that allows educational professionals to know at a glance the goals for an activity and what the student needs to successfully engage in it. Completed by a team, CAPS can also facilitate student independence across settings, activities, and people. Further, this breakthrough tool supports compliance with the student's IEP and current legislation while reducing teachers' workload. That is, the structure of this programming tool gives it broad applicability for autistic children, youth, and adults.

Bibliography

Aspy, Ruth & Barry Grossman. *Designing Comprehensive Interventions for High-Functioning Individuals with Autism Spectrum Disorders: The Ziggurat Model* (Release 2.0). Ziggurat Group (2022).

Frost, L., & Bondy, A. *The Picture Exchange Communication System Training Manual*. Pyramid (2002).

CHAPTER 4

A Brief Review of Evidence-Based Practices in Autism

Selecting effective and appropriate instructional, communication, and behavioral supports for autistic students can be difficult given the myriad strategies available in books, articles, and on the Internet. Fortunately, researchers in the field of autism have established a set of practices that are supported by high-quality research findings that can serve as the starting point for providing supports. These practices, deemed evidence based (EBPs), offer educational professionals and families alternatives to the many fads and potentially harmful practices they might encounter

Certainly, no EBP works for every child, but educators and parents should consider EBP a logical starting place in the design of educational supports. The important work in establishing EBP help us answer important questions regarding "What is the research behind this practice?" or "Given my student/child's need, which interventions are most likely to be effective?" Of course, with any practice, including EBP, we must collect data and evaluate a student's progress to ensure they are not exposed to ineffective practices for extended periods of time. A plan language guide for embedding EBPS into CAPS and brief description of interventions that meet the existing EBP criteria follow.

Plain Language Guide for Embedding EBP Into CAPS

The following list is not exhaustive but provides an example for educational teams as they consider how to support the student with EPBs embedded throughout the day. A description of these interventions follows.

Making sure your student understands what is expected
- Visual supports
- Antecedent-based intervention, such as priming
- Video modeling
- Social narratives, such as social descriptions and Social Stories
- Task analysis
- Modeling

Making sure your student is successful
- Antecedent-based intervention
- Direct instruction
- Discrete trial
- Prompting
- Time delay
- Technology-aided instruction and intervention
- Peer-based instruction and intervention
- Modeling
- Visual supports
- Response interruption/redirection

Making sure your student can express themselves
- Functional communication training
- Picture Exchange Communication System
- Augmentative and alternative communication
- Naturalistic intervention

Make sure your student is motivated
- Reinforcement
- Behavioral momentum intervention
- Social narratives, such as the Power Card Strategy
- Antecedent-based interventions, such as using special interests and highly preferred activities

Making sure your students has coping strategies
- Ayres Sensory Integration®
- Self-management
- Social narratives, such as the Power Card Strategy and Social Stories
- Antecedent-based interventions, such as self-calming before activity
- Exercise and movement
- Cognitive behavioral-instructional strategies

Evidence-Based Practices

The most recent set of EBP identified by the National Clearinghouse on Autism Evidence and Practice (NCAEP, 2021) includes 28 practices selected based on the findings of a rigorous review of over 50,000 research articles using stringent criteria for determining whether a practice qualified as evidence based.

Antecedent-Based Interventions (ABI)

When events or circumstances that occur before an activity or demand are structured to change the occurrence of a behavior, this is called an antecedent-based intervention (ABI) (Radley & Dart, 2022). Interventions included in this category are:
- Using highly preferred activities/special interest items to increase interest level
- Teaching rules and routines to facilitate ease of moving through the environment
- Priming for an upcoming event, including showing a visual schedule
- Offering choices
- Providing advance notice of a schedule change
- Altering the way instruction is provided to promote learning
- Enriching the environment with sensory supports that meet the individual's needs

- Providing self-calming interventions before an activity
- Providing a signal that a lesson is about to end
- Arranging the environment to promote engagement
- Teaching the skills needed to function in a group or activity before becoming a part of the situation

Most visual supports and sensory supports are antecedent-based interventions. Additional information about ABI may be found in Chapter 5: Structure/Modifications and Chapter 7: Sensory/Regulation.

Augmentative and Alternative Communication

Augmentative and alternative communication (AAC) interventions use and/or teach the use of a communication system. ACC can be aided or unaided. Aided AAC includes any device, either electronic or non-electronic, that transmits or receives messages. Communication boards; communication books; language boards; computers; handheld devices, such as tablets; and speech-generating devices are examples of aided AAC. Aided AAC is further divided into two categories: low-tech (aids that are not battery- or electrically powered) and high-tech aids (aids that rely on battery or electricity).

Table 4.1. Low- and High-Tech Aided AAC Examples.

Low-Tech	High-Tech
Pictures/picture communication symbols	Speech-generating devices
Objects	Single-message devices
Photographs	Eye-gaze devices
Written words/sentences	Tactile symbol buttons
Gestures/posture/facial expressions	Tablets/smartphones/hand-held devices with dynamic software
Communication boards/books	Computers with dynamic software
Manual signing	

Unaided communication includes unspoken means of natural communication, including gestures, posture, facial expressions, and manual signing. Unaided modes of communication often require adequate motor control and communication partners who can interpret the intended message. AAC is discussed further in Chapter 8: Communication/Social Skills.

Ayres Sensory Integration® (SI)

Occupational therapy using Ayres' Sensory Integration® (Ayres, 1979) is an effective EBP for autistic children. The intervention targets a person's ability to integrate sensory information (visual, auditory, gustatory, olfactory, tactile, proprioceptive, vestibular, interoception) from their body and surroundings to respond in a manner that matches the environment (Hume et al., 2021).

Sensory integration interventions address sensory needs that may be negatively impacting a student's academic performance or social skills. The intervention is generally play-based, emphasizing the active involvement of the student. Activities often involve the use of specialized equipment such as trampolines, hanging swings, scooters, weighted vests, and ball pools. Outcome data are collected at regular intervals to allow for adjustments in the program (Mailloux et al., 2018; Schoen et al., 2019). Additional information may be found in Chapter 7: Sensory/Regulation.

Behavioral Momentum Intervention (BMI)

When a student completes tasks that are easy for them, they are usually motivated to complete other tasks that may be more difficult. Using BMI, tasks and activities are sequenced from easy to difficult and the student is directed to complete two-to-three tasks they can do without much effort. The student is then presented with the more difficult task. Students are more likely to complete the more difficult task as they have experienced success. For example, to support a student following multiple-step directions, start by giving two easy directions. Reinforcement, key to BMI, is made available throughout the process.

Cognitive Behavioral-Instructional Strategies (CBIS)

This type of intervention focuses on self-awareness and self-management. Through instruction and practice, students learn to detect when there is a mismatch between their behavior and the environment. This analysis is followed by making changes to the behavior.

The following are steps of CBIS: (a) recognize the problem (b) define the problem; (c) develop a solution to solve the problem; (d) identify alternate solutions to the problem, just in case; (e) evaluate the consequences of the solutions; (f) decide which alternative is best; (g) practice the selected solution until the individual is comfortable in implementing it; (h) implement the solution; and (i) evaluate the effectiveness (Texas Educational Association, 2019).

Prerequisite skills for CBIS are cognitive development and expressive and receptive language at or above the 6-year-old level (TRIAD Consultants, 2023). Situation, Options Consequences, Choices, Strategies, Simulation (SOCCSS; Roosa, 1995), a CBIS, is described in Chapter 11: Instruction Often Occurring in Specialized Settings.

Differential Reinforcement of Alternative (DRA), Incompatible (DRI) or Other Behavior (DRO)

Differential reinforcement, a systematic way to reinforce one behavior while extinguishing another, can take three forms.

1. **DRA.** The teacher selects a behavior and a replacement behavior when using DRA. The behaviors can be occurring at the same time. When the student uses the replacement behavior, reinforcement is provided. For example, if a student uses a disruptive behavior to gain attention, such as pounding on the desk, the teacher reinforces appropriate behavior, such as raising a hand or asking for attention in a polite manner. The learner is reinforced to increase the occurrence of the alternative behavior.
2. **DRI.** This strategy involves identifying a behavior that is not compatible with the target behavior. For example, if a child uses physical aggression to gain access to toys, the teacher reinforces the child for engaging in nonaggressive behavior, such as (a) asking to play with toys or (b) playing with a puzzle or coloring book. The teacher then uses positive reinforcement to increase the occurrence of the incompatible behavior.
3. **DRO.** In DRO, the instructor identifies a behavior and when that behavior does not occur, reinforcement is provided. For example, if the target behavior is hitting, the learner is reinforced when hitting does not occur. What the "other" behavior looks like does not necessarily matter, as long as it is positive and meets the individual's needs (ABA Exam Review, 2024).

Direct Instruction (DI)

Direct instruction (DI) is a systematic approach that uses scripted protocols or lessons. This teacher-led approach emphasizes teacher and student dialogue through choral and independent student responses and employs systematic and explicit error correction to promote mastery and generalization. The following steps occur in DI:

1. **Introduction.** The goals of the introduction are to (a) engage the student, (b) get their attention, and (c) activate prior knowledge. In addition, the student is provided with lesson objectives so that they know what they are responsible for learning.

2. **Presentation and Demonstration.** During this step, the teacher introduces the main concept to be learned, uses examples to explain the concept, provides multiple practice opportunities, demonstrates what the concept looks like, and offers a summary of the process.

3. **Guided Practice.** The student attempts the tasks under the direction of the teacher. The purpose of guided practice is to (a) support initial practice; (b) provide correction, as needed; (c) reteach, if necessary; and (d) provide enough practice so that the student can use the skill independently.

4. **Feedback.** The student is given information about their implementation of the strategy. The feedback may be reinforcement for completing the task correctly or further instruction, if needed.

5. **Independent practice.** Students need enough practice to use a given skill without assistance. The goal is for the student to reach the "automatic" stage where they no longer need to think through each step of the task and can use it across settings, materials, and individuals (Main, 2021; Renard, 2023).

Discrete Trial Training (DTT)

Discrete trial training (DTT) is based on the theory that clear instructions eliminate misinterpretation and accelerate learning (National Institute on Direct Instruction, 2024). It is used most often as a one-to-one instructional approach for skills that are best taught in small, repeated steps. The process can also be used in group settings.

Each trial or teaching opportunity has a definite beginning and end. The instructional sequence typically includes teacher instruction/presentation, the student's response, a carefully planned consequence of the response, and a pause prior to presentation of the next step/instruction. Multiple practice opportunities are provided. The structure is designed to ensure content mastery. Students learn gradually, giving them an opportunity to learn and apply skills before new skills are introduced. Ten percent of each lesson is devoted to new content. The other 90% is review and application of previously-learned skills. Skills are first taught in isolation and then integrated into other skills.

Exercise and Movement (EXM)

The category of exercise and movement (EXM) includes interventions that use physical exertion, specific motor skills/techniques, or mindful movement to target a variety of skills and behaviors. Physical activity has many benefits, including reducing stress, improving physical health, reducing stereotypic behavior, and creating opportunities to communicate and socialize with others (Bremer et al., 2016; Steinbrenner et al., 2020; Tarr et al., 2020). A key to success with this practice is to proactively and regularly schedule physical activity breaks rather than waiting until students are becoming dysregulated (Bremer et al., 2016).

Even small exercise breaks throughout the day can make a difference. For example, Canella-Malone et al. (2011) found that two 20-min breaks in the morning and 1-to 5-minute breaks every hour reduced challenging behavior in the classroom. Another study found that giving autistic students 12-minute jogging/walking breaks around the school gym three times a week improved academic engagement upon returning to class (Nicholson et al., 2011).

Extinction (EXT)

If a problem behavior no longer occurs, it is said to be extinct, and the process of accomplishing this is referred to as extinction (EXT). When extinction occurs, the reinforcement that was previously available for the behavior is no longer provided. The goal is to make a behavior occur less often or stop altogether (Fisher et al., 2023). From the perspective of the child, the behavior no longer works to get what they want. Sometimes a behavior targeted with an extinction procedure does not decrease but instead increases. This is known as an "extinction burst"—a temporary increase in the frequency, duration, or magnitude of a behavior (Lerman et al., 1999).

Functional Behavioral Assessment (FBA)

Functional behavior assessment (FBA) "is the process of identifying the variables that reliably predict and maintain problem behaviors" (Horner & Carr, 1997). That is, an FBA is a systematic way of determining the underlying function or purpose of a challenging behavior so that an effective intervention plan can be developed. An FBA consists of the following steps: (a) identify and define the challenging behavior and replacement behaviors, (b) collect data, (c) identify the function of the behavior, (d) design an intervention, (e) implement the intervention, and (f) evaluate the effectiveness of the intervention (IRIS Center, 2024).

The most comprehensive FBA, in our opinion, is contained in the Ziggurat Model. Its consideration of patterns of behavior in addition to underlying characteristics leads to a better understanding of specific behavioral concerns and their unseen causes (Aspy & Grossman, 2022).

Functional Communication Training (FCT)

Introduced by Carr and Durand (1985), functional communication training (FCT) is a set of practices that replace a challenging behavior with more appropriate and effective communication behaviors or skills. The following are guidelines for conducting FCT:

- Identify the challenging behavior and the reinforcer that maintains it and complete an FBA to determine the function of the behavior
- Select a replacement behavior/communicative response that is easily and quickly recognized and meets the needs of the learner and the environment
- Create a data collection system
- Initiate FCT in a safe and controlled environment; arrange multiple opportunities to prompt and reinforce the communication response to promote skill acquisition; use most-to-least or least-to-most prompting procedures; and reinforce each occurrence of the communicative response
- Program for generalization by (a) thinning the reinforcement schedule; (b) fading prompts; (c) teaching the replacement behavior with multiple communication partners and environments; (d) teaching caregivers to respond to the individual's response; and (e) arranging learning situations in the natural environment
- Increase the complexity of the response over time and continue to monitor progress (Franzone, 2009; Griffin & AFIRM Team, 2017).

Modeling (MD)

In modeling (MD), an adult or peer provides a demonstration of the desired target behavior that results in the learner exhibiting the behavior. The demonstration of the behavior before the individual is expected to imitate it primes or prepares them to do so. Modeling is most effective when accompanied by reinforcement and prompting (Cox, 2013). MD can be used effectively to address social, communication, joint attention, play, school readiness, as well as academic and vocational skills (Sam & AFIRM TEAM, 2015a).

Music-Mediated Intervention (MMI)

Music-mediated interventions (MMI) incorporate songs, melodic intonation, and/or rhythm to support learning or performance of skills/behaviors, including communication, socialization, play, motor, adaptive skills, self-awareness, and personal fulfillment (Janzen & Thaut, 2018; Sharda et al., 2018). It includes music therapy, as well as other interventions that incorporate music to address target skills.

The structure and predictability of music creates an environment that eases anxiety and creates opportunities for successful participation. Music allows for the target goal to be repeated many times yet remain novel with changes in melody, rhythm, or dynamics. The intervention is delivered by a certified music therapist (MT); parents, educators, and others can provide the intervention with training/guidance from a MT. MMI can be used as a structured intervention or to support other EBP, such as using MMI and modeling to teach a student to line up for recess (Sharda et al., 2018).

Naturalistic Intervention (NI)

Naturalistic intervention (NI) strategies are a collection of techniques and strategies that are embedded in typical activities and/or routines in which the learner participates to naturally promote, support, and encourage target skills/behaviors. Its focus is to provide functional skills that can be used in the learner's natural environments. NI was developed from concerns related to applied behavior analysis instruction (ABA) resulting in (a) lack of spontaneous use and generalization of skills and (b) behavior instruction divorced from communication (Schreibman, et al., 2015). Studies using NI have shown increases in the expressive language, play skills, and social engagement of autistic children (Tiede & Walton, 2019).

NI typically consists of short instructional sessions that are learner-directed and embedded into activities. Four commonly used instructional strategies used in NI are: (a) modeling a response and correcting or expanding a child's interaction; (b) providing a verbal label that is supported in a desired object or activity; (c) using time delay, shaping, chaining, prompting, as needed; and (d) using incidental teaching that emphasizes intentionality by arranging the environment around preplanned learning objectives that include learner preferences and "teachable moments" initiated by the learner (Dubin et al., 2020). NI can be used to build more elaborate behaviors that are naturally reinforcing in the individual's typical environment (Schreibman et al., 2015).

Parent-Implemented Intervention (PII)

Using parent-implemented interventions (PII), a caregiver provides individualized interventions with their child to increase positive learning opportunities and acquisition of important skills, as well as decrease challenging behavior. The history of autism intervention contains multiple examples of parents as teachers for their children on the spectrum (Schopler et al., 1971). According to a meta-analysis conducted by Cheng et al. (2023), caregivers can effectively teach their children a variety of skills, including (a) language/communication, (b) social skills, (c) positive behaviors, (d) academics and pre-academics, and (e) daily living skills.

Peer-Based Instruction and Intervention (PBII)

Peers directly promote autistic children's social interactions and/or other individual learning goals in peer-based instruction and intervention (PBII) (Odom, 2019). There are typically four steps in this process:

1. **Identify and recruit peers.** The following peer characteristics are recommended: (a) of similar age with similar interests, if possible; (b) motivated to participate; (c) strong communication and social skills; and (d) dependability and consistency in participation.
2. **Train peers.** Peers learn what the Vanderbilt Kennedy Center for Excellence in Developmental Disabilities (2022) calls "disability etiquette" that includes understanding (a) autism and its terminology, (b) what the autistic student likes and dislikes, and (c) the student's strengths and challenges. In addition, the goal of the intervention is

shared with peers, and peers learn what they can gain from the intervention. Peers are systematically taught to initiate and maintain interactions with the autistic individual.

3. **Facilitate interactions in a structured setting.** The adult organizes the environment and structures simple social activities that are designed to build the confidence of the peer and autistic student in interacting with each other. Peers and autistics are prompted and reinforced for their interactions with each other. Simple board games and motor activities are often used to begin interactions; over time, activities that require more complex interactions, such as classroom projects, school-based extra-curricular activities, lunch, or recess, may be added.

4. **Fade support and structure.** At this stage, the adult assumes a more passive stance as individuals gain additional skills and confidence in interacting with each other. Eventually, the adult is present but intervenes only when necessary, ensuring that the autistic student and peer have enough time to address the issue independently. It should be noted that all supports except reinforcement can be faded (Vanderbilt Kennedy Center for Excellence in Developmental Disabilities, 2022).

Prompting (PP)

Prompting (PP) is a method of assisting a student to use a skill or behavior. Prompts can be provided during instruction or offered when a student has difficulty responding to an instruction or cue. They can also be used to create errorless learning by ensuring that the student responds correctly. Prompting helps a student learn new skills more efficiently, promotes independence, and reduces frustration.

There are several types of prompts. They are briefly described here from most intrusive to least intrusive. In this context, "intrusiveness" refers to the amount of assistance provided.

- **Physical prompt.** This intrusive prompt is seen in two forms: (a) the full physical prompt, also known as hand-over-hand assistance, which involves physically guiding the individual through the entire task; and (b) the partial physical prompt wherein physical assistance is provided for some of the steps of a task or activity.

- **Verbal prompt.** Telling the learner an answer or giving a direction more than once are forms of a full verbal prompt. Voicing the beginning sound of the answer or providing the first word in a sequence are examples of partial verbal prompts.

- **Gestural prompt.** Using pointing, reaching, nodding, or other type of movement or nonverbal action to give information to the learner about the correct response are gestural prompts.
- **Model prompt.** The adult demonstrates or models the task or activity. The student then imitates the teacher.
- **Positional prompt.** A positional prompt occurs when an instructor places the correct response closer to the learner than the incorrect response options. The closeness of the item indicates that it is the correct response
- **Visual prompt.** This is a visual cue that provides information about a correct response or task. Visual prompts can take many forms: visual schedule, video, photograph, drawing, or a card that supports the individual to change their (e.g., "raise your hand" card) (Chicago ABA Therapy, 2024; Sam & AFIRM Team, 2015b).

While prompts are an important part of instruction, it is important to fade their use so that the learner becomes independent. Using a prompt hierarchy is an efficient means of accomplishing this. At least three prompts are used in the hierarchy: (a) independent: when no prompt occurs; (b) intermediate: more assistance than independent and less than controlling; (c) controlling: the prompt that results in the individual completing the task (Neitzel & Woolery, 2009a).

- Least-to-most prompting begins with the most intrusive prompt to ensure the learner provides the correct response, and reinforcement, while also reducing errors. The intrusiveness of the prompts is systematically faded if the learner demonstrates success (Cengher et al., 2016). The criterion for reducing the level of assistance must be specified. For example, how many correct responses are required to move to a less intrusive prompt? How many errors lead to increasing the intrusiveness of the prompt (Libby et al., 2008)?
- With least-to-most prompting the learner is given an opportunity to independently respond to the instruction. If the learner engages in no response or gives an incorrect response, a more intrusive prompt is provided. The intrusiveness of the prompt systematically increases until the learner engages in a correct response (Cengher et al., 2018).

Reinforcement (R)

A reinforcer (R) is something that increases the likelihood that a specific behavior or response will occur again. Simply speaking, reinforcement is adding or taking away something after a behavior occurs to try to ensure that the behavior will occur again. Because reinforcement is considered one of the most powerful interventions, an entire chapter is devoted to it (see Chapter 6: Reinforcement).

Response Interruption/Redirection (RIR)

Response interruption/redirection (RIR) can be used when the learner's attention is away from the activity at hand or to direct the learner to the correct response. RIR contains three main components. First, during the response interruption component, the practitioner stops the learner from engaging in the interfering behavior through a prompt, comment, a gentle block, or other distractor. The second step, redirection, focuses on prompting the learner to engage in an alternative behavior that will better meet their needs. The third component is reinforcement.

"A teacher places a bowl of goldfish crackers on a table in the dramatic play area during free play. When an autistic learner attempts to pick up a piece of dirt off the floor and put it in her mouth, the teacher says, 'Molly, don't,' and puts her hand in front of the learner's mouth to stop her from ingesting it. The teacher waits until eye contact has been established and then points to the bowl of goldfish on the table. When the learner tries to pick up another piece of dirt and put it in her mouth, the teacher gently guides her to the table and says, 'Goldfish'" (Neitzel, 2009).

Self-Management (SM)

Self-management (SM) interventions place the student in charge of changing their behavior and monitoring that change. Behaviors targeted for SM intervention include students getting up from their seat during instructional time, touching or otherwise "bothering" others, attending to task, completing classwork, or turning in homework (IRIS Center, n.d.; Mattson & Pinkelman, 2020; Sam & AFIRM Team, 2016a).

SM includes several components, some or all of which may be part of an intervention package. Self-monitoring does not create new skills; instead, it is intended to increase or decrease the frequency, intensity, or duration of an existing behavior. It also saves teachers time spent monitoring students' behavior (IRIS Center, 2024). Individual components of SM are identified for use with a student based on that individual's strengths, needs, and abilities (Li et al., 2023).

- **Goal setting** occurs when the individual selects a standard that they want to achieve. While practitioners, parents, or others may support an individual in goal setting, ultimately, the goal should be one that the individual believes will improve their quality of life.
- **Self-monitoring** involves an individual observing their own behavior and recording, or in some way responding to, the occurrences of that behavior. Individuals are responsible for taking their own data and recording it, typically using a checklist.
- **Self-evaluation** takes into consideration the accuracy of the data. During self-evaluation, students learn if their data matched that of their teachers. Disparities may indicate that additional instruction and support in SM are needed.
- **Self-reinforcement** refers to the individual selecting a desirable object, event, or activity after they have met the predetermined goal (see goal setting above) for their target behavior.
- **Self-instruction** involves the individual providing themselves with instructions (in any form [e.g., spoken, written, video]) that increase the likelihood that they will engage in the target behavior. A self-reminder and positive affirmation are forms of self-instruction (Marshall & Rohrer, 2023; Sulu et al., 2023).

Social Narratives (SN)

Social narratives (SN) are written and/or pictorial interventions that describe social situations by providing relevant cues, an explanation of the feelings and thoughts of others, and descriptions of behavior expectations. A response or response options are often presented. They can be used to address social skills, challenging behavior, generalization, choice making, play, and on-task behavior. SN include Social StoriesTM (Gray & Garand, 1993), social scripts, the Power Card strategy (Gagnon, 2023), and social descriptions. A social narrative typically contains the following parts:

- A brief description of the situation
- What the autistic individuals thinks, feels, does, or says in the situation
- What others may think, feel, do, or say in the situation
- Description of the response or behavior that best matches the environment
- Explanation of why that behavior or response will benefit the autistic person (Southern, 2017).

Additional information about social narratives is provided in Chapter 11: Instruction Often Occurring in Specialized Settings.

Social Skills Training (SST)

Social skills training (SST) includes group or individual instruction designed to teach learners multiple ways to successfully interact with others. Led by an adult, SST may also include practice or review sessions in classroom settings. PMII, social narratives, and video modeling are some of the EBP that may co-occur with SST (Griffin et al., 2015). Social skills training typically includes instruction, role-play or practice, and feedback to help autistic learners acquire and practice communication, play, or social skills to promote positive interactions with peers.

A recent meta-analysis revealed that autistic individuals who participated in SST had increased social knowledge, social skills, and social contacts, and loneliness and mental health challenges decreased (Dubreucq et al., 2022). The authors noted that SST should occur real-life environments that promote skill generalization. Social skills can be situational and environment-specific; thus, it is essential that students understand which environments and which social skills go together. Additional information about SST may be found in Chapter 11: Instruction Often Occurring in Specialized Settings.

Task Analysis (TA)

Task analysis (TA) is a process in which a skill/behavior is divided into small, manageable steps to assess and teach the skill. It is used with behaviors that consist of several steps, such as tying shoes, safety, grocery shopping, writing a paper, turning in homework, or cooking (Sam & Affirm Team, 2016b). Once behaviors or skills are broken into smaller steps, team members work with the learner to systematically teach the individual steps. As the learner masters the individual steps, they gradually become more independent using the target skill or behavior (McConomy, 2022).

Technology-Aided Instruction and Intervention (TAII)

Technology-aided instruction and intervention (TAII) refers to instruction/intervention in which technology is the central feature and is specifically designed or employed to support the learning of a behavior or skill for the learner (Hedges & AFIRM Team, 2018; Heng et al., 2021). Technology is "any electronic item, equipment, application, or virtual network that is used intentionally to increase/maintain, and/or improve daily living, work/productivity, and recreation/leisure capabilities" of autistic children (Odom et al., 2015). Smart phones, tablets, laptops, desktop computers, interactive white boards, computer software, speech-generating devices, and the Internet are examples of TAII (Heng et al., 2021).

Time Delay (TD)

Time delay (TD) focuses on fading prompts while delivering reinforcement to increase the likelihood that target skills/behaviors will occur in the future. With this procedure, a brief delay occurs between the instruction and the prompt (Neitzel & Woolery, 2009b). The evidence-based research focuses on two types of time delay procedures: progressive and constant:

- **Progressive time delay.** The teacher gradually increases wait time between an instruction/cue and any prompts that might be used to elicit a response from a learner.
- **Constant time delay.** When a student is first learning a skill, a specific amount of time (e.g., 3 to 5 seconds) occurs between instruction and prompt. This continues until the student is reliably giving the correct response (Horn et al., 2023; Walker, 2008).

Video Modeling (VM)

Video modeling (VM) is defined as a video-recorded demonstration of a targeted behavior or skill shown to the learner to assist them in learning or engaging in the desired behavior or skill. Videos can feature the individual who is learning a new skill or can include a peer model. It was the most frequently researched intervention from 1998 to 2018 (Radley et al., 2020). Video modeling has been used to teach a variety of skills, including (a) commenting, (b) seeking help, (c) abduction prevention, and (d) job skills (Abadir et al., 2021; Bross et al., 2021).

Benefits of video modeling include its use to safely simulate environments and situations that could otherwise be anxiety-provoking or dangerous. In addition, video modeling is an easy and time efficient intervention that is compatible with the student's learning style and capitalizes on their use of imitation skills (Bross et al., 2021). Additional information about video modeling is provided in Chapter 11: Instruction Often Occurring in Specialized Settings.

Visual Supports (VS)

Visual supports (VS) are tools that visually support the learner to engage in a desired behavior or skill independent of additional prompts. Visual supports provide structure and routine. When autistic people use VS, they experience increased (a) independence, (b) confidence, and (c) improved understanding. In addition, VS help prevent frustration and anxiety, and provide opportunities for interaction with others (National Autistic Society, n.d.).

Visual supports can be used in most situations and are adaptable and portable. They can (a) show sequential steps, such as how to turn in papers; (b) demonstrate units of time; (c) show a to-do list; and (d) offer choices. VS can explain situations using objects, photographs, line drawings, and/or written words (Bennie, 2017). Additional information about VS may be found in Chapter 5: Structure/Modifications.

Summary

The 28 EBP identified by the NAECP (2021) provide important guidance on how to teach and support autistic people in school, home, and community. Proper implementation of these interventions has been linked to improved outcomes for autistics (Hume et al., 2021). Thus, it is essential that practitioners understand how to use and evaluate outcomes associated with these strategies.

Learning how to teach and support autistics is an evolving field. Over time, more practices will be identified and individual outcomes will continue to improve. However, problems exist in the application of EBP. For example, social skills training programs have been identified as EBP. Does that mean that any social skills program is effective?

Can you select any social skills training program and count on it to include best practices? Unfortunately, just because a social skills curriculum exists does not mean that it is effective. On the other hand, just because a curriculum has not been researched does not mean that it is ineffective.

In light of limited guidance on the effectiveness of specific materials, how will we know if a given curriculum is effective? The answer: We take data. Data showing learner progress using a specific intervention allow us to state, "This practice is evidence-based for this individual in this situation."

Resources such as *Taming the Data Monster: Collecting and Analyzing Classroom Data to Improve Student Progress* (Reeve & Kabot, 2015) and *The Data Collection Toolkit: Everything You Need to Organize, Manage, and Monitor Classroom Data* (Golden, 2017) can be helpful in developing data collection systems.

Bibliography

ABA Exam Review. Differential reinforcement: DRO, DRA, DRI, DRL Explained. (2024). Accessed December 18, 2023 from https://btexamreview.com/differential-reinforcement-dro-dra-dri-drl-explained-simply/.

Abadir, Christina M., Ruth M. DeBar, Jason C. Vladescu, Sharon A. Reeve, and Douglas M. Kupferman. "Effects of Video Modeling on Abduction-Prevention Skills by Individuals With Autism Spectrum Disorder." *Journal of Applied Behavior Analysis* 54, no. 3 (2021): 1139-1156.

Aspy, Ruth & Barry Grossman. *Designing Comprehensive Interventions for High-Functioning Individuals with Autism Spectrum Disorders: The Ziggurat Model* (Release 2.0). Ziggurat Group (2022).

Ayres, A. Jean. *Sensory Integration and the Child.* Los Angeles, Western Psychological Services. (1979).

Bennie, Maureen. *Visual Supports for Autism: A Step-by-Step Guide.* (October 8, 2017). Accessed Feb 10, 2024 from https://autismawarenesscentre.com/visual-supports-best-way-use/.

Bremer, Emily, Michael Crozier, and Meghann Lloyd. "A Systematic Review of the Behavioral Outcomes Following Exercise Interventions for Children and Youth With Autism Spectrum Disorder." *Autism* 20, no. 8 (2016): 899-915.

Bross, Leslie Ann, Jason C. Travers, Jonathan M. Huffman, John L. Davis, and Rose A. Mason. "A Meta-Analysis of Video Modeling Interventions to Enhance Job Skills of Autistic Adolescents and adults." *Autism in Adulthood* 3, no. 4 (2021): 356-369.

Cannella-Malone, Helen I., Christopher A. Tullis, and Aline R. Kazee. "Using Antecedent Exercise to Decrease Challenging Behavior in Boys With Developmental Disabilities and an Emotional Disorder." *Journal of Positive Behavior Interventions* 13, no. 4 (2011): 230-239.

Carr, Edward G., and V. Mark Durand. "Reducing Behavior Problems Through Functional Communication Training." *Journal of Applied Behavior Analysis* 18, no. 2 (1985): 111-126.

Cengher, Mirela, Anna Budd, Nicole Farrell, and Daniel M. Fienup. "A Review of Prompt-Fading Procedures: Implications for Effective And Efficient Skill Acquisition." *Journal of Developmental and Physical Disabilities* 30 (2018): 155-173.

Cengher, Mirela, Kimberly Shamoun, Patricia Moss, David Roll, Gina Feliciano, and Daniel M. Fienup. "A Comparison of the Effects of Two Prompt-Fading Strategies on Skill Acquisition in Children With Autism Spectrum Disorders." *Behavior Analysis in Practice* 9 (2016): 115-125.

Cheng, Wai Man, Timothy B. Smith, Marshall Butler, Tina M. Taylor, and Devan Clayton. "Effects of Parent-Implemented Interventions on Outcomes of Children With Autism: A Meta-Analysis." *Journal of Autism and Developmental Disorders* 53, no. 11 (2023): 4147-4163.

Chicago ABA Therapy. "What Is a Prompt." (2024). Accessed January 10, 2024 from https://chicagoabatherapy.com/articles/6-types-of-prompts-used-in-aba-therapy/.

Cox, A. W. *Modeling Fact Sheet.* The National Professional Development Center on Autism Spectrum Disorders, Frank Porter Graham Child Development Institute, The University of North Carolina (2013).

Dubin, A.H., Lieberman-Betz, R.G. "Naturalistic Interventions to Improve Prelinguistic Communication for Children with Autism Spectrum Disorder: A Systematic Review." *Journal of Autism and Developmental Disorders* 7, 151–167 (2020).

Dubreucq, J., F. Haesebaert, J. Plasse, M. Dubreucq, and N. Franck. "A Systematic Review and Meta-Analysis of Social Skills Training for Adults With Autism Spectrum Disorder." *Journal of Autism and Developmental Disorders* 52, no. 4 (2022): 1598-1609.

Fisher, Wayne W., Brian D. Greer, Timothy A. Shahan, and Halle M. Norris. "Basic and Applied Research on Extinction Bursts." *Journal of Applied Behavior Analysis* 56, no. 1 (2023): 4-28.

Franzone, E. *Steps for implementation: Functional communication training.* The National Professional Development Center on Autism Spectrum Disorders, Waisman Center, University of Wisconsin (2009).

Gagnon, Elisa. *Power Cards: Using Interests and Enthusiasms to Teach Social Problem Solving and Emotional Regulation Skills to Autistic Students.* 5 Point Publishing (2023).

Golden, Cinda. *The Data Collection Toolkit: Everything You Need to Organize, Manage, and Monitor Classroom Data.* Brookes (2017).

Gray, Carol, and Joy D. Garand. "Social Stories: Improving Responses of Students With Autism With Accurate Social Information." *Focus on Autistic Behavior,* 8(1), (1993): 1–10.

Griffin, W., and AFIRM Team. Functional Communication Training. (2017). Accessed January 10, 2024 from https://afirm.fpg.unc.edu/functional-communication-training.

Griffin, W., Sam, A., and AFIRM Team. Social Skills Training. (2017). Accessed December 10, 2023 from http://afirm.fpg.unc.edu/Social-skills-training.

Hedges, S. and AFIRM Team. Technology-Aided Instruction and Intervention (2018). Accessed December 20, 2023 from http://afirm.fpg.unc.edu/Technology-aided-instruction-and-intervention.

Heng, Emily, Marc J. Lanovaz, and Alexia Beauregard. "Research on Technological Interventions for Young Children With Autism Spectrum Disorders: A Scoping Review." *Journal of Autism and Developmental Disorders* 8 (2021): 253-263.

Hume, Kara, Jessica R. Steinbrenner, Samuel L. Odom, Kristi L. Morin, Sallie W. Nowell, Brianne Tomaszewski, Susan Szendrey, Nancy S. McIntyre, Serife Yücesoy-Özkan, and Melissa N. Savage. "Evidence-Based Practices for Children, Youth, and Young Adults With Autism: Third Generation Review." *Journal of Autism and Developmental Disorders* (2021): 1-20.

Horn, Annemarie L., Jane Roitsch, and Kimberly A. Murphy. "Constant Time Delay to Teach Reading to Students with Intellectual Disability and Autism: A Review." *International Journal of Developmental Disabilities* 69, no. 2 (2023): 123-133.

Horner, Robert H., and Edward G. Carr. "Behavioral Support for Students with Severe Disabilities: Functional Assessment and Comprehensive Intervention." *The Journal of Special Education* 31, no. 1 (1997): 84-104.

IRIS Center Peabody College Vanderbilt University, Nashville. Conducting a Functional Behavior Analysis. (2024). Accessed January 2, 2024 from https://iris.peabody.vanderbilt.edu/module/fba/cresource/q2/p04/.

IRIS Center Peabody College Vanderbilt University, Nashville. SOS: Helping Students Become Independent Learners. (nd). Accessed January 6, 2024 from https://iris.peabody.vanderbilt.edu/module/sr/#content.

Janzen, Thenille Braun, and Michael H. Thaut. "Rethinking the Role of Music in the Neurodevelopment of Autism Spectrum Disorder." *Music & Science* 1 (2018): 2059204318769639.

Lerman, Dorothea C., Brian A. Iwata, and Michele D. Wallace. "Side Effects of Extinction: Prevalence of Bursting and Aggression During the Treatment of Self-Injurious Behavior." *Journal of Applied Behavior Analysis* 32, no. 1 (1999): 1-8.

Li, Yi-Fan, Suzanne Byrne, Wei Yan, and Kathy B. Ewoldt. "Self-Monitoring Intervention for Adolescents and Adults with Autism: A Research Review." *Behavioral Sciences* 13, no. 2 (2023): 138.

Libby, Myrna E., Julie S. Weiss, Stacie Bancroft, and William H. Ahearn. "A Comparison of Most-to-Least and Least-to-Most Prompting on the Acquisition of Solitary Play Skills." *Behavior Analysis in Practice* 1 (2008): 37-43.

Mailloux, Zoe, L. Diane Parham, Susanne Smith Roley, Laura Ruzzano, and Roseann C. Schaaf. "Introduction to the Evaluation in Ayres Sensory Integration®(EASI)." *The American Journal of Occupational Therapy* 72, no. 1 (2018): 7201195030p1-7201195030p7.

Main, P. Direct Instruction: A Teacher's Guide. November 18, 2021. Retrieved February 10, 2024 from https://www.structural-learning.com/post/direct-instruction-a-teachers-guide.

Marshall, Kimberly B., and Jessica L. Rohrer, J. L. "Self-Management Interventions: A Treatment Summary." *Science in Autism Treatment*. (2002). Accessed December 29, 2023 from https://asatonline.org/for-parents/learn-more-about-specific-treatments/applied-behavior-analysis-aba/aba-techniques/self-management/.

Mattson, Stephanie L., and Sarah E. Pinkelman. "Improving On-Task Behavior in Middle School Students With Disabilities Using Activity Schedules." *Behavior Analysis in Practice* 13 (2020): 104-113.

McConomy, M. Addie, Jenny Root, and Taryn Wade. "Using Task Analysis to Support Inclusion and Assessment in the Classroom." *TEACHING Exceptional Children* 54, no. 6 (2022): 414-422.

National Autistic Society. Visual Supports. (nd). Accessed January 1, 2024 from https://www.autism.org.uk/advice-and-guidance/topics/communication/communication-tools/visual-supports.

National Clearinghouse on Autism Evidence and Practice. Why a Clearinghouse? Frank Porter Graham Child Development Institute, The University of North Carolina. (2021). Accessed December 22, 2023 from https://ncaep.fpg.unc.edu.

National Institute on Direct Instruction. Implementing Direct Instruction Successfully. Accessed December 26, 2023 from https://nifdi-tutorial-76ba.thinkific.com/courses/nifdi-tutorial (2024).

Neitzel, J. *Steps for Implementation: Response Interruption/Redirection*. The National Professional Development Center on Autism Spectrum Disorders, Frank Porter Graham Child Development Institute, The University of North Carolina (2009).

Neitzel, J., and Woolery, M. *Steps for Implementation: Least-to-Most Prompts*. National Professional Development Center on Autism Spectrum Disorders, Frank Porter Graham Child Development Institute, The University of North Carolina (2009a).

Neitzel, J., and Wolery, M. (2009). *Steps for Implementation: Time Delay*. The National Professional Development Center on Autism Spectrum Disorders, Frank Porter Graham Child Development Institute, The University of North Carolina (2009b).

Nicholson, Heather, Thomas J. Kehle, Melissa A. Bray, and Jaci Van Heest. "The Effects of Antecedent Physical Activity on the Academic Engagement of Children with Autism Spectrum Disorder." *Psychology in the Schools* 48, no. 2 (2011): 198-213.

Odom, Samuel L., Julie L. Thompson, Susan Hedges, Brian A. Boyd, Jessica R. Dykstra, Michelle A. Duda, Kathrine L. Szidon, Leann E. Smith, and Aimee Bord. "Technology-Aided Interventions and Instruction for Adolescents with Autism Spectrum Disorder." *Journal of Autism and Developmental Disorders* 45 (2015): 3805-3819.

Odom, Samuel L. "Peer-Based Interventions for Children and Youth With Autism Spectrum Disorder: History and Effects." *School Psychology Review* 48, no. 2 (2019): 170-176.

Radley, Keith C., and Evan H. Dart. "Antecedent Interventions." *Social Skills Teaching for Individuals with Autism: Integrating Research into Practice*. (2022): 75-86.

Radley, Keith C., Evan H. Dart, Kayleigh J. Brennan, Kate A. Helbig, Erica L. Lehman, Magenta Silberman, and Kai Mendanhall. "Social Skills Teaching for Individuals with Autism Spectrum Disorder: A Systematic Review." *Advances in Neurodevelopmental Disorders* 4 (2020): 215-226.

Reeve, Chris and Sue Kabot. *Taming the Data Monster: Collecting and Analyzing Classroom Data to Improve Student Progress*. AAPC Publishing (2015).

Renard, Lucie. Direct Instruction: A Practical Guide to Effective Teaching. (2023). Accessed February 10, 2024 from https://docs.google.com/document/d/1xt15YBkOeuOXNipK-PYGXPhA7J4fCRBe/edit.

Roosa, J. B. *Men on the Move: Competence and Cooperation: Conflict Resolution and Beyond*. Author (1995).

Sam, A., and AFIRM Team. "Modeling." National Professional Development Center on Autism Spectrum Disorder, FPG Child Development Center, University of North Carolina. (2015a).

Sam, A., and AFIRM Team. "Prompting." National Professional Development Center on Autism Spectrum Disorder, FPG Child Development Center, University of North Carolina. (2015b).

Sam, A., and AFIRM Team. "Self-Management." National Professional Development Center on Autism Spectrum Disorder, FPG Child Development Center, University of North Carolina." (2016a).

Sam, A., and AFIRM Team. "Task Analysis." Chapel Hill, NC: National Professional Development Center on Autism Spectrum Disorder, FPG Child Development Center, University of North Carolina." (2016b).

Schoen, Sarah A., Shelly J. Lane, Zoe Mailloux, Teresa May-Benson, L. Dianne Parham, Susanne Smith Roley, and Roseann C. Schaaf. "A Systematic Review of Ayres Sensory Integration Intervention for Children with Autism." *Autism Research* 12, no. 1 (2019): 6-19.

Schopler, Eric. "Behavioral Priorities for Autism and Related Developmental Disorders." In *Behavioral Issues in Autism*, pp. 55-77. Springer US (1994).

Schopler, Eric, Sharon S. Brehm, Marcel Kinsbourne, and Robert J. Reichler. "Effect of Treatment Structure on Development in Autistic Children." *Archives of General Psychiatry* 24, no. 5 (1971): 415-421.

Schreibman, Laura, Geraldine Dawson, Aubyn C. Stahmer, Rebecca Landa, Sally J. Rogers, Gail G. McGee, Connie Kasari et al. "Naturalistic Developmental Behavioral Interventions: Empirically Validated Treatments for Autism Spectrum Disorder." *Journal of Autism and Developmental Disorders* 45 (2015): 2411-2428.

Sharda, Megha, Carola Tuerk, Rakhee Chowdhury, Kevin Jamey, Nicholas Foster, Melanie Custo-Blanch, Melissa Tan, Aparna Nadig, and Krista Hyde. "Music Improves Social Communication and Auditory-Motor Connectivity in Children with Autism." *Translational Psychiatry* 8, no. 1 (2018): 231.

Southern, Louise. Social Narratives Support Individuals with Autism. Autism Society of North Carolina. (2017). Accessed December 12, 2023 from https://www.autismsociety-nc.org/social-narratives-guidelines/.

Steinbrenner, Jessica R., Kara Hume, Samuel L. Odom, Kristi L. Morin, Sallie W. Nowell, Brianne Tomaszewski, Susan Szendrey, Nancy S. McIntyre, Serife Yücesoy-Özkan, and Melissa N. Savage. "Evidence-Based Practices for Children, Youth, and Young Adults with Autism." FPG Child Development Institute (2020).

Sulu, Mehmet D., Ronald C. Martella, Kharon Grimmet, Amanda M. Borosh, and Emine Erden. "Investigating the Effects of Self-Monitoring Interventions With Students With Disabilities on the Maintenance and Generalization of On-Task Behavior: A Systematic Literature Review." Review *Journal of Autism and Developmental Disorders* 10, no. 3 (2023): 458-476.

Tarr, Christopher W., Ashlea Rineer-Hershey, and Karen Larwin. "The Effects of Physical Exercise on Stereotypic Behaviors in Autism: Small-n Meta-Analyses." *Focus on Autism and Other Developmental Disabilities* 35, no. 1 (2020): 26-35.

Texas Educational Association. Cognitive Behavior/Instructional Strategy. (2019). Accessed December 10, 2024 from https://www.txautism.net/interventions/cognitive-behavioral-instructional-strategies#:~:text=Role%2Dplaying%2C%20 case%20studies%2C,problem%20occurred%2C%20and%20what%20happened.

Tiede, Gabrielle, and Katherine M. Walton. "Meta-Analysis of Naturalistic Developmental Behavioral Interventions for Young Children with Autism Spectrum Disorder." *Autism* 23, no. 8 (2019): 2080-2095.

TRIAD Consultants. "Overview of Cognitive Behavioral Instructional Strategies." (2023). Accessed 2/1/24 from https://vkc.vumc.org/assets/files/triad/tips/CBIS.pdf.

Walker, Gabriela. "Constant and Progressive Time Delay Procedures for Teaching Children with Autism: A Literature Review." *Journal of Autism and Developmental Disorders* 38 (2008): 261-275.

Vanderbilt Kennedy Center for Excellence in Developmental Disabilities, Peer-Based Intervention and Autism Spectrum Disorders. (2022). Accessed December 16, 2023 from https://vkc.vumc.org/assets/files/tipsheets/peerinterventionasdtips.pdf.

CHAPTER 5

Structure/Modifications

*Brenda Smith Myles, PhD, Amy Moore Gaffney, MA, CCC-SLP
and Cathy Pratt, PhD, BCBA-D*

The potential of autistic students is often not realized because their learning style is not taken into consideration when planning and implementing educational programs. In addition, research has shown that most autistic students require environmental as well as academic supports to be successful. Research further supports that no one methodology is appropriate for all autistic individuals (Steinbrenner et al., 2020).

This chapter explores the intent behind CAPS's Structure/Modifications column that incorporates these considerations and thereby enhances the possibility that the student's potential is fully realized. All of the structure/modifications described in this chapter meet the criteria for evidence-based practices (EBP) under the category of antecedent-based interventions; most meet the criteria for visual supports.

Environmental Considerations

It is well documented that autistic students benefit from structure (Meindl, 2020), especially when that structure is visual (Carrington et al., 2020). Therefore, it is important to ensure that the environment is well organized and has a strong visual component.

Providing students with a well-organized, visual classroom is only a starting point in instruction. Each of the components described in this chapter, including classroom layout, must be taught to and practiced by the autistic student until they have reached mastery. Such instruction should occur when the student is calm as it is difficult if not impossible for students to learn when they are not well regulated.

Classroom Layout

All students benefit from a well-organized classroom. Indeed, a well-planned classroom can be as central to a student's success as other interventions. Therefore, to create a classroom that is conducive to learning, teachers need to start by examining how the classroom space is organized.

Components of a well-organized classroom include:

- Clearly defined areas for each activity—break area, independent work, small-group work, large-group area
- Visual reminders of classroom expectations, including rules and schedules
- Adequate spacing to allow for personal space preferences
- Flexible seating options, such as stools, rocking chairs, etc.
- Clear and consistent organization of materials, for example, by color coding and labeling (with written words, pictures, or both) (TEACCH Staff, nd).

A well-organized environment is particularly beneficial for autistic students as it provides the structure, predictability, and visual supports that many need. It informs them where to be, where to obtain items, where to return items, and what the classroom and learning expectations are. In addition, it adds meaning and context to the area/environment and helps to minimize distractions (TEACCH Staff, nd; Zwilling & Levy, 2022).

It's important to limit visual "clutter." This can be done by using curtains to cover shelves or storage containers with lids or containers that are not transparent. Carpets and colored tape are good ways to define spaces (Long, nd).

Some students may benefit from separate independent work areas that reduce distractions, thereby, increasing focus. A separate work area does not take the place of the student's individual desk. This area is one that anyone can use if they need help focusing (TEACCH Staff, nd).

Figure 5.1. Components of Well-Organized Classrooms.*

Karla Dennis & Lezli Carson

Rhonda Bowen, Marita Burrow, Jennifer Stanley, & Lisa Toler

Katie Lents

* Used with permission from a classroom teacher (anonymous).

Home Base/Break Room

A home base or break room is a quiet place in the school where students can go to (a) plan or review information or (b) cope with stress and behavioral challenges (Kreibich et al., 2020). It also serves as a place the student can go if (a) the classroom is becoming overwhelming, (b) a teacher thinks a meltdown may be on the way, or (c) the student otherwise needs a place to calm. There are no specific criteria for the location of a home base.

Home base is not a time-out, nor is it somewhere a student goes to escape work. Primarily, it should be a positive place for the student, located anywhere that is quiet and comfortable, such as a resource room, a favorite teacher's classroom, or an ancillary staff member's office.

Use of home base is individually determined. Some students primarily use it to address stress and behavioral challenges, whereas others use it on a regular basis to plan and review information. Time at home base can be scheduled into a student's school day and may be especially helpful if scheduled immediately following a class period or activity that proves stressful for the autistic student. A home base/break card is often used to prompt the student to take a break.

Figure 5.2. Sample Home Base/Break Card.

Visual Schedules

Visual schedules offer a sequential presentation of upcoming activities in a concrete format. As such, they allow students to (a) anticipate upcoming events and activities; (b) develop an understanding of time; (c) satisfy their need for predictability; and (d) experience a greater sense of confidence and decreased anxiety about an upcoming event (Vermeulen, 2022). Further, visual schedules can be utilized to stimulate conversation through a discussion of past, present, and future events; increase on-task behavior; and facilitate transition between activities.

Most classrooms display a daily schedule that the entire class will follow. Although these classroom schedules are helpful, they often do not allow for the individualization that many students need, such as showing when a speech therapy session will occur, when Lunch Bunch occurs, or when a student is taking a test in the resource room. To capture all these unique events, an individualized visual schedule is needed (TEACCH Staff, nd).

Individualized visual schedules show the student where they will be going throughout the day and/or activities they will be participating in, such as music class, the blue table, or math. Times may or may not be included on the schedule, depending on the student's needs (Long, nd).

The information listed in each schedule may be presented solely through words, through words and pictures, entirely with pictures, or incorporate objects that represent different locations and activities. The length of individual visual schedules can vary from a few activities to a partial day to a whole day schedule (Zimmerman, 2017). The decision on how the information is presented should be based on the specific student's comprehension and preferences. For some students, adding reinforcement and breaks into the schedule is beneficial (Rutherford et al., 2020).

Participation by the autistic individual in preparing the schedule is often helpful. For example, a student can assist in assembling their schedule, copying it, or adding their own personal touch in some manner. This interactive time can also be used to review the daily routine, discuss changes, and review expectations. Various formats and materials can be used to develop individual schedules, as illustrated in the following.

Figure 5.3. Sample Visual Schedule.

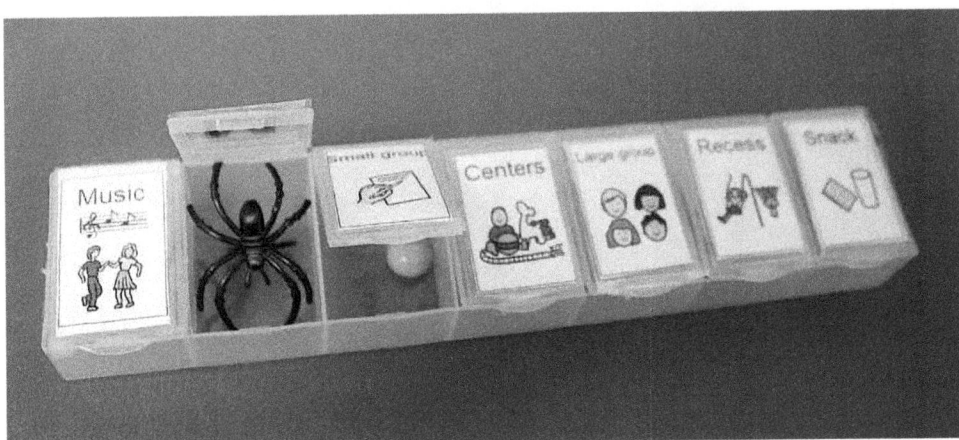

https://sharingkindergarten.com/classroom-management-tips/visual schedule using pictures. Objects inside the dispenser represent the reinforcer the individual earns after the activity.

Figure 5.4. Sample Visual Schedule.

Boardmaker by Mayer-Johnson LLC. (1981-2005). *The Picture Communication Symbols*. All Rights Reserved Worldwide. Used with permission.

Figure 5.5. Sample Visual Schedule.*

*Used with permission from a classroom teacher (anonymous).

Figure 5.6. Sample Visual Schedule.*

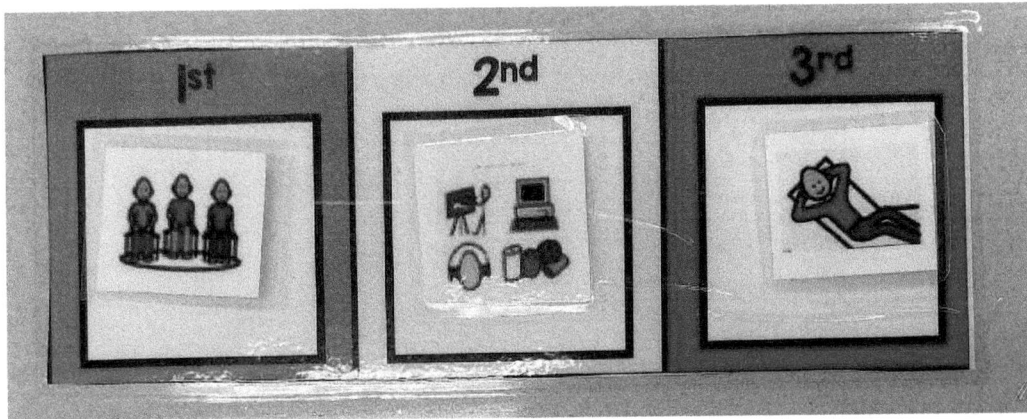

*Used with permission from a classroom teacher (anonymous).

Figure 5.7. Sample Visual Schedule.*

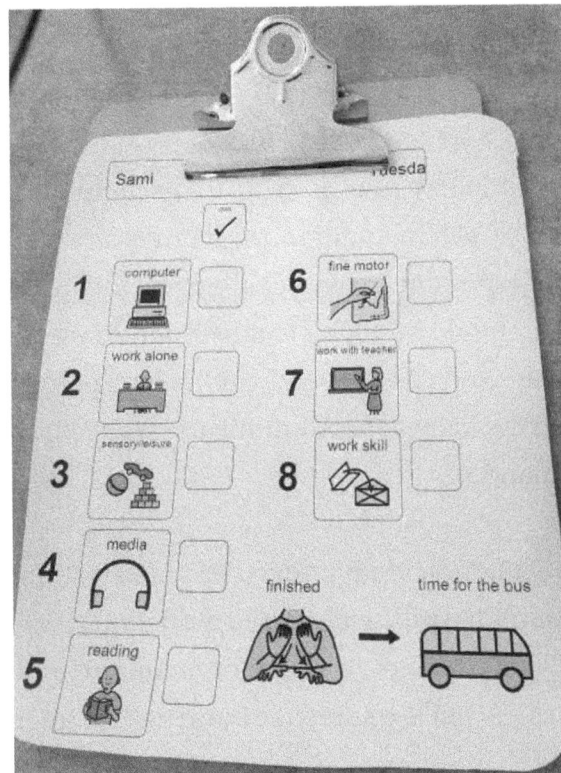

*Used with permission from a classroom teacher (anonymous).

Figure 5.8. Sample Visual Schedule.

Phyl's Schedule for Monday, Sept 5	
*Means that a change is happening.	
8:30-8:45	Morning Routine
8:45-9:00	Morning Work
9:00-10:15	Math
10:15-10:30	Bathroom Break
10:30-11:00	Recess
11:30-12:00	Specials: Music Art (circle one)
12:00-12:30	Independent Work* (Ms. Johnson is not here for PE. You will work in the classroom)
12:30-1:00	Lunch
1:00-1:30	Recess
1:30-1:45	Bathroom Break
1:45-2:30	Language Arts/Reading
2:30-3:00	Science Social Studies (circle one)
3:00-3:15	Pack to Go Home
Remember: Sometimes things change and that is okay!	

Posted Rules

The ability to understand and follow rules is critical to school and life success (Nuske et al., 2019; Silveira-Zaldivar et al., 2021). In addition, when rules are stated positively, taught, and used consistently, students experience fewer challenges, including meltdowns (as do their neuromajority peers). Rules should be stated in a manner that lets students concretely know what to do. For example, rules such as "Be safe" can be interpreted many ways. Instead, stating the rules as "Walk down the hallway" communicates what students are supposed to do in a very clear and concrete manner.

Stated positively, rules help an individual understand expectations and how to be safe. Students are more likely to respond to positively stated guidelines than to negatively stated ones. In addition, rules that only tell what not to do are often not helpful. For example, a rule that says, "No blurting out" does not tell the student how to get the attention of the teacher.

Table 5.1. Sample Rules.

- Listen to the teacher when they speak
- Ask for help when you need it
- Bring necessary materials to class: paper, pencil, book, assignment notebook
- If you want to touch other people's materials, ask first
- Listen and follow directions
- Raise your hand before speaking
- Keep hands, feet, and objects to yourself.

Routine Cards

According to Kathy Quill (personal communication, August 4, 2005), if educational professionals spend the first two weeks of the school year teaching routines, students would have fewer challenges. Research supports this: one of the elements of a well-run and emotionally supportive classroom is the use of routines (Meindl et al., 2020).

Routines should be created and taught for commonly occurring activities across the school day. A simple guideline: Any regularly occurring direction that begins with "Get ready to" or "Clean out/up" should have a routine card.

Table 5.2. Examples of Routines to Teach.

How and When To ...

- Obtain forgotten supplies
- Ask for help
- Sharpen your pencil
- Pass out papers
- Hand in work
- Make up missed work
- Organize materials so that they are accessible in a locker, backpack, desk, or cubby
- Clean out locker, backpack, desk, or cubby
- Line up for various activities
- Walk down the hall with others
- Get ready to move to another activity within the same environment
- Get ready to move to another activity in a different environment
- Get ready to start the day
- Get ready to go home
- Navigate lunchtime
- Ask to go to the bathroom

Figure 5.9. Sample Routine Card.

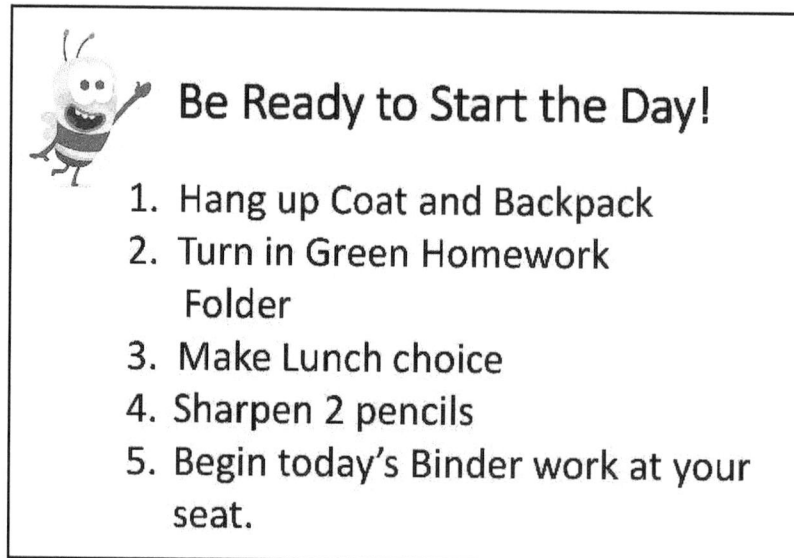

Be Ready to Start the Day!

1. Hang up Coat and Backpack
2. Turn in Green Homework Folder
3. Make Lunch choice
4. Sharpen 2 pencils
5. Begin today's Binder work at your seat.

Work Systems/To-Do Lists

A work system or to-do list gives the student a systematic way to complete work. An effective system visually conveys the work that needs to be completed, a clear finish point, and directions on how to move to the next activity. A work system helps support the student's organization skills by creating a routine of working left to right. In addition, the concept of "finished" is reinforced by having the student place completed work in a designated place, such as a finished tray or finished folder (MacDonald et al., 2018; Mesibov, 2015; Sreckovic, 2020).

Gigi's teacher set up a work system for her to use to complete her morning work. She has a hanging file box by her desk. Each morning, Gigi starts with File #1. She completes the work in File #1 and places it into the classroom's All Done Tray. She then moves to File #2, and so on, until all of her work is complete. On occasion, one of Gigi's folders may contain a direction for a task to complete, such as to go to the board and make a lunch choice. The last folder contains choices of independent activities (i.e., read a book, draw) that she can do until morning work time is over.

Figure 5.10. Sample Work System.*

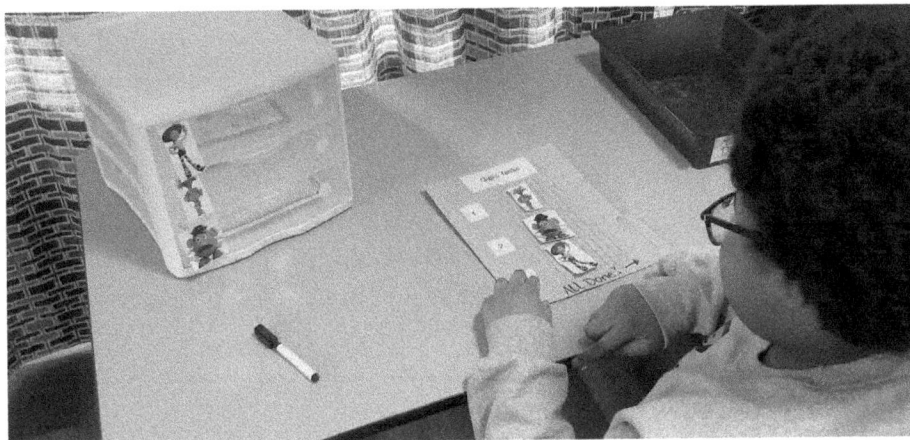

*Used with permission from a classroom teacher (anonymous).

A to-do list can use pictures, written words, or a combination of both. The student is taught to follow the list to complete the designated work. To-do lists may be used individually by students or as a support for a group of students, such as a to-do list for calendar time activities. Students can either use a picture matching system to move through the list or cross off an item after it is completed.

Change Card

Because it is difficult for the autism neurology to tolerate and predict change, it is important to provide advance notice when student expectations and the schedule do not match (Vermeulen, 2022). One way to prepare students in advance of changes is to use a change card—a visual cue that introduces an unexpected event. It may be a colored cue card, or feature a "surprise" icon, a "lightning bolt," a specific photograph, or a written word depending on the needs of the student.

Figure 5.11. Sample To-Do List.

*Used with permission from classroom teacher (anonymous).

Figure 5.12. Examples of Change Icons.

To teach this support, the selected change cue is first placed on top of the scheduled activity that will not be occurring. Then a visual of the new activity is placed on top of the change cue. When teaching the change concept, it is helpful to go to the visual schedule with the student, look at the change card together, and then assist with the transition to the new activity.

It is helpful to introduce change in a positive manner by first changing activities that are typically non-preferred by the student to activities that are preferred (e.g., changing a student's schedule from math to extra computer time). Then change can be introduced as a neutral event (e.g., changing math to language arts), and finally as something that may be difficult to accept (e.g., changing free time to work time). Systematically presenting change and novelty as a positive experience and providing a supportive routine around change can increase student flexibility and participation in new activities.

Make Another Choice Card

When teaching this type of visual support, it is important that the student understands that this is a helpful card. is support is designed to help them not get "in trouble"—to help them be successful. This simple two-sided card is subtly given to the student when they need redirection in the classroom, hallway, workplace, community, or home.

Figure 5.13. Make Another Choice Card.

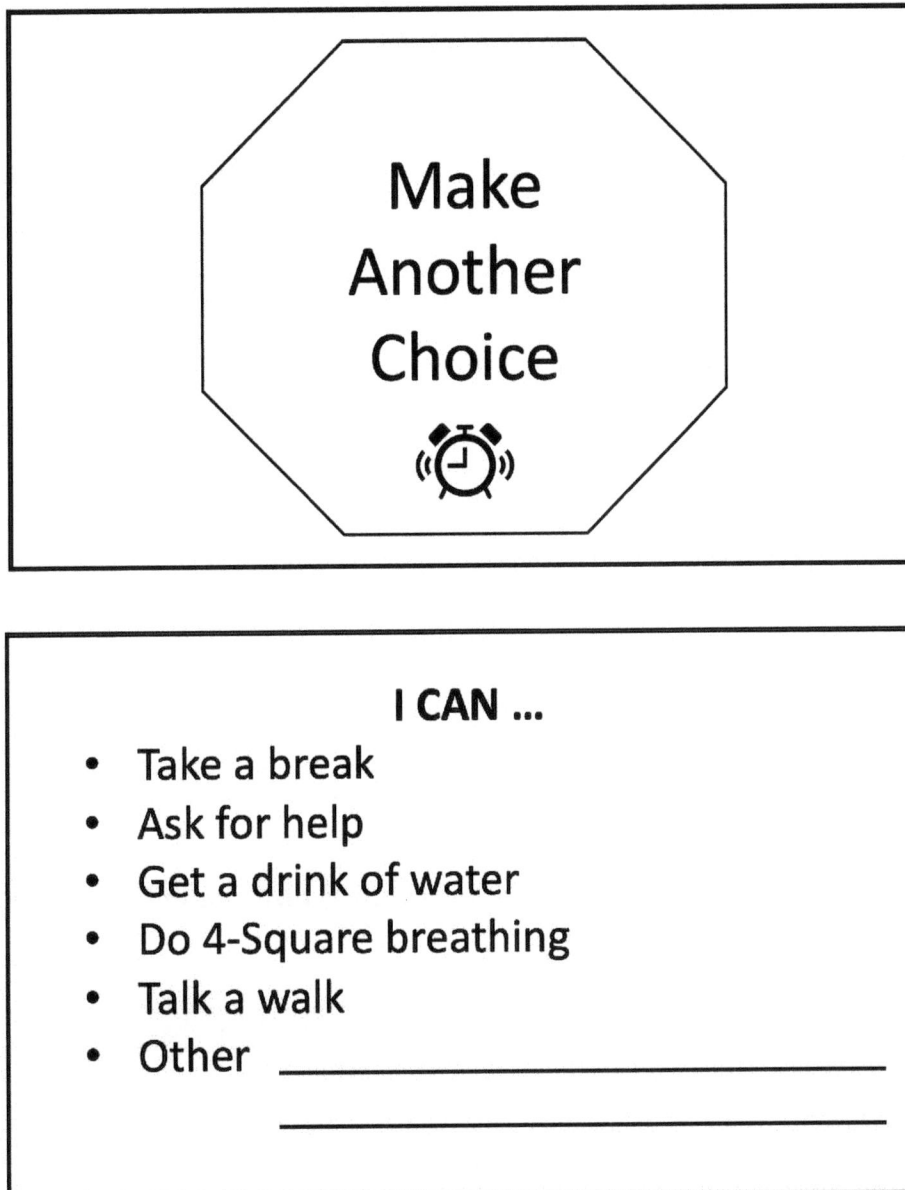

```
                    Make
                   Another
                    Choice
                     ⏰
```

```
                  I CAN ...
   •  Take a break
   •  Ask for help
   •  Get a drink of water
   •  Do 4-Square breathing
   •  Talk a walk
   •  Other _____
      _____
```

Signals/Cues

Signals and cues are subtle methods used to prompt students to attend and respond. In addition, they can provide students with time needed to process information presented verbally.

John and Mrs. Wilcox have agreed that when the class discusses the answers to assignments and Mrs. Wilcox would like to call on John, she will:

- Walk by John's desk and tap his hand while saying, "Now let's talk about the answer for question number three."
- Pause.
- Call on John to share his answer to question number three from last night's homework assignment.

Signals and cues come in a wide variety. For example, turning the lights off can signal that quieter voices are needed during group work. Music can also be an effective signal or cue. Transition time between activities can be a good time to use soft music or a Tibetan singing bowl to prepare students for a new activity. Playing a consistent clean-up time song can help keep young students focused on the expectation that it's time to put their toys and/or materials away.

Choice Boards

A verbal presentation of choices is often not effective for highly visual learners, such as autistic students. One way to make choice more visual is to create a choice board. A choice board typically identifies the reason for the choice—calming, recess, so forth—and the choice options using pictures, words, objects, or a combination thereof.

Choice boards aid and support the student's comprehension of a verbal message and indicate what options are available. Use of this type of visual display affords the student time to (a) process the possible choices, (b) consider a response, and (c) check choice options as frequently as needed

Figure 5.14. Sample Choice Board.

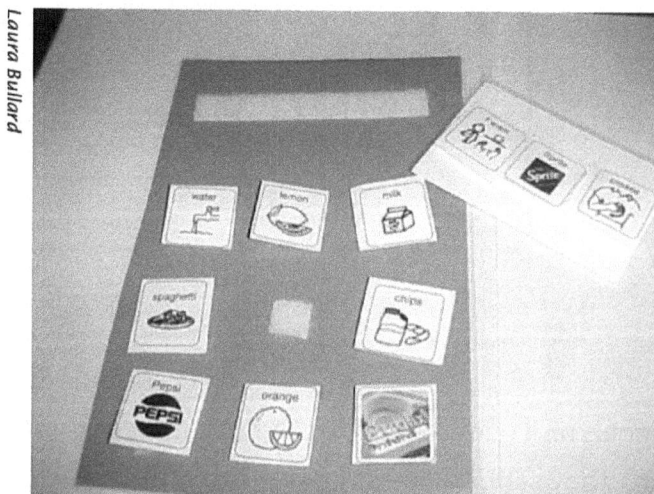

Laura Bullard

Boardmaker by Mayer-Johnson LLC. (1981-2005). *The Picture Communication Symbols*. All Rights Reserved Worldwide. Used with permission.

before making a decision (Deel et al., 2021). Because a choice board allows the student more control over an activity, its use often leads to a reduction in behavior challenges.

Choice boards are also helpful in communicating the acceptable options for a situation, such as available indoor recess activities or supports that can create a sense of calm. The following example shows a list of choice options the student can select from when feeling "stuck" on an assignment.

Figure 5.15. Sample Choice Board.

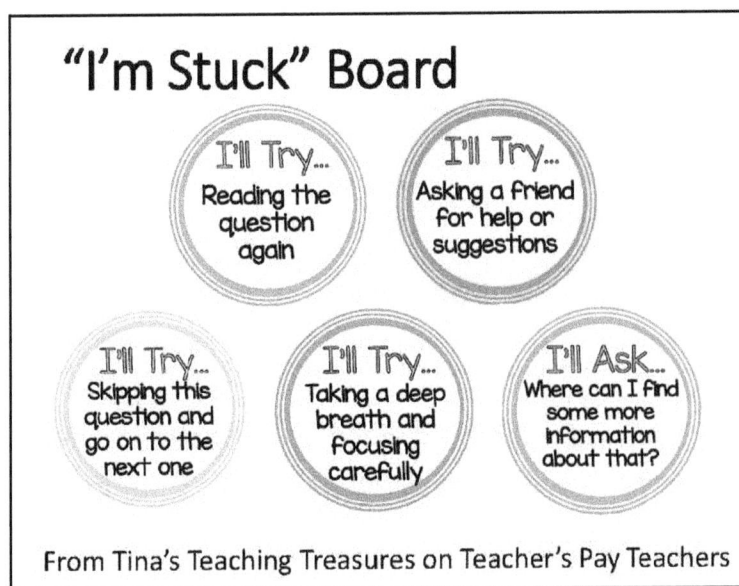

"I'm Stuck" Board

I'll Try...
Reading the question again

I'll Try...
Asking a friend for help or suggestions

I'll Try...
Skipping this question and go on to the next one

I'll Try...
Taking a deep breath and focusing carefully

I'll Ask...
Where can I find some more information about that?

From Tina's Teaching Treasures on Teacher's Pay Teachers

Problem-Solving Rubric

To address the problem-solving difficulties experienced by many autistics (Herrero & Lorenzo, 2020), Mataya and Owens (2013) created the Problem-Solving Rubric and Curriculum. Using these materials, educational professionals teach learners how to identify a problem and then use a special chart to decide how to approach the situation. Typically, solutions include the following options: (a) ignore it and move on, (b) let it bother you, or (c) seek help from an adult. As illustrated in the following, an advanced option is introduced later: (d) talk it out and compromise. Finally, there is a scale with pictures for nonreaders who have not yet learned to compromise and a version for students who need to remove themselves to calm before participating in problem solving.

Figure 5.16. Problem-Solving Rubric.

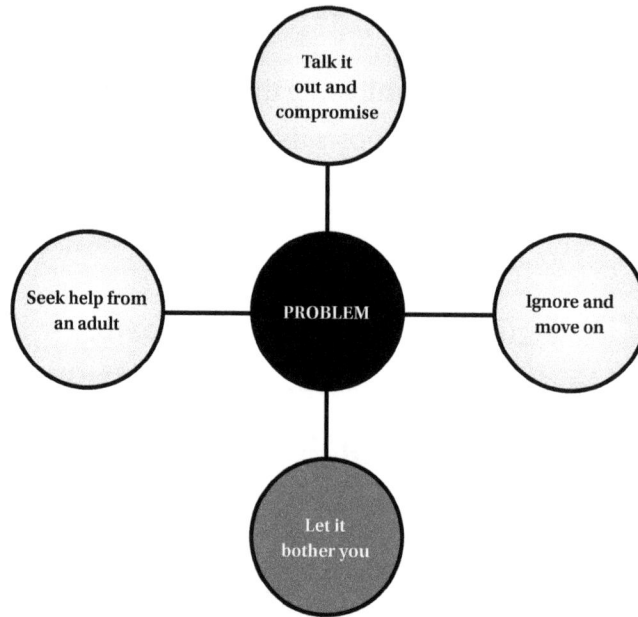

From Mataya, K., & Owens, P. (2013).

Figure 5.17. Problem-Solving Rubric for Nonreaders and/or Those Who Have Not Learned to Compromise.

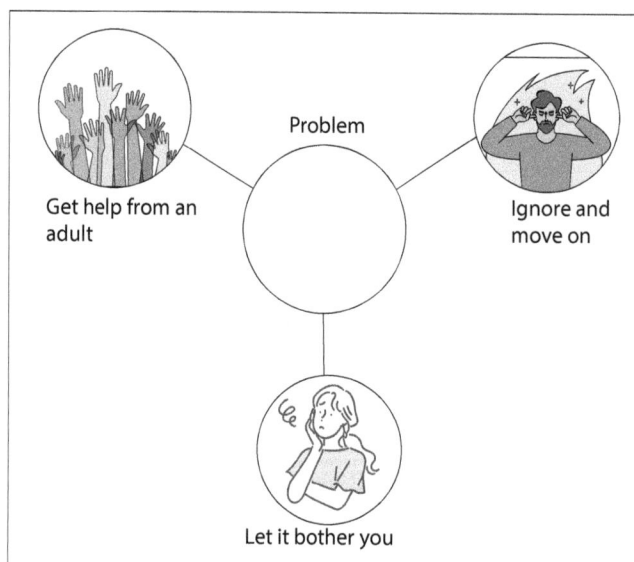

Modified from Mataya & Owens (2013).

Figure 5.18. Problem-Solving Rubric With Calming Activity.

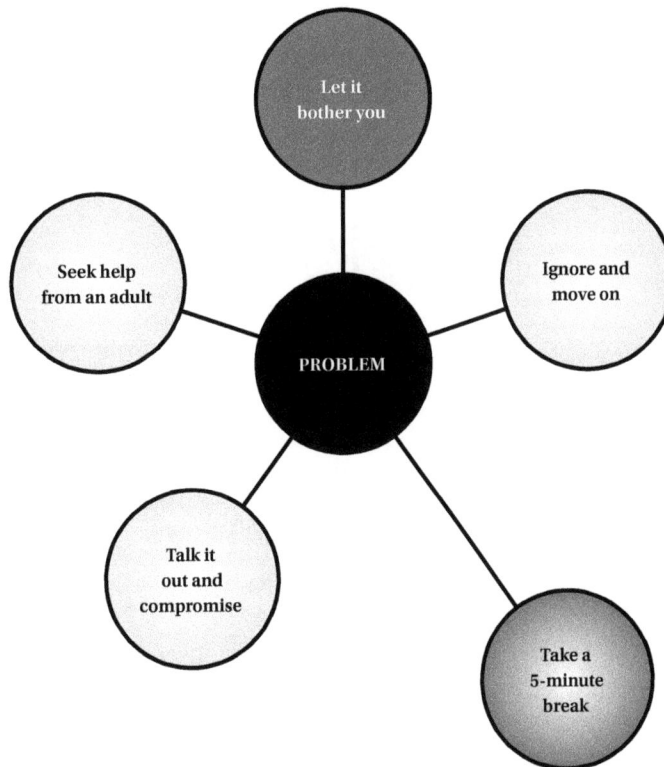

Modified from Mataya & Owens (2013).

Check-In Chart

As learners enter the classroom or some other environment, they can "sign in" on a posted chart to indicate how they are feeling. Students can Velcro™ their name or picture, or write their name on the chart next to the corresponding emotion. This allows the teacher, at a glance, to identify those who may need additional support as well as those whose "mood" may not match their self-report. These learners may need instruction and ongoing support on how to identify their feelings.

Sometimes students feel shy or uncomfortable about publicly sharing how they feel. When that's the case, a small set of emotion icons or a color strip on the student's desk can serve the same function. The teacher can take a moment to stop at the student's desk and the student can point to or mark how they are feeling. The teacher can also talk privately check in with the student. Some students may need additional support to identify how they feel. Often, a reference card that labels emotions with real-life examples is helpful.

Figure 5.19. Check-In Chart.

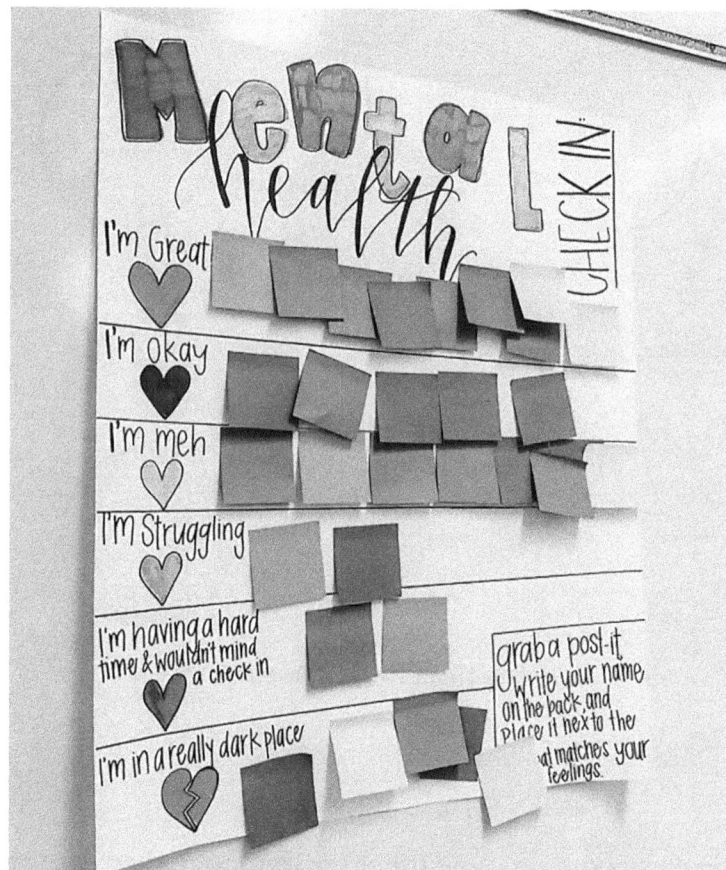

Retrieved from: https://www.boredpanda.com/students-health-check-board-erin-castillo/?utm_source=google&utm_medium=organic&utm_campaign=organic.

Boundary Markers

Boundary markers are visual cues posted throughout the classroom that guide students through physical spaces. Visual boundaries are all around us—cubicles in an office, cashier stations in grocery stores, booths in restaurants, lanes on a highway. Boundary markers not only help students understand their environment, but they often provide a feeling of safety and comfort (Young et al., 2019). With boundaries, learners know (a) where things begin and end, and (b) what they can access without supervision.

Boundaries can be created through furniture arrangement, labels, and color-coding. For example, a boundary for sitting could be a bean bag or pillow and tape on the floor can show where to line up or where to place a chair. Other boundary markers include rugs, bookcases, other furniture, or colored tape on the floor that represent boundaries of areas for play and study. The following are examples of boundary markers indicating where to do work and where to wait, as well as the demarcation of a calming area.

Figure 5.20. Sample Boundary Marker on a Desk.*

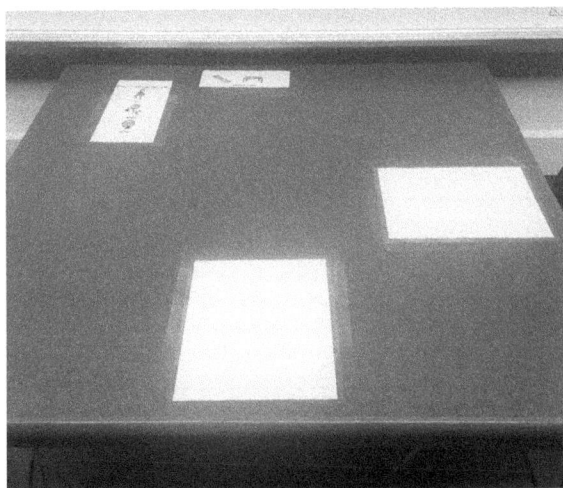

*Used with permission from a classroom teacher (anonymous).

Figure 5.21. Sample Boundary Marker Showing Where to Wait.*

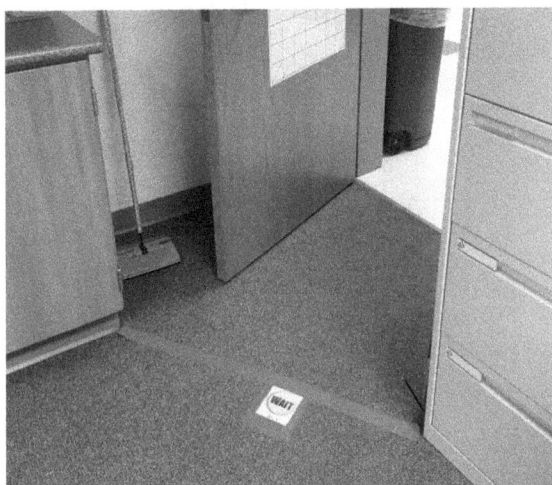

*Used with permission from a classroom teacher (anonymous).

Figure 5.22. Sample Boundary Marker of a Calming Area.*

*Used with permission from a classroom teacher (anonymous).

Because it can be difficult for autistic students to identify their need for and understand boundaries (Uherek-Bradecka, 2020), teaching them to understand (and eventually establish their own boundaries) is part of daily instruction.

Travel Card

The Travel Card is visual support especially for middle or high school youth to ensure that all teachers and the student's parents are attuned to the student's needs on a daily basis. Specifically, the Travel Card is designed to (a) increase productive behavior across environments; (b) facilitate collaboration between teachers; (c) increase teacher awareness of the student's academic, behavior, and social goals; and (d) improve home-school communication (Carpenter, 2001; Riden et al., 2020).

Figure 5.23. Sample Travel Card.

Travel Card
Rocky

Date _____

Key   +=Yes   0=No   NA=Not Applicable

	Did student follow class rules?	Did student participate in class?	Did student complete assignments?	Did student turn in homework?	Teacher's initials
Reading					
Science					
Social Studies					
Study Skills					
English					
Spanish					
Bonus Points	Went to nurse after getting off bus?			Has assignment book?	
Total	**+**	0			

Teacher Comments/Suggestions/Announcements:

The Travel Card lists four to five of the student's target behaviors across the top and the classes the student attends along the left-hand side. At the end of each period, the teacher indicates whether the student performed the desired behaviors by marking a + (yes), 0 (no), or NA (not applicable) on the card. At the end of the day, the positive notations are tallied and graphed, and points are accumulated toward a menu of reinforcers that have been jointly negotiated by the student and the adult responsible for the card. Rocky's Travel Card below shows the skills he is working on: (a) following class rules, (b) participating in class, (c) completing assignments, and (d) turning in homework.

Transition/Time Supports

Time is an abstract concept, and students with only an emerging sense of time can be surprised when it is time to end an activity. Consequently, some may benefit from an extra warning to help them prepare to stop what they are doing and ready themselves for the next activity.

Visual timers are helpful because they show the passage of time. A student who may not respond to the cue "5 more minutes" may better understand the cue "when the red is gone", it will be time to stop." Other cues include playing a clean-up song, using a buddy system, or using a countdown visual. To support a student's transition to another activity or location in the building, an object, such as a lunchbox for cafeteria, a book for the library, or a paintbrush for art class, can be given to the student to carry with them.

Figure 5.24. Transition/Time Support.

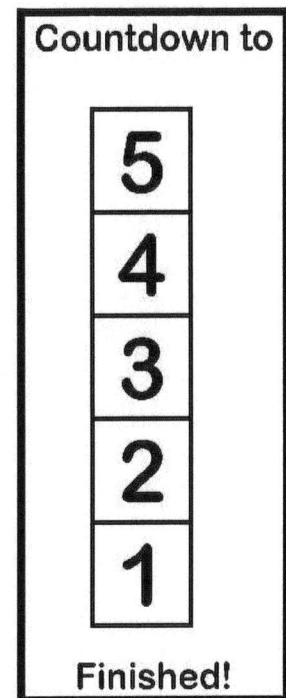

Academic Considerations

Most autistic students require some sort of instructional modifications. Modifications are diverse, ranging from altering the way in which materials are presented to modifying how students are to indicate competence of academic concepts. The following EBP have been found particularly useful when programming for autistic students.

Graphic Organizers

Graphic organizers, such as semantic maps, Venn diagrams, outlines, and compare/contrast charts, provide visual, holistic representations of facts and concepts and their relationships within an organized framework. That is, these strategies arrange key terms to show their relationship to each other, presenting abstract or implicit information in a concrete manner. They are particularly useful with content-area material such as social studies, science, and so on, or tasks related to areas such as cooking, interviewing, and dating.

Graphic organizers often enhance the learning of autistics because:
- They are visual—a frequent area of strength.
- They are static; they remain consistent and constant.
- They allow for processing time; the individual can reflect on the material at their own pace.
- They are concrete and are more easily understood than a verbal-only presentation.

The following are examples of graphic organizers that (a) help an employee understand the hidden meaning of what their boss said, (b) describe the water cycle, and (c) show the characteristics of a dog, respectively.

Figure 5.25. Graphic Organizer of the Hidden Meaning of Supervisor's Comments.

Friendly Thins My Boss Says	Purely Friendly Comment	Comment With Hidden Meaning	Hidden Meaning
When you have time, please ...		X	You have no choice but to do whatever you are asked.
Good morning.	X		
It would be great if you could ...		X	This is usually a directive, meaning you will do whatever it is.

Myles et al. (2013).

Figure 5.26. Graphic Organizer That Explains the Water Cycle.

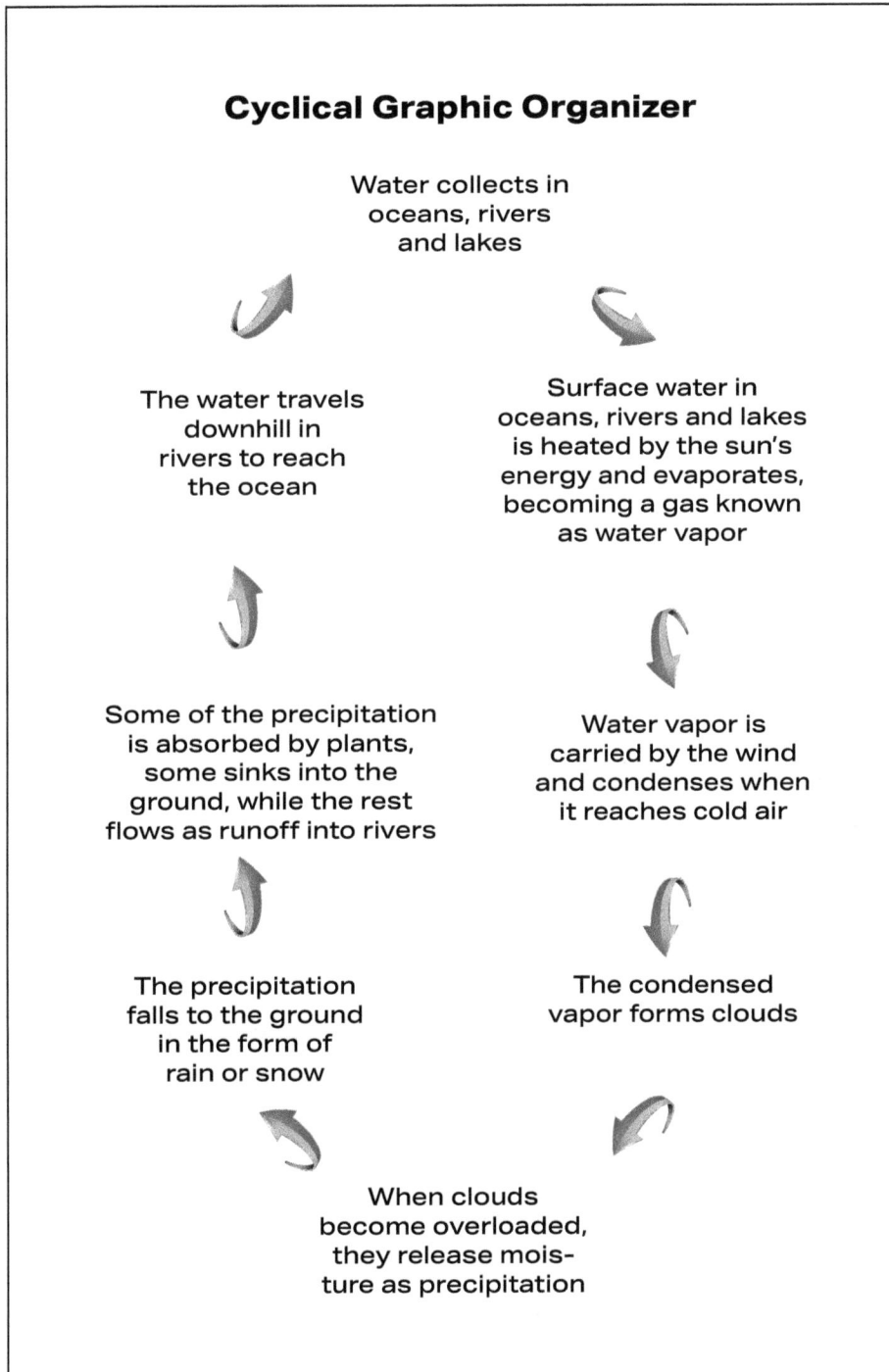

Cyclical Graphic Organizer

Water collects in
oceans, rivers
and lakes

The water travels
downhill in
rivers to reach
the ocean

Surface water in
oceans, rivers and lakes
is heated by the sun's
energy and evaporates,
becoming a gas known
as water vapor

Some of the precipitation
is absorbed by plants,
some sinks into the
ground, while the rest
flows as runoff into rivers

Water vapor is
carried by the wind
and condenses when
it reaches cold air

The precipitation
falls to the ground
in the form of
rain or snow

The condensed
vapor forms clouds

When clouds
become overloaded,
they release mois-
ture as precipitation

Figure 5.27. Graphic Organizer of the Characteristics of a Dog.

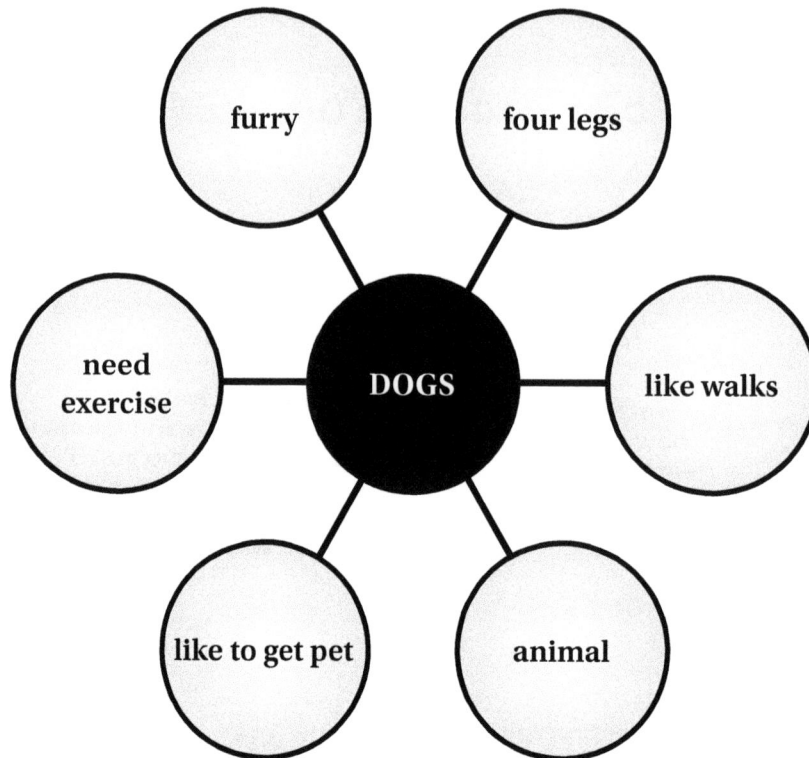

furry

four legs

need exercise

DOGS

like walks

like to get pet

animal

Handwriting Modifications

Many autistic students have challenges with handwriting, which prevent them from adequately expressing in writing what they know (Handle et al., 2022). The rule of thumb for identifying student competence has been stated as follows: "If you wish to know what an autistic student knows, do not ask them to write it down. A pencil in the hand typically means a concentration on the task of letter formation rather than the knowledge that the student needs to impart."

Alternatives to having the student write responses include (a) responding orally, (b) typing out answers, (c) answering questions in a true/false or multiple-choice format instead of an essay format, (d) reading answers into a recorder, (e) using a scribe, or (f) using speech-to-text technology. In addition, occupational therapists can suggest accommodations for students who experience problems with handwriting.

Mrs. Brewer gave Josh cards with addition problems on them. Each card contained 3 answer choices. Josh clipped a small clothespin on the correct answer for each card.

Figure 5.28. Josh's Math Work.

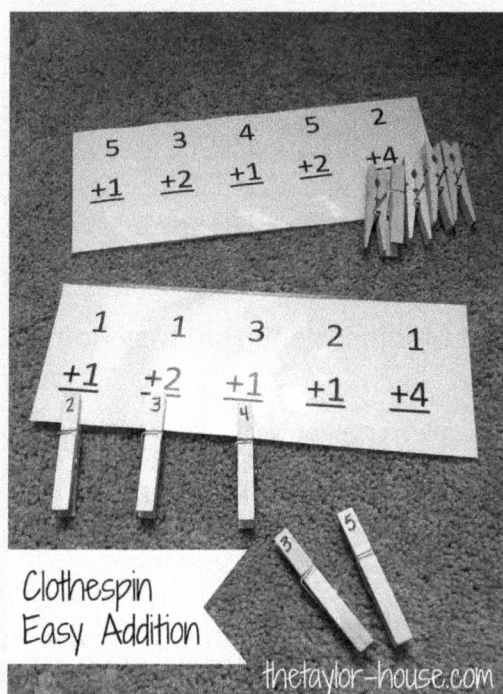

Retrieved from https://evatnvftezo.exactdn.com/wp-content/uploads/2013/11/
Clothespin-Easy-Addition-Image-4.jpg?strip=all&lossy=1&w=2560&ssl=1.

Assignment and Test Modifications

Similar to all other modifications, assignment and test modifications should match the student's needs. For example, a student who works more slowly and methodically than peers may be allowed to complete fewer items. A student with handwriting issues may be allowed to do assignments or take tests verbally.

Many ways other than traditional assignment and test formats exist to assess students' knowledge. Examples include collages, crossword puzzles, interviews, posters, video presentations, and so on.

Table 5.3. Alternatives to Traditional Assignments and Tests.

Comic strip	Map
Graph or chart	Comic book
Riddles	Newspaper story
Scroll	Mural
Song or dance	Poem
Telegram	Timeline
Radio broadcast	Letter
Webcast	Banner
Webpage	Game

Table 5.4. Sample Test Modifications That May Benefit Autistic Students.

Give a copy of the test beforehand	Allow responses to be drawn
Provide a practice test	Accept cursive handwriting or print
Test state/school objectives only	Have student tape record responses
Read test to the student	Give test in a quiet area
Allow the student to respond orally	Have the student rephrase incomplete answers
Use untimed tests	Allow the student to write on the test
Reduce number of items on the test	Avoid "bubble" tests that require answers to be transferred to a separate sheet of paper
Work a sample problem with the student	Allow the student to keyboard responses
Use a multiple-choice instead of essay format	Grade content, not mechanics

Note-Taking Strategies

Many autistic students have difficulty when required to take notes in class. Often motor problems preclude them from getting important content onto paper in a timely manner. In addition, some students have difficulty listening and writing at the same time. Thus, note-taking alternatives are needed, such as those below.

Table 5.5. Note-Taking Alternatives.

- A teacher-developed complete outline that includes main ideas and supporting details
- A teacher-developed skeletal outline that includes the main ideas and provides spaces for the student to fill in supporting details as they are discussed in class
- A peer-constructed outline developed by a fellow student
- Outlining software that allows the computer-adept student to take notes on main ideas and details

As a prerequisite for teaching note-taking skills, teachers must first determine whether the student knows how to identify main ideas and supporting details. This is important, because quite often these skills are not directly taught, but assumed to be in place when students reach middle school.

Leah had struggled to recognize main ideas and supporting details in social studies during the first nine weeks. When her teacher, Mr. Hardesty, decided to reintroduce these concepts to Leah using materials on her special interest, horses, she easily learned to identify main ideas and details.

Once this step has been accomplished, students can begin the progression from using a teacher-developed complete outline to a skeletal outline. As mastery occurs, students gradually take more and more responsibility for outlining. The teacher facilitates this growing independence by teaching the student to recognize direct verbal cues that signal information that is important for the student to memorize and understand, such as in the examples below.

Mrs. Johnson taught Sam that when she said, "This is important," the item that followed was going to be on the weekly quiz.

Table 5.6. Sample Phrases That Indicate That Information Is Important.

These Mean IMPORTANT!
They will probably be on a test or assignment!
• "This is important."
• "You need to remember ..."
• "The first main idea ..."
• "This is what started ..."
• "Remember these ..."
• "You need to understand ..."
• "Write this down."
• "This will be on the test."

Priming

Priming refers to the act of preparing the student for an activity that they will be expected to complete in the near future. Priming is strictly a preview of activities and an overview of assignments or schedule changes—it is not a time to teach academic content. During priming, the learning is presented with a visual schedule so that the structure of the day is understood. The student may also be shown the actual materials that will be used in class, such as a worksheet or outline for a group project, so they can predict what will likely happen in each upcoming class (Canon et al., 2021; Koegel et al., 2003).

Given an opportunity to preview activities before they will occur, the learner is often less likely to experience anxiety about what lies ahead. With anxiety and stress at a minimum they can focus their efforts on successfully completing assignments and other activities.

Priming should occur close to when the target activity will occur. It may occur on the day before an activity, the morning of the activity, the class period before, or even at the beginning of the class period during which the activity will be completed. It can occur in school or at home. Anyone can prime the student—a teacher, a parent, or peer. Priming should occur in short, concise time periods in an environment that is relaxing for the student (Canon et al., 2021; Koegel et al., 2003).

Task Cards

Task cards present information that often would typically be presented only verbally, such as instructions, or information that would not be presented at all because it is assumed knowledge, such as the steps for handing in homework. The task card is concrete and provides a reference point for the student. They may include classroom rules, teacher expectations, or test reminders.

Task cards can also be used to break down tasks, such as dividing assignments into their component parts, and set deadlines for their completion. They may be written in a variety of formats, from checklists to numbered lists of steps to be taken to complete a task.

Figure 5.29. Sample Task Cards.

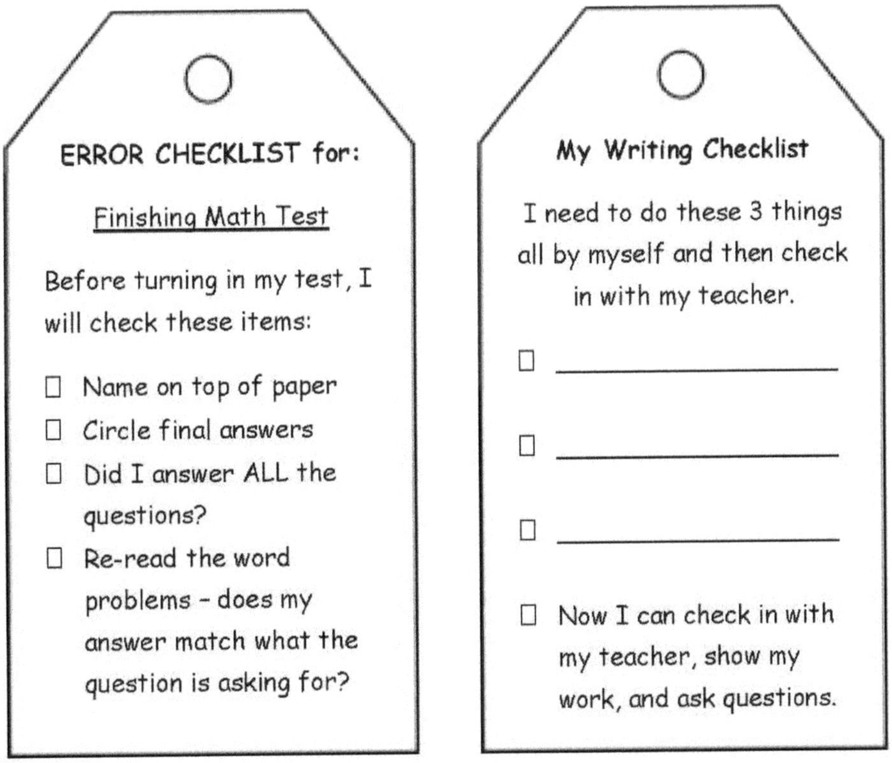

ERROR CHECKLIST for:

Finishing Math Test

Before turning in my test, I will check these items:

☐ Name on top of paper
☐ Circle final answers
☐ Did I answer ALL the questions?
☐ Re-read the word problems – does my answer match what the question is asking for?

My Writing Checklist

I need to do these 3 things all by myself and then check in with my teacher.

☐ _____
☐ _____
☐ _____

☐ Now I can check in with my teacher, show my work, and ask questions.

*Used with permission from a classroom teacher (anonymous).

Jack was working on a poster project on the history of Lego. His teacher provided a template that listed the components to include and how to present them on the poster. Jack's teacher worked with him to create a list of materials he needed. Jack then wrote all of the components he needed to include on his poster and set dates for when each part had to be completed.

Color Coding/Highlighting

The use of color can draw attention to an important concept. For example, if a student is having difficulty switching between addition and subtraction, highlighting the operation sign can help draw the student's eye to slow down and identify the needed operation. Directions and key vocabulary words can be highlighted, especially if there is a significant amount of text on a page.

When teaching a student to answer WH-questions based on a text, for example, it can be helpful to highlight the WH-question, such as WHO, and then highlight the sentence in the text where the answer can be found in the same color. When first teaching the strategy, the teacher may color code/highlight with the student. As the student learns the strategy, they can take additional ownership and highlight independently, as appropriate.

Figure 5.30. Highlight Text for Reading Comprehension.

Highlighting text for Reading Comprehension

On Saturday, Jack and Jill went up the hill to fill up a bucket of water. Jack tripped on a rock and fell down. He started to roll down the hill. When Jill tried to help him, she started to roll down the hill too. Jack and Jill decided to go home. They will try again tomorrow.

• Where did Jack and Jill go on Saturday?

• Why did Jill start to roll down the hill?

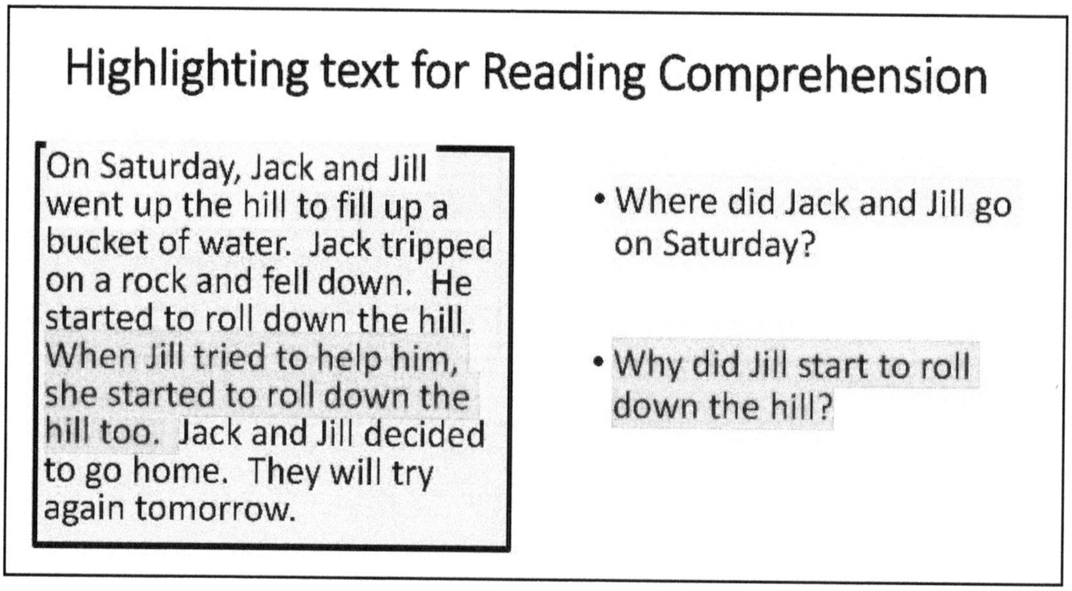

Vocabulary Supports

Vocabulary supports can be useful for a student who has challenges finding words. Examples include:

- A word bank of vocabulary to include while writing
- A visual support with science vocabulary and definitions that the student can reference when reading an article
- A word bank card to use for fill-in-the blank activities and tests
- A word wall that contains words for an activity and/or tests is accessible to all students

Vocabulary supports can also be useful when completing an activity, such as a science experiment that requires a variety of steps, including defining a hypothesis, observation, data, and conclusion. A student may benefit from a reference card with these steps defined, explained, and/or an example.

When it was time to write a short story in class, Emma used her list of emotion vocabulary to help her choose words that would invoke the intensity of the emotion the character was feeling, such as fine or elated.

Summary

Structure/modifications are essential components of the CAPS model. Environmental and academic supports can help students across the spectrum learn, minimize behavioral challenges, and show their many talents.

Bibliography

Canon, Jonathan, Amanda M. O'Brien, Lindsay Bungert, and Pawan Sinha. "Prediction in Autism Spectrum Disorder: A Systematic Review of Empirical Evidence." *Autism Research* 14, no. 4 (2021): 604-630.

Carpenter, L. "The Travel Card." In B. S. Myles & D. Adreon (Eds.), *Asperger Syndrome and Adolescence: Practical Solutions for School Success* (pp. 92-96). AAPC Publishing (2001).

Carrington, Suzanne, Beth Saggers, Amanda Webster, Keely Harper-Hill, and Julie Nickerson. "What Universal Design for Learning Principles, Guidelines, and Checkpoints are Evident in Educators' Descriptions of their Practice When Supporting Students on the Autism Spectrum?." *International Journal of Educational Research* 102 (2020): 101583.

Deel, Nicole M., Matthew T. Brodhead, Jessica S. Akers, Allison N. White, and David Ray G. Miranda. "Teaching Choice-Making within Activity Schedules to Children With Autism." *Behavioral Interventions* 36, no. 4 (2021): 731-744.

Handle, Henriette C., Marcus Feldin, and Artur Pilacinski. "Handwriting in Autism Spectrum Disorder: A Literature Review." *Neuroscience* 3, no. 4 (2022): 558-565.

Herrero, Jorge Fernández, and Gonzalo Lorenzo. "An Immersive Virtual Reality Educational Intervention on People With Autism Spectrum Disorders (ASD) for the Development of Communication Skills and Problem Solving." *Education and Information Technologies* 25 (2020): 1689-1722.

Koegel, Lynn Kern, Robert L. Koegel, William Frea, and Israel Green-Hopkins. "Priming as a Method of Coordinating Educational Services for Students With Autism." *Language Speech and Hearing Services in the School* 35, no. 3 (2003) 228-235.

Kreibich, Shelley R., Mo Chen, and Joe Reichle. "Teaching a Child with Autism to Request Breaks While Concurrently Increasing Task Engagement." *Language, Speech, and Hearing Services in Schools* 46, no. 3 (2015): 256-265.

Long, Sasha. "Seven Steps for Setting up a stellar Autism Classroom: Classroom Structure." (n.d.). Accessed February 25, 2024 from https://theautismhelper.com/steps-setting-stellar-autism-classroom-classroom-structure/#:~:text=The%20 structure%20of%20your%20classroom,break%20time%2C%20etc.).

Macdonald, Libby, David Trembath, Jill Ashburner, Debra Costley, and Deb Keen. "The Use of Visual Schedules and Work Systems to Increase the On-Task Behavior of Students on the Autism Spectrum in Mainstream Classrooms." *Journal of Research in Special Educational Needs* 18, no. 4 (2018): 254-266.

Mataya, Kerry, and Penny Owens. *Successful Problem-Solving for High-Functioning Students with Autism Spectrum Disorder*. Future Horizons (2012).

Meindl, James N., Diana Delgado, and Laura B. Casey. "Increasing Engagement in Students with Autism in Inclusion Classrooms." *Children and Youth Services Review* 111 (2020): 104854.

Mesibov, Gary, Marie Howley, and Signe Naftel. "Accessing the Curriculum for Learners with Autism Spectrum Disorders: Using the TEACCH Programme to Help Inclusion." Routledge (2015).

Nuske, Heather Joy, Elizabeth McGhee Hassrick, Briana Bronstein, Lindsay Hauptman, Courtney Aponte, Lynne Levato, Aubyn Stahmer et al. "Broken Bridges—New School Transitions for Students With Autism Spectrum Disorder: A Systematic Review on Difficulties and Strategies for Success." *Autism* 23, no. 2 (2019): 306-325.

Riden, Benjamin S., Jonté C. Taylor, Sal Ruiz, David L. Lee, and Mary Catherine Scheeler. "Using a Daily Report Card to Reduce Off-Task Behaviors for a Student with Autism Spectrum Disorder." *Journal of Behavioral Education* 30 (2021): 397-416.

Rutherford, Marion, Julie Baxter, Zoe Grayson, Lorna Johnston, and Anne O'Hare. "Visual Supports at Home and in the Community for Individuals with Autism Spectrum Disorders: A Scoping Review." *Autism* 24, no. 2 (2020): 447-469.

Silveira-Zaldivar, Tracey, Kamil Ö, and Gül Özerk. "Developing Social Skills and Social Competence in Children with Autism." *International Electronic Journal of Elementary Education* 13, no. 3 (2021): 341-363.

Sreckovic, Melissa A., Kara A. Hume, and Tara E. Regan. "Use of Work Systems to Increase the Independence of Adolescents with Autism Spectrum Disorder." *Career Development and Transition for Exceptional Individuals* 43, no. 4 (2020): 240-256.

Steinbrenner, Jessica R., Kara Hume, Samuel L. Odom, Kristi L. Morin, Sallie W. Nowell, Brianne Tomaszewski, Susan Szendrey, Nancy S. McIntyre, Serife Yücesoy-Özkan, and Melissa N. Savage. "Evidence-Based Practices for Children, Youth, and Young Adults with Autism." FPG Child Development Institute (2020).

TEACCH Staff. "Structured Teaching." (n.d.). Accessed January 21, 2024 from https://teacch.com/structured-teaching-teacch-staff/.

Uherek-Bradecka, B. "Classroom Design for Children with an Autism Spectrum Disorder." IOP Conference Series: Materials Science and Engineering (Vol. 960, No. 2, p. 022100). IOP, 2020.

Vermeulen, Peter. *Autism and the Predictive Brain: Absolute Thinking in a Relative World.* Future Horizons (2022).

Young, Nicholas B. Angela C., Fain, and Teresa A. Citro. *Creating Compassionate Classrooms: Understanding the Continuum of Disabilities and Effective Educational Interventions.* Vernon Press (2019).

Zwilling, Moti, and Beni R. Levy. "How Well Environmental Design is and Can be Suited to People With Autism Spectrum Disorder (ASD): A Natural Language Processing Analysis." *International Journal of Environmental Research and Public Health* 19, no. 9 (2022): 5037.

CHAPTER 6

Reinforcement

Joyce Anderson Downing, PhD

What is reinforcement? When and how do we use it? Teachers and parents often use the term "reinforcement" informally, describing a variety of ways to reward children for completing their assigned tasks or chores. This chapter will discuss how to identify and use reinforcement effectively as part of the Comprehensive Autism Planning System (CAPS).

Definition of Reinforcement

Based in the well-researched fields of experimental analysis of behavior (EAB) and applied behavior analysis (ABA; cf. Cooper et al., 2019), reinforcement is more than just a reward; it is a powerful tool for teaching, strengthening, and maintaining desirable academic, communicative, and social behaviors. For the purposes of this book, reinforcement involves delivering a specific consequence when a student demonstrates a target behavior to increase the likelihood that the behavior will occur again when requested.

Selecting Reinforcers

Natural environments provide a variety of potential reinforcers, including the approval of peers and adults, access to preferred activities or objects, and opportunities to make choices.

"Commonly used classroom reinforcement strategies include verbal praise, approving gestures (nods, smiles, winks, thumbs-up), positive physical touch (pat on shoulder, high-five), individual feedback and recognition, positive individual attention, and individual and group tangibles" (Downing, 2007).

As part of CAPS, reinforcers must be selected carefully, based on the student's needs, interests, and characteristics. For example, Billy may find a high-five for completing his work very reinforcing, but for Adrienne, who is preoccupied with germs and avoids casual physical contact, a high-five would likely have an adverse effect.

A reinforcer can be positive (giving a reward) or negative (taking away or reducing something aversive). In the previous example, Billy's teacher has determined that he finds a high-five to be a positive reinforcer for work completion; that is, using social praise and a high-five increases the likelihood that Billy will continue to complete his work in the future. Adrienne struggles to complete written assignments and avoids physical contact. Based on observation, Adrienne's teacher chooses both a positive and a negative reinforcer to address her work completion. If Adrienne completes 8 out of 10 tasks, she can skip the last two items (taking away something she does not like) and choose a quiet individual activity for five minutes (providing a short break with a preferred activity).

Reinforcers can be social, or tangible, or part of a generalized system that is used for the entire class. Regardless of type, it must be something the student considers rewarding and is willing to work for. The reinforcer should be selected in advance by student choice, and delivered as soon as the student has demonstrated the requested behavior (Scheithauer et al., 2022).

While some students will work for the same reinforcer every day, most prefer to make choices from a range of options. A reinforcer menu for individual students or groups can be developed in a variety of informal ways, including:
- Observing the student's preferences and choices in natural settings,
- Asking the student what they would like to work for
- Interviewing parents or teachers to determine what has worked in the past
- Conducting formal or informal assessments using an assortment of potential reinforcers to determine student preferences (cf. DeLeon & Iwata, 1996; Fernandez et al., 2022)

Table 6.1. Potential Reinforcers by Category.

Social/Leisure/Activity	Tangible/Edible	Generalized/Token System*
• Take a break • Play a game or engage in a physical activity (running, shooting hoops) • Use an iPad or preferred electronic device • Spend time with a preferred individual • Talk about or research a favorite topic/special interest • Earn 5-minute break for the whole class • Skip one assignment • Obtain a high-status privilege (feed the goldfish for the day)	• Healthy snack or beverage (e.g., grapes, raisins, fruit jerky, popcorn, cereal) • "Cool" school supplies (e.g., superhero eraser, animal pencil toppers, glitter pens) • Small/mini toy or fidget • Baseball card, gaming, or other hobby trading card • Inexpensive jewelry, temporary tattoos, light sticks • Certificates, ribbons, badges, stickers • Access to music, video games, technology	• Point sheets • Play money or scrip • Stars on a chart • Stickers • Tickets, coupons • Poker chips • Marbles in a jar to earn class pizza party

* In a token system, the tokens are placeholders for the actual reinforcers, which are selected from a token store or a menu of items.

Another way to select reinforcers, as well as to identify replacement behaviors (i.e., desired behaviors to replace undesirable ones), is to consider the function of the student's problem behavior. Most behaviors are instrumental; that is, they represent an attempt to either "get" or "get out of" something. For example, students may attempt to secure the attention of their peers or adults, obtain a tangible object, or gain access to a desired activity. They may refuse to engage in activities they find stressful or difficult, or they may avoid interaction with specific individuals.

For students with limited communication skills, including those who are autistic who in times of stress have a limited ability to communicate, behavior may be an effort to address their needs and wants. In some cases, problem behavior is also related to sensory processing, as students attempt to manage their sensory input (for further information, see Chapter 7: Sensory/ Regulation).

The role of the educational team is to develop a hypothesis for why a challenging behavior occurs based on patterns of behavior. The hypothesis can be used to structure an effective learning environment and select replacement behaviors and reinforcers that address the function—or purpose—of the behavior in more acceptable ways.

Yao routinely fell to the floor during science class. To determine the reason for this behavior, the autism specialist, Ms. Teen, observed Yao during science class as well as during other classes. A careful analysis of the environment led her to believe that his behavior might be related to the teacher writing on the whiteboard with a squeaky marker. Ms. Teen met with the team, and they hypothesized that the sound of the marker on the board might be discomforting to Yao. The occupational therapist (OT) suggested providing Yao with earplugs during the times the teacher wrote on the board; the teacher suggested that she could try to do all writing on the board before class began. Both strategies were evaluated and were determined to be effective, with the former being most consistently effective.

Yao was also regularly disruptive on the school bus, leaving his seat and yelling at other students to be quiet. The team thought it was likely that Yao's bus behavior was also related to auditory stimuli and provided him with an iPod with headphones preloaded with Yao's chosen playlist. Yao happily listened to his music on the bus and no longer exhibited the behavior that had previously disrupted both his learning and socialization.

In this example, the team's primary focus was on designing an environment in which Yao could be successful. They were able to eliminate most of the problem behaviors in the classroom and on the bus by a combination of techniques that reinforced appropriate behaviors. The teacher modified her own behavior and avoided the squeaky marker noises (negative reinforcement), Yao could use his earplugs any time noise was bothering him (negative reinforcement), and use of the iPod provided a pleasant alternative to the noises on the bus (positive reinforcement).

Many reinforcers are available for students whose behavior appears to represent an effort to gain sensory input, including the following.

Table 6.2. Potential Sensory Reinforcers.

Auditory	Visual	Olfactory
• Bells, chimes • Recorded music • Animal sounds • Running or bubbling water (e.g., fountain, fish tank) • Whistles, flutes, rain sticks, musical instruments • White noise	• Battery-operated or wind-up toys • Nature videos • Animated computer screensavers • Kaleidoscopes, prisms, mirrors • Colorful pinwheels • Adjust lights (brighter, dimmer, colored)	• Potpourri • Hand lotion • Body oil • Perfume • Air freshener • Scented crayons or markers • Scented play dough • Scratch and sniff stickers
Taste/Oral Motor	**Tactile**	**Proprioception/Vestibular**
• Crunchy foods • Chewy snacks or gum • Sweet or sour snacks or liquids • Suckers • Blowing bubbles, whistles, straws, balloons	• Tickles and bear hugs • Petting an animal • Holding something cold or warm • Stroking or rubbing skin with textured materials (e.g., fur, chenille, baby hairbrush) • Playing with sand, water, playdoh, or slime	• Rocking chair • Sit-and-SpinTM • Swing • Trampoline, pogo stick • Structured exercise (weights, bicycle, aerobics) • Grip-strengthening tools (stress balls, etc.)

For a more detailed listing of potential sensory reinforcers by function, see Helpful Handy Hints: Finding Reinforcers (© 2005 Pyramid Educational Consultants UK Ltd and Pyramid Educational Consultants) a downloadable form available at https://pecsusa.com/download/PECSDATAFORMCD-USA.zipf

Special Interests: Reinforcers of High Interest

Most people have some sort of hobby, interest, or area of expertise. So do autistic people. The interests of autistic people, often referred to as "circumscribed or restricted interests," can be very intense and sometimes all-consuming. They can include common topics, such as video games and movies, or unique subjects, such as solar energy and pythons. (Kim et al., 2024).

Up to 90% of autistics develop deep and intense interests compared to 30% of their neuromajority peers. And these interests may occur as early as 1 to 2 years of age and last throughout the lifespan, often increasing in adulthood. Interests are so important to autistic children and adults that they spend approximately three hours per day or 21 hours per week with their special interests (Nowell, 2020).

Boyd et al. (2007) identified four major characteristics of special interests. The person
- Accumulates large amounts of information
- Would rather engage in the interest over almost all other activities
- Has difficulty being redirected from physically interacting with or conversing about the interest
- Typically has a lengthy fascination with the interest

While special interests vary across autistics, topics are generally centered on specific categories (Nowell, 2020).

Figure 6.1. Categories of Special Interests.

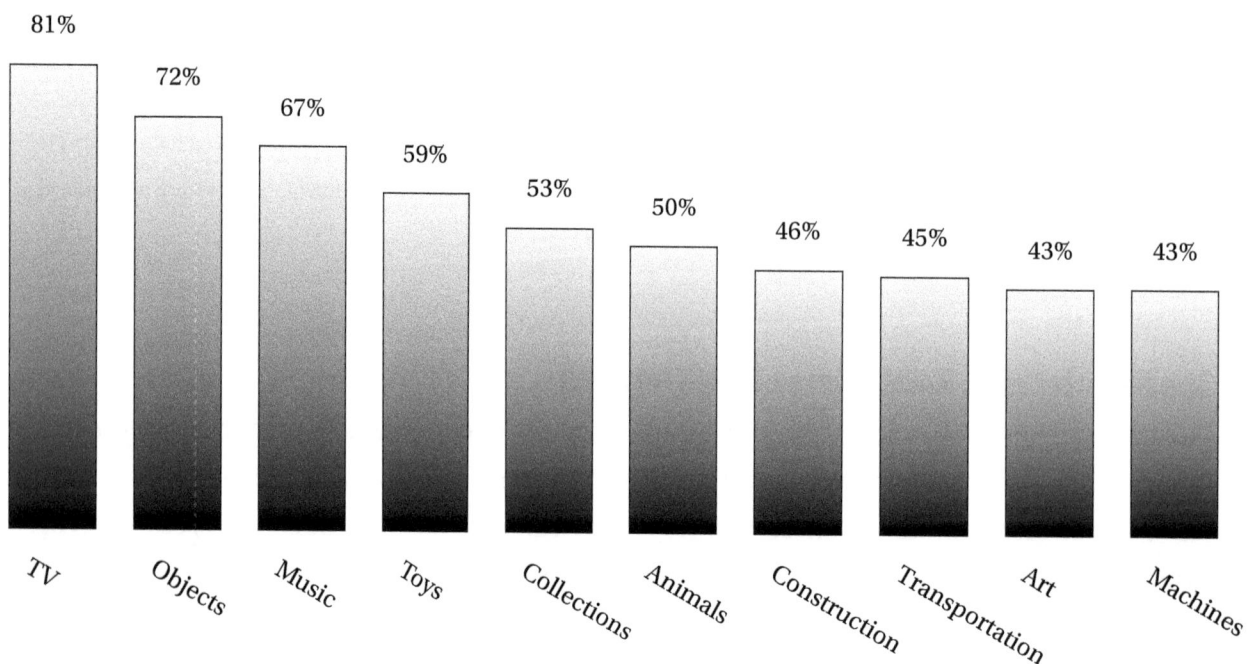

Adapted from Nowell et al., 2020.

Some people have interests that are not based in the above categories and are distinctly unique. Examples include: medieval dress, vacuum cleaners, carnivorous houseplants, constructing imaginative objects, brooms, and bodily injuries.

The Power of Special Interests in Learning

The power of special interests, referred to as restricted patterns of behavior and interests in the *Diagnostic and Statistical Manual of Mental Disorders* (American Psychiatric Association [APA], 2013), on the lives of autistics should not be underestimated. Winter-Messiers and colleagues (2007), in their seminal study, interviewed autistic children, adolescents, and adults about the role their special interests played in their lives. Autistics reported that, overall, that the world made more sense and they felt a greater sense of confidence and positivity when engaged with their areas of special interest. Almost every aspect of life improves when special interests are a part of the individual's day (Goldfarb et al., 2019; Patten & Williams, 2017; Winter-Messiers et al., 2007; Wood, 2021).

Using Special Interests as Reinforcers

Clearly, a student's special interest can play an important role in reinforcement. There are many ways to use special interests in the classroom, including:

- **Use on first/then schedules.** The first/then schedule is often the student's first schedule. The student *first* learns to complete a task and *then* engages in an activity related to their special interests—first puzzle, then Blippi.
- **In individualized tasks and reinforcers.** The special interest can be incorporated into activities, worksheets, and reinforcers. For example, writing a math word problem that includes the superhero interest or giving a sticker that contains a picture of a honey bee are both reinforcing.
- **Embedded into activities.** Students can be allowed/encouraged to explore their special interests in reading, writing, spelling, and/or multimedia presentations. Learning to sequence is easier when the student practices with cards showing Thomas the Tank Engine pulling into the station. It is easier to remember the four elements of speech when presenting on Thomas Edison's cruelty to animals.
- **Time to talk about their interests.** Allowing the student to earn time to discuss their special interest with somebody else who also enjoys or maximally tolerates the topic has multiple benefits. Neurological research has shown that autistic individuals do

not respond well to social reinforcers—those that involve another person (Bottini, 2018). But when a special interest is paired with social praise (verbal and nonverbal) over a significant period of time, a change can occur: social becomes a reinforcer for the individual.

- **Classroom displays.** Wharmby (2022) suggests setting aside a section of classroom for the student to populate with their interest if they'd like. More than one student remarked positively about Rae's bulletin board on dog breeds.
- **The Power Card Strategy.** As discussed in Chapter 11: Instruction in Specialized Settings, the Power Card strategy (Gagnon, 2023) is a visual support that uses the individual's special interest to teach and/or reinforce the use of a behavior or activity. For example, Ing's Power Card featured Spiderman, who provided directions on how he reacted when bumped. Ing tried to remember to be like his hero in the hallways.

Summary

Clearly, special interests are important to and positively impact autistic children, adolescents, and adults. As such, they should be embedded into their daily activities. Special interests are not only one of the strongest reinforcers for autistics, they may lead to great enjoyment, social interactions with like-minded people (e.g., stamp collecting club, Pokémon Club, community theater group), and perhaps even a vocation.

Their unswerving determination and penetrating intellectual powers, part of their spontaneous and original mental activity, their narrowness and single-mindedness, as manifested in their special interests, can be immensely valuable and can lead to outstanding achievements in their chosen areas (Asperger, 1944/1991).

Delivering Reinforcement

Reinforcement must be contingent on the target behavior—that is, depend on the target behavior. Thus, in contingent reinforcement, the student only earns the predetermined consequence when she performs the requested behavior. The target behavior must also be clearly defined and include a measurable criterion that easily determines whether the student has earned the reinforcer.

Vaguely defined target behaviors and unclear criteria, on the other hand, are likely to result in confusion and power struggles as the student and adult attempt to negotiate their interpretation of the plan. In the sample CAPS in Chapter 3, Ginny can earn a break when she has completed five math problems. If she refuses to complete the assignment, or only completes three math problems, she does not earn the reward. In that example, "Completing math problems" is the target behavior and "five problems" is the criterion.

Measuring Criteria

The criterion can be measured by a variety of methods. In the example with Ginny, her success was determined by the number of math problems she completed. Sometimes the criterion is expressed as duration, or the length of time necessary to complete the task. For example, "Using her visual schedule, Ginny will transition to her reading group in less than 3 minutes."

For some behaviors, success may be expressed as a percent correct or a percentage of time elapsed. For example, "Ginny will remain in her seat at least 80% of the time during independent seatwork."

The initial criterion should be based on the student's present level of performance and adjusted incrementally only after the student has demonstrated mastery of the desired behavior. For Ginny, that might mean rewarding transition to reading group at the 3-minute level for five consecutive days, then adjusting the criteria to 2.75 minutes for five days, and so on.

> Vaguely defined target behaviors and unclear criteria are likely to result in confusion and power struggles as the student and adult attempt to negotiate their interpretation of the plan.

Schedules of Reinforcement

Another important consideration is the schedule of reinforcement used. When teaching a new behavior to mastery, or introducing a replacement behavior to address a problem, reinforcement is generally delivered on a fixed ratio, often one-to-one (1:1) basis. This means that for every instance of the target behavior, the student receives the reinforcer. For behaviors that occur over time, the reinforcer may be delivered at a fixed interval of time, for example, after 1 minute on the timer. After the student has demonstrated fluency in the new skill, the ratio of behaviors to reinforcer or interval of reinforcement can be raised gradually in a fixed or a variable manner, based on the performance level of the new skill and the student's tolerance level for change. We generally use five types of reinforcement schedules.

Table 6.3. Possible Reinforcement Schedules.

Schedule	Definition	Example
Continuous	One token for every behavior demonstrated	Each time Wei raises his hand he gets a token.
Fixed ratio	One token for a predetermined number of trials	Every five times Suzy raises her hand, she gets a token.
Variable ratio	One token for a differing number of behaviors based on routine	Chanelle receives a token approximately every five times she raises her hand four times. The second time she receives a token after she raises her hand six times. The average of these two occurrences is five target responses (raises hand) per token.
Fixed interval	One token for a predetermined time	For every 5 minutes, Luis stays in his seat, he gets a token.
Variable interval	One token for differing time periods based on a mean	Raj receives a token approximately every 5 minutes he remains in his seat. The first time, he receives a token for remaining in his seat for 6 minutes. The average of these two occurrences is 5 minutes display of the target behavior (remaining in seat) per token.

Token Economies

In a token economy, rather than receiving reinforcement immediately, students earn tokens that have no actual value (points, coupons, play money) that can be exchanged later for their choice of a reinforcer from a menu including items similar to those in Table 6.1 and Table 6.2.

Neurological research (Bottini, 2018) reveals that because of the abstraction of token economies, they may not be the first reinforcement delivery system that is used with an autistic student. Therefore, several things must be taken into consideration to ensure students benefit from this system of reinforcement.

Figure 6.2. Token Economy Checklist.

Token Economy Checklist

Identifying Target Behaviors

YES	No	Are the target behaviors defined in measurable terms?
YES	No	Are the behaviors based on positive outcomes?

Specifying Reinforcers

YES	No	Are the reinforcers age-appropriate?
YES	No	Was student input allowed?
YES	No	Is there a variety of items likely to appeal to all students?
YES	No	Are token reinforcers combined with other forms of praise? (verbal, physical, or differential forms)
YES	No	Is the token economy flexible enough to allow for student growth beyond specific reinforcers? (e.g., moving from social reinforcers to academic reinforcers)

Planning Token Distribution and Redemption Strategies

YES	No	Do students understand the token-dispensing system?
YES	No	Are students given the opportunity to earn "bonus" or "extra" points?
Yes	**NO**	Do students ever lose points for behaviors?
Yes	**NO**	Is there a "point-of-no-return" where students cannot earn enough points to receive a reinforcer? When? _____
Yes	**NO**	Do students begin with a previously specified number of points each day?

Record-keeping Procedures

YES	No	Is a record-keeping plan developed?
YES	No	Is the record of tokens earned visible and accessible to students?

(**Boldface** answers represent the optimal response)

When the teacher has determined that the student is ready to learn token economies, the first introduction to this concept should include the special interest. This will help the autistic neurology transition to token economies (Bottini, 2018; Kohls et al., 2013). As the student earns a token, they are given a token that depicts the special interest: an interest-specific sticker, chip, or coin. Jo enjoys dinosaurs. His teacher has cut into thirds and laminated a picture of a stegosaurus. Jo knows that each time he turns in his homework, he earns one of the three pictures. When he receives the three pictures—the complete stegosaurus—he exchanges them for an item on his reinforcer menu.

Troubleshooting

The purpose of reinforcement is to teach and support appropriate behavior. Therefore, if the desired behavior does not occur when requested using a particular reinforcement system, the team needs to consider the following questions and adjust the plan based on their conclusions.

Were the task requirements and the selected consequence clearly stated by the adult and understood by the student?

If not, then reteach or restructure the task, and check for understanding. Example: Ginny begins whining when asked to begin her math problems. Use a visual support to cue Ginny that when she finishes her five problems, she will earn a break. As she finishes each problem, the icon can be checked off or covered with a sticker.

Figure 6.3. Ginny's Work System.

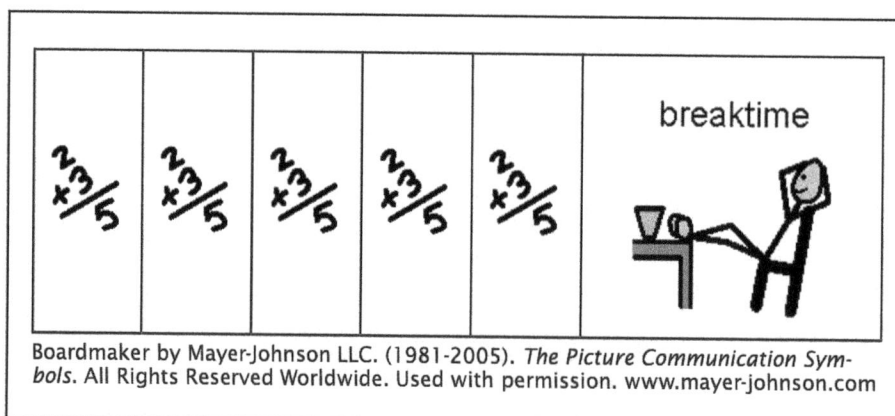

Boardmaker by Mayer-Johnson LLC. (1981-2005). *The Picture Communication Symbols*. All Rights Reserved Worldwide. Used with permission. www.mayer-johnson.com

Was the target behavior a task the student could perform without prompting?

If not, consider adding a verbal prompt or precorrection to your request. Example: Ginny sometimes becomes confused and agitated when it is time for her to transition to her reading group. Use a visual cue to remind Ginny to refer to her visual schedule. When Ginny brings you her schedule, say, "What's next? Reading. Good job."

Figure 6.4. Cue to Check Visual Schedule.

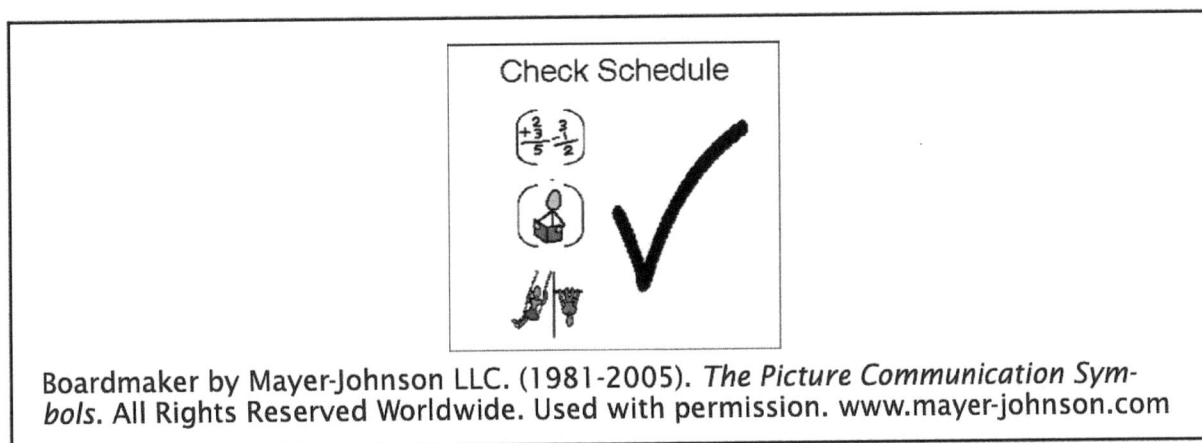

Boardmaker by Mayer-Johnson LLC. (1981-2005). *The Picture Communication Symbols*. All Rights Reserved Worldwide. Used with permission. www.mayer-johnson.com

Did the student choose the reinforcer and was it sufficiently desirable?

If not, work with the student to identify a reinforcer that is stronger or allow them a choice between two options. Example: Ginny does not respond to a teacher's request. Present Ginny with pictures or icons representing two preferred activities or tangibles. Ask, "Ginny, what do you want to work for?" Place the picture she has selected next to her break icon.

Was the reinforcer delivered immediately following the target behavior?

If not, consider strategies to either reduce the student's wait time or increase the student's tolerance for waiting. Example: Ginny finishes her math problems, but the teacher is busy with another student and cannot tend to Ginny right away. Ginny becomes agitated. Teach Ginny to use a Wait Card and get to her as quickly as possible. Hand her the card and say, "Wait, please."

Figure 6.5. Visual Cue for Wait.

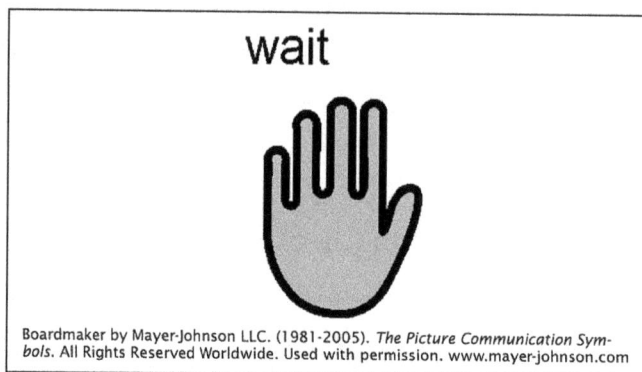

If the desired behavior replaced a problem behavior, did the replacement behavior and reinforcer address the function of the student's original behavior?

If not, consider adjusting the plan to find a better fit for the functional hypothesis. Example: Ginny can earn raisins for moving between classrooms using a typical volume of voice (i.e., without screeching). The team believes the screeching is Ginny's way of communicating her anxiety about the noise and proximity of other students in the hall. Neither the desired behavior (walking down the hall quietly) nor the reinforcer (raisins) has addressed Ginny's need to communicate or her anxiety. Stress-reduction strategies may include (a) providing a passing time (i.e., early or late) that reduces the number of other students in the hall, (b) developing a visual cue card that allows Ginny to communicate her concerns to an adult, or (c) giving Ginny a stress ball to squeeze when she feels like screeching. Another reinforcer might be for Ginny to sit on a beanbag listening to music through headphones after reaching her destination.

Figure 6.6. Visual Cue for Noisy.

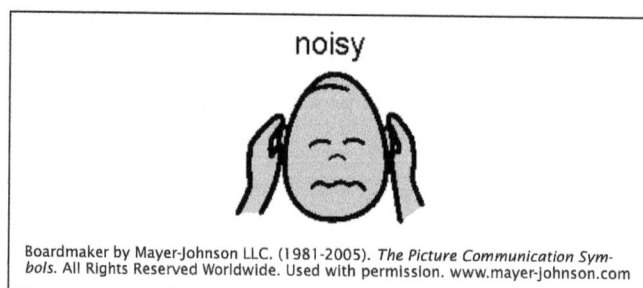

Summary

Research has unequivocally shown that reinforcement is an essential component in learning to function in a complex society for autistic individuals and, indeed, for all (cf. Cooper et al., 2019; Deleon & Iwata, 1996). According to Aspy and Grossman (2022), without reinforcement, there often is no learning. CAPS supports this reality by ensuring that reinforcement is considered systematically throughout the student's day.

Bibliography

American Psychiatric Association. *Diagnostic and Statistical Manual for Mental Disorders* (5th ed., text revision). Author. (2013).

Asperger, Hans. "'Autistic Psychopathy' in Childhood," in Autism and Asperger Syndrome, edited by Uta Frith. Cambridge (1991), 37-92. Originally published as "Die 'Autistischen Psychopathen' im Kindesalter," *Archiv für Psychiatrie und Nervenkrankenheiten* 117 (1944):76-136.

Aspy, Ruth., & Barry Grossman. *The Ziggurat Model: A Framework for Designing Comprehensive Strategies and Supports for Autistic Individuals—Rel. 2.1* [4th ed.]. Dallas, TX: Ziggurat Group, (2022).

Bottini, Summer. "Social Reward Processing in Individuals with Autism Spectrum Disorder: A Systematic Review of the Social Motivation Hypothesis." *Research in Autism Spectrum Disorders* 45 (2018): 9-26.

Boyd, Brian A., Maureen A. Conroy, G. Richmond Mancil, Taketo Nakao, and Peter J. Alter. "Effects of Circumscribed Interests on the Social Behaviors of Children With Autism Spectrum Disorders." *Journal of Autism and Developmental Disorders* 37 (2007): 1550-1561.

Cooper, J. O., T.E. Heron, & W. L. Heward, W. *Applied Behavior Analysis* (3rd ed.). Pearson Education. (2021).

DeLeon, Iser G., and Brian A. Iwata. "Evaluation of a Multiple-Stimulus Presentation Format for Assessing Reinforcer Preferences." *Journal of Applied Behavior Analysis* 29, no. 4 (1996): 519-533.

Downing, Joyce Anderson. *Students with Emotional and Behavioral Problems: Assessment, Management, and Intervention Strategies*. Prentice Hall. (2007).

Fernandez, Nathalie, Iser G. DeLeon, Elizabeth Schieber, and Tracy Argueta. "Preference Among Array Sizes for Backup Reinforcers: An Evaluation of "Choice Overload" in Token Economies." *Behavior Analysis: Research and Practice* 22, no. 2 (2022): 179.

Gagnon, Elisa. "Power Cards: Using Interests and Enthusiasms to Teach Social Problem Solving and Emotional Regulation Skills to Autistic Students." 5 Point Publishing. (2023).

Goldfarb, Yael, Eynat Gal, and Ofer Golan. "A Conflict of Interests: A Motivational Perspective on Special Interests and Employment Success of Adults with ASD." *Journal of Autism and Developmental Disorders* 49 (2019): 3915-3923.

Kim, Gospel Y., Lee SoHyun, Kathleen N. Tuck, and Jose R. Martinez. "Effects of Embedding Special Interest Area in Instruction on the Engagement and Out-of-Seat Behaviors of Children With Autism Spectrum Disorder." *Focus on Autism and Other Developmental Disabilities* (2024): 10883576241232894.

Kohls, G., Schulte-Rüther, M., Nehrkorn, B., Müller, K., Fink, G.R., Kamp-Becker, I., Herpertz-Dahlmann, B., Schultz, R.T. and Konrad, K., 2013. "Reward System Dysfunction in Autism Spectrum Disorders." *Social Cognitive and Affective Neuroscience*, 8, no. 5 (2013). pp.565-572.

Nowell, Kerri P., Courtney J. Bernardin, Cynthia Brown, and Stephen Kanne. "Characterization of Special Interests in Autism Spectrum Disorder: A Brief Review and Pilot Study Using the Special Interests Survey." *Journal of Autism and Developmental Disorders* 51 (2021): 2711-2724.

Patten Koenig, Kristie, and Lauren Hough Williams. "Characterization and Utilization of Preferred Interests: A Survey of Adults on the Autism Spectrum." *Occupational Therapy in Mental Health* 33, no. 2 (2017): 129-140.

Scheithauer, Mindy, Clarissa Martin, and Summer Bottini. "Preferences for Edible and Electronic Leisure Items: A Systematic Replication." *Focus on Autism and Other Developmental Disabilities* 37, no. 3 (2022): 135-145.

Wharmby, Pete. "Special Interests and Their Role in Keeping the Teacher in the Classroom." *Learning From Autistic Teachers: How to Be a Neurodiversity-Inclusive School* (2022): 29.

Winter-Messiers, Mary Ann, Cynthia M. Herr, Casey E. Wood, Amy P. Brooks, Mary Anne M. Gates, Tasker L. Houston, and Kelly I. Tingstad. "How Far Can Brian Ride the Daylight 4449 Express? A Strength-Based Model of Asperger Syndrome Based on Special Interest Areas." *Focus on Autism and Other Developmental Disabilities* 22, no. 2 (2007): 67-79.

Wood, Rebecca. "Autism, Intense Interests, and Support in School: From Wasted Efforts to Shared Understandings." *Educational Review* 73, no. 1 (2021): 34-54.

CHAPTER 7

Sensory Regulation

Elizabeth Grant, OTD, OTRL, and Jocelyn Warren, MEd, OT/L

Ever wonder why you go to the same store to buy the same shirts year after year, or why you go into the same coffee shop again and again? What is it that you like about the store or the shirts or the coffee shop?

We call these behaviors preferences. Why do we have them? Our preferences can be attributed to our ability to organize or interpret sensory information as something we like, dislike, or crave. Do you like the store because they play your favorite genre of music or maybe it's no music at all. Do you like the clothing because of the feel of the fabric and the way it clings to your body or maybe because it fits loosely on your body?

Take a minute to think about what happens to you each morning when you wake. How did you alert yourself from sleep? Was it by a loud beeping alarm, your favorite music, someone nudging you, or do you wake on your own? What do you need to alert yourself to begin your day? Once awake, do you take a shower, use the bathroom, or just get dressed? What clothing did you choose and why? Was it the color, fabric or fit you preferred?

These individual choices and responses continue to tell the story of how we alert, calm, and organize ourselves. We make individual choices that will likely control the kind and amount of input we receive. These choices support our learning and help us to manage sensations and generate adaptive responses for participation in community. This process is mostly unconscious and generally true for everybody—if our sensory systems function optimally. However, for many autistics, this is not the case. Hence this chapter on how to support students who have difficulties with sensory regulation.

Sensory Processing

Sensory processing occurs when our brain registers internal or external stimuli from our senses. Our brain orients to the stimuli, interprets the information, and decides if it is important or can be ignored. The final step is execution, or lack of execution. If action does not need to occur, then we ignore the stimulus, but if it is determined to be important, we respond. That is, our response is determined by our interpretation of the incoming stimuli (Mallory & Keehn, 2021).

Figure 7.1. The Sensory Processing Process.

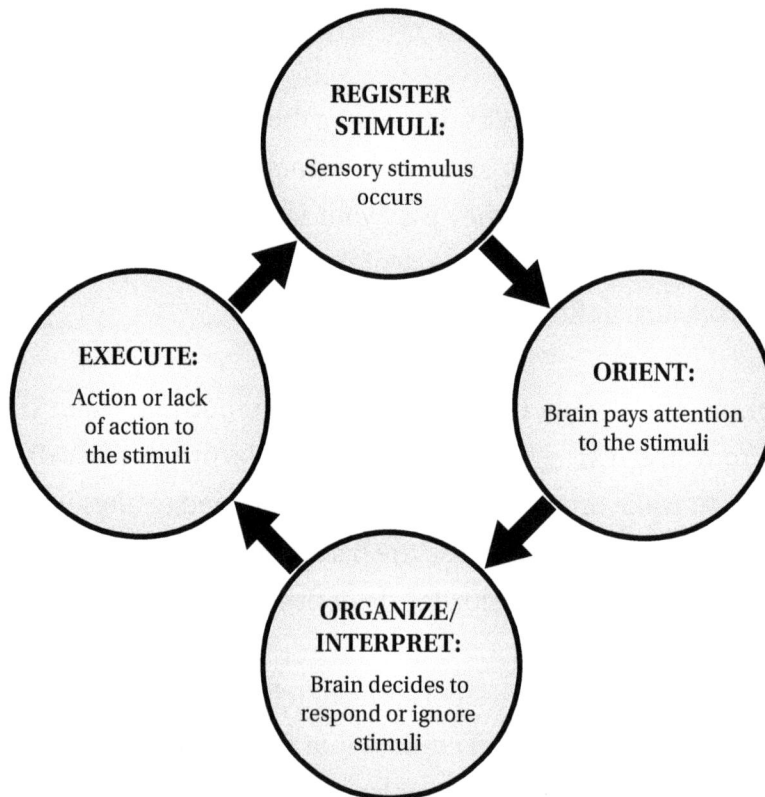

The ability to register, orient, organize, and execute adaptive responses—desired or successful responses; fitting a given situation—to sensory information varies across individuals and diagnoses (Bodison & Parham, 2018). In school, an *adaptive response* usually means engaging in learning or a desired behavior, such as raising hand to ask a question or using a mindfulness strategy to self-calm before responding. But sometimes a student may respond with a diminished or exaggerated response and, consequently, the desired—or the adaptive—response does not occur (Mallor & Keehn, 2021; Neufeld, 2021).

The Eight Senses

The sensory information we constantly receive comes to us through the following eight senses: tactile, vestibular, proprioception, visual, auditory, gustatory, olfactory, and interoception (see table 7.1 on the next page).

In the classroom, sensory stimuli are constantly present, including:
- **Visual:** bulletin boards, lights, and peers
- **Auditory:** the hum of overhead lights, people talking, and pencils being sharpened
- **Olfactory:** cafeteria smells and peers who may not have bathed
- **Tactile:** the smooth surface of desks, irritating clothing tags, and occasional bumps from peers

Students also receive sensory information internally through their proprioception, vestibular and interoception systems:

- **Vestibular** information is crucial for maintaining balance when changing body positions, such as sitting in a chair or playing on playground equipment.
- **Proprioceptive** refers to knowing where your body is in place. This input is necessary for navigating the school environment without bumping into doorways, desks, people, standing in line to wait your turn or playing on playground equipment.
- **Interoceptive** information helps students to understand their own needs, like need to use the bathroom, eat, nap, or take a break to calm down.

How our brain interprets these stimuli can differ for students, especially those who are autistic.

Table 7.1. The Eight Senses.

System	Location	Function
Tactile *(touch)*	Skin – density of cell distribution varies throughout the body. Areas of greatest density include mouth, hands, and genitals.	Provides information about the environment and object qualities (touch, pressure, texture, hard, soft, sharp, dull, heat, cold, pain).
Vestibular *(balance)*	Inner ear – stimulated by head movements and input from other senses, especially visual.	Provides information about where our body is in space, and whether or not we or our surroundings are moving. Tells about speed and direction of movement.
Proprioception *(body awareness)*	Muscles and joints – activated by muscle contractions and movement.	Provides information about where a certain body part is and how it is moving.
Visual *(sight)*	Retina of the eye – stimulated by light.	Provides information about objects and persons. Helps us define boundaries as we move through time and space.
Auditory *(hearing)*	Inner ear – stimulated by air/ sound waves.	Provides information about sounds in the environment (loud, soft, high, low, near, far).
Gustatory *(taste)*	Chemical receptors in the tongue – closely entwined with the olfactory (smell) system.	Provides information about different types of taste (sweet, sour, bitter, salty, spicy).
Olfactory *(smell)*	Chemical receptors in the nasal structure – closely associated with the gustatory system.	Provides information about different types of smell (musty, acrid, putrid, flowery, pungent).
Interoception *(inside body)*	Inside of your body – helps the body "feel" the internal state or conditions of the body.	Provides information such as pain, body temperature, itch, sexual arousal, hunger and thirst. It also helps bring in information regarding heart and breathing rates and when we need to use the bathroom.

DSM-5 Definition of Autism and Sensory Features

Reactivity to sensory input has been related to autism for a long time, and finally the latest DSM-V definition of autism includes sensory issues as one of the four restricted/repetitive behavior features defined as hyper- or hyporeactivity to sensory input or unusual interest in sensory aspects of the environment (American Psychiatric Association [APA, 2013]). While sensory challenges impact the lives of up to 96% autistics (Bodison & Parham, 2018; Sibeoni et al., 2022), some sensory features can be identified as both strengths and barriers depending on the environment, tasks, activity demands and impact on participation.

Hyporeactivity

Someone who is hyporeactive is under-responsive to sensory input compared to the neuro-majority. For example, they may not register or attend to certain stimuli in their environment (Narvekar, 2024).

- **Hyporeactivity to sound** may look as if the person is not listening, responding to directions or their name being called.
- **Hyporeactivity to movement, pressure, or touch** may look like a student that slouches in their chair, clothing may be twisted, have an overall clumsy appearance, high tolerance of pain and wait until the last minute to address bathroom needs or has accidents and unaware.

Research has shown that these children may have lower communication skills and daily living skills (Watling & Spitzer, 2018).

Hyperreactivity

Those who experience hyperreactivity are likely to have an exaggerated or negative response to certain sensory input compared to the neuromajority. For example, they may be cautious with movements and heights, be very specific about clothing and foods, and may detect or notice things in the environment more readily than others.

- **Hyperreactivity to sounds** may look like a child that is covering their ears, running away to get away from the sound or avoiding environments that are loud like gymnasiums, grocery stores, or sporting events.
- **Hyperreactivity to touch** may look like an individual who avoids certain textures of clothing, not like to be touched during play, avoid getting hands dirty during play, or have difficult time with self-care activities such as haircuts, bathing, and grooming tasks.

Hyperresponsiveness is also evident in the student who eludes playground equipment that spins or swings; eats only a limited number of foods; or has a negative reaction to fluorescent lights, perfume odors, and various sounds.

Research has shown that hyperresponsive children may participate less in activities, prefer quieter and less stimulating activities, and demonstrate decreased academic and social competence (Watling & Spitzer, 2018).

Variable Reactions

Although a person may tend to be either hypo- or hyperresponsive to sensory stimuli, their responses can vary daily across settings and activities. How somebody responds to stimuli can be influenced by factors, such as (a) internal state (e.g., sick, tired, anxious), (b) whether the task is easy or difficult, (c) whether the activity is preferred or not, or (d) the classroom's level of busy-ness.

When a student can organize and interpret sensory information as either important to respond to or to ignore, they can execute an adaptive response and learning can occur.

Regulation

For autistic students to function successfully and be ready to learn, they need to be able to regulate their reactions to the stimuli around them. "Regulation" here refers to the ability to maintain an appropriate level of alertness. If regulation does not occur, a meltdown may happen. The meltdown is "supported" by the autistic neurology. That is, research shows that there is underactivity in the parts of the brain associated with regulation (Richey et al., 2015), leading to greater likelihood of a meltdown.

Not only is the autistic brain not wired for regulation, it often does not recognize that the individual is in the early stages of becoming upset, overwhelmed, or anxious because their interoception sense does not communicate this. Thus, the individual may not even be aware that that a meltdown is potentially on the horizon (see Chapter 11: Instruction Often Occurring in Specialized Settings for strategies to support interoception). Since challenges in regulation are brain based—not purposeful behavior (Ni et al., 2020; Phung, 2021)—helping students regulate is an instructional issue.

Figure 7.2. Sensory Processing Resulting in an Adaptive Response.

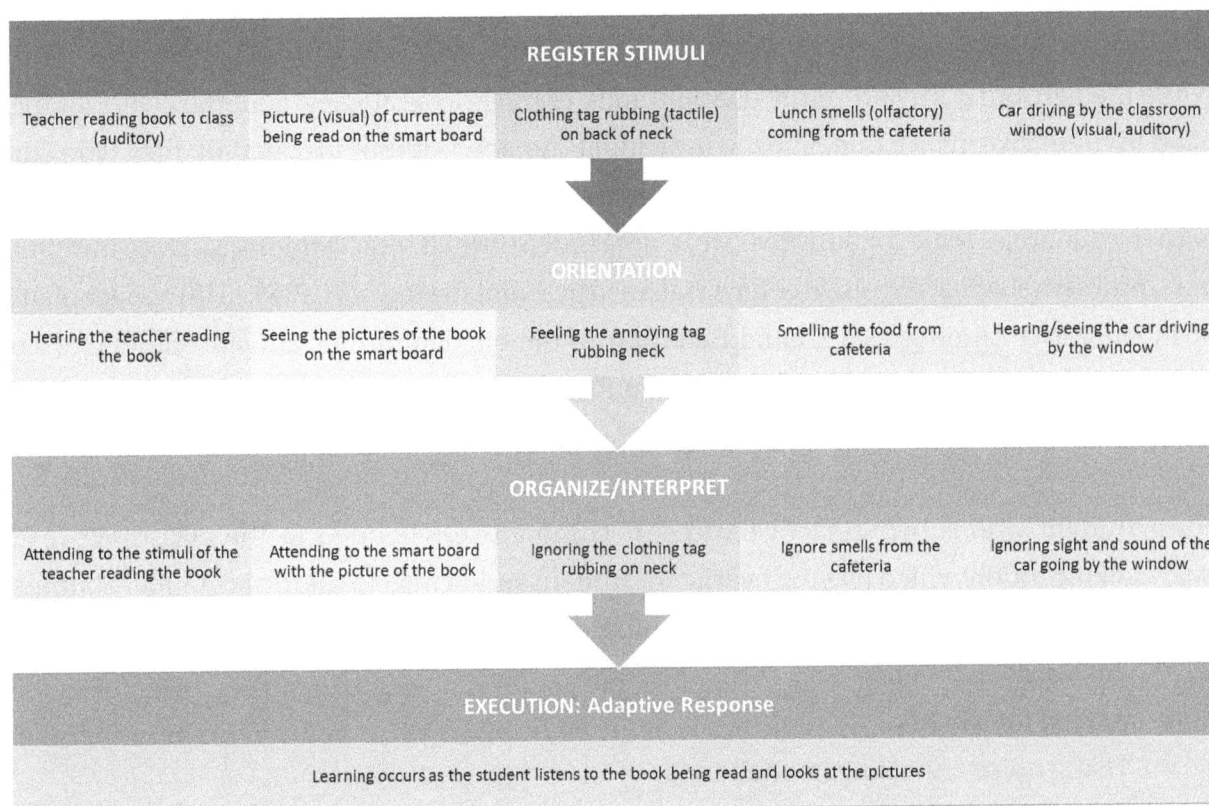

REGISTER STIMULI				
Teacher reading book to class (auditory)	Picture (visual) of current page being read on the smart board	Clothing tag rubbing (tactile) on back of neck	Lunch smells (olfactory) coming from the cafeteria	Car driving by the classroom window (visual, auditory)

ORIENTATION				
Hearing the teacher reading the book	Seeing the pictures of the book on the smart board	Feeling the annoying tag rubbing neck	Smelling the food from cafeteria	Hearing/seeing the car driving by the window

ORGANIZE/INTERPRET				
Attending to the stimuli of the teacher reading the book	Attending to the smart board with the picture of the book	Ignoring the clothing tag rubbing on neck	Ignore smells from the cafeteria	Ignoring sight and sound of the car going by the window

EXECUTION: Adaptive Response
Learning occurs as the student listens to the book being read and looks at the pictures

When difficulties in regulation occur, generally, there are two types of responses: voluntary or involuntary.

- **Voluntary regulation strategies** actively focus on changing the environment or adapting to the situation. These interventions, such as problem solving, cognitive behavioral/ instructional strategies (CBIS), or self-management strategies can be successful when regulation is a challenge.
- **Involuntary regulation strategies** are unconscious strategies that often do not directly relate to the problem and most often do not result in solving the challenge. These include (a) intrusive thoughts: constantly thinking/having bad dreams about the problem and associated feelings; (b) physiological arousal: having feelings in the body, such as racing heart, muscle tightening; (c) emotional arousal: getting upset by

situations that normally would not be problematic; and (d) involuntary action: being unable to control words or actions (Cai et al., 2018; Mazefsky et al., 2014).

While the neuromajority primarily use voluntary regulation strategies, generally without the need for intensive instruction, autistic individuals do not. Without instruction, they typically default to involuntary strategies, which are generally nonproductive. As a result, regulation is an instructional issue for autistics. Thus, antecedent-based interventions, such as mindfulness, problem solving, cognitive behavioral/instructional strategies (CBIS), self-management, or moving to a calming area should be a part of the curriculum for autistic students. (see Chapter 4: A Brief Review of Evidence-Based Practices in Autism and Chapter 5: Structure/Modifications for additional information).

For a student who is hyperreactive and is becoming overwhelmed in the classroom (e.g., peers talking loudly, video playing overhead, student sitting next to them accidentally bumps their leg, sock seams rubbing toe), self-calming strategies to reduce the stimuli may include

- Taking deep breaths
- Asking for a break
- Using noise-canceling headphones
- Engaging with sensory tools like fidgets.

For a student who hyporeactive—inattentive, lacking in energy, falling asleep, or daydreaming—strategies to assist with regulation may occur by trying to increase the sensory stimuli include:

- Chewing gum/chewy tube/chewy foods
- Drinking ice water
- Playing upbeat music
- Taking a movement break
- Sitting on a ball chair or seat cushion that allows movement or playing with fidgets.

The overall goal is for students to recognize what they need so they can achieve regulation independently. When a student is regulated, they are alert and attentive, enabling effective learning.

Evidence-Based Practices (EBP)

Although up to 96% of autistic children demonstrate sensory challenges (Sibeoni et al., 2022), research findings aimed at determining the most effective interventions are diverse (Tomchek et al., 2023). Nonetheless, there is clear and compelling evidence supporting interventions that focus on enhancing participation in school and everyday activities and supporting regulation. These findings are corroborated by the National Clearinghouse on Autism Evidence and Practice (NCAEP; 2021). See Chapter 4: A Brief Review of Evidence-Based Practices in Autism.

Many of these accepted EBPs may be described as sensory strategies/supports, using sensory stimuli to assist with learning or desired behaviors. And although some EBPs would be described as behavioral interventions, they have a strong sensory component that can support autistic learners. The following links sensory systems to EBP. Chapter 4 provides additional information on these interventions.

Table 7.2. Linking Sensory Systems to EBP.

Sensory System	Evidence-Based Practices
Auditory	• Music-Mediated Intervention (MMI) incorporates songs, melodic intonation, and/or rhythm to support learning and performance of skills/behaviors. It also includes music therapy. This intervention utilizes auditory stimuli to assist with learning.
Auditory, Visual, and Tactile	• Augmentative and Alternative Communication (AAC) interventions are systems of communication that include language boards, sign language, and speech-generating devices. They combine tactile, visual, and auditory sensory input to assist with communication. • Functional Communication (FCT) is a set of practices that support the replacement of a challenging behavior with more effective communication strategies. They include tactile, visual and/or auditory sensory stimuli. • Prompting (PP) occurs when verbal, gestural, or physical assistance is provided to students to support skill acquisition. Prompts can be visual, auditory, tactile, or proprioceptive. • Technology-Aided Instruction and Intervention (TAII), in which technology is the central feature of instruction or support, includes the use of visual, auditory, tactile, and proprioceptive stimuli. • Video Modeling (VM), a video-recorded demonstration of behavior or skills, can provide both visual and auditory sensory input to assist with learning.

Table 7.2 (continued)

Sensory System	Evidence-Based Practices
Auditory, Visual, and Tactile (continued)	• Visual Supports (VS), visual displays that support the learner across settings, has a visual and often also a tactile component. • Modeling (DM), the demonstration of skills, uses visual and auditory sensory input to teach skills.
Proprioceptive/ Vestibular	• Exercise and Movement (EXM) interventions that incorporate physical exertion, motor skills, and/or mindful movement in instruction, are replete with proprioceptive and vestibular stimuli.
Interoceptive	• Cognitive Behavioral/Instructional Strategies (CBIS) that focus on self-awareness and self-management require an understanding how the body feels internally to regulate behaviors. • Self-Management (SM) Instruction that places the student in charge of changing their behavior and monitoring that change relies on an understanding of the body's internal state.
Multisensory	• Ayres Sensory Integration® (ASI) targets a person's ability to integrate sensory information from their body and environment to interact in a way that is considered appropriate. This involves the visual, auditory, tactile, proprioceptive, and vestibular systems.

From Steinbrenner, Jessica R., et al. "Evidence-based practices for children, youth, and young adults with autism." Frank Porter Graham Child Development Institute (2020).

Overall, there is clear evidence that sensory supports and interventions can be utilized within the school environment to support student learning.

Interventions

An occupational therapist (OT) can be effective in identifying and designing sensory supports to meet the needs of an autistic student, such as attending to the teacher, completing assignments, or playing on playground equipment. Following an assessment of (a) the student's sensory needs, (b) the behavior the child exhibits, and (c) what the student is expected to do in each environment, the OT can plan interventions that fit into the student's CAPS.

It is important that an OT trained in designing sensory interventions be part of the individualized education program (IEP) team to ensure the supports match the student's sensory needs and are embedded into their schedule. For example, if a student's attention is enhanced through oral-motor input, they might need chewy or crunchy foods throughout the day. An OT can consult with a student's teacher to ensure these supports are available when needed.

Ginny's school team used a variety of strategies that she was ready to learn:

- Ginny used a slant board with textured paper so that she could better feel her writing.
- To prevent Ginny from being overwhelmed from excessive stimuli, Ginny's teacher created a paper frame that allowed Ginny to see one problem at a time.
- Sensory items, such as lotion, a koosh ball, and sticky string help Ginny stay focused.
- It is often easier for Ginny to learn in small, structured settings. Computer, library, and video activities have been structured to meet this need.

Several sensory strategies and interventions have been researched and contribute to our ongoing learning of sensory processing and integration. However, to date, extensive research has not been conducted on sensory interventions for autistic individuals. While not considered by some (cf. Steinbrenner et al., 2020) as EBPs, it can be argued that sensory-based strategies can at least be identified as promising, and as shown earlier, sensory interventions fit under many of the established categories of EBP, including antecedent-based interventions. Table 7.3 (on the next page) shows various sensory challenges a student may have and potential interventions tailored to the individual's needs.

Table 7.3. Sensory Interventions That an OT Might Suggest for an Autistic Student.

Challenge	Possible Interventions
Difficulty transitioning between activities	• Provide a visual schedule (pictures and/or written words) of the sequence of daily activities. • Provide a social narrative for the different kinds of transitions, how to respond, and what to expect. This offers a visual and sequential script of what to expect. • Provide a colored circle for where to stand in line or tape boundaries on the floor. • Allow the student to leave class just before the transition so they can miss the transition in the classroom and already be settled when the rest of the class transitions to the new activity. • Allow the student to be first or last in line. • Offer a visual a few minutes before the transition to give prior warning of the change. • Use a visual timer for a transition to support a warning that transition is coming. • Dim lights at the time of the transition. • Provide headphones with a favorite song playing during the transition. • Provide a peer, visual list, or video for following the steps in a task.
Constantly moving: in and out of the chair, around the room, fidgeting in the chair, or squirming on the floor during circle time	• Provide alternate seating: ball chair, seat cushions, floor chairs, rocking chairs, and wobble chairs. • Offer a lap weight during seated activities. • Provide deep pressure through the shoulders when seated upright in a chair. • Embed functional movement breaks during the day that include pushing in chairs, sharpening pencils, wiping tables, carrying books, taking a note to the office, sweeping the floor, etc. • Give responsibilities such as handing out books or papers. • Wrap a large exercise band around the legs of the student's chair so they can get input through pushing and pulling the band with their feet or legs while sitting in the chair. • Place weights under the student's chair so when scooting or moving the chair they get heavy work built in. • Conduct whole-class structured movement/exercises: jumping jacks, jumping up and down, grape vines, animal walks or jumps, yoga, following a dance or yoga video.

Table 7.3 (continued)

Challenge	Possible Interventions
Leans on peers while in line, sitting in groups, or sitting at a table.	• Provide opportunities for large-motor activities such as jumping, pulling, and pushing prior to these activities. • Allow the child to stand during activities. • Embed opportunities to get up and move, such as sharpening pencils or throwing away trash. • Place rubberized shelf-lining or DycemTM on the seat of the student's chair. • Place a tennis ball on chair legs (diagonal) to allow for continual small movements.
Talking self through a task, but it appears that the student is simply talking loudly and disrupting others	• Use a social narrative for working independently. Pictures and words describe expected behaviors of the entire class. • Allow the student to talk out loud if it does not disrupt other students. • Offer a lap weight or deep pressure through the shoulders. • Provide a check-off list for each step in the process. • Provide a space that is away from others during longer times of independent work.
Difficulty organizing materials; frequent misplacing of materials	• Color-code folders, notebooks, and book covers and mark with name or sticker to identify that it belongs to the student. • Use a calendar or daily schedule to list classes to attend, homework assignments, tests, major projects. • Use different-colored writing tools for different kinds of assignments. • Place all books, folders, and classroom materials in a box with the student's name on it. • When beginning a specific class, post a visual list of the materials needed for the subject matter on the student's desk and a larger pictorial representation on the board for all class members. • Decrease visual distractions. • Use colored overlays or colored paper. • Provide a reader line guide to block text during reading.

Table 7.3 (continued)

Challenge	Possible Interventions
Chews on writing tools, utensils, clothing and other inedible objects	• Provide a chew toy or chew necklace. • Provide resistive foods: gummy bears, licorice, gum, or chewy candies. They can be either calming or alerting for organizing. • Incorporate blowing activities: bubbles, cotton balls, feathers, whistles, bazooka, harmonica. • Provide sucking opportunities – candies, pudding through straws, milkshakes, cotton balls/paper on the end of a straw.
Chews on writing tools, utensils, clothing and other inedible objects (continued)	• Provide licking activities – ice cream, lollipops. • Have student drink through straws of varying diameters and lengths. • Use sports bottles filled with water for student to sip. • Offer a variety of chewy toys and teethers, such as Thera-tubing or refrigerator tubing. • Teach the student to take deep breaths. • Have student use a vibrating toothbrush to brush teeth during scheduled times throughout the school day.
Seems impulsive or hurries through things, including being unaware of safety issues	• Break the activity into steps and ask the student to perform one step at a time, completing each step before moving on. • Have someone model the activity first. • Use a visual for each step. • Reinforce completion of each step instead of just the final project. • Consider tactile sensitivity or avoidance and provide an alternate material with less threatening sensory features (e.g., use a cotton swab to glue on small pieces of the art activity instead of getting glue on fingers). • Consider a cooperative assignment where different steps can be distributed among students.
Has difficulty regulating reactions in the lunchroom, including having meltdowns, screaming, or refusing to cooperate	• Allow the student to go to the cafeteria early. • Allow the student to eat in the classroom or other nonstimulating environment. • Decrease time in the lunchroom. • Assist the student in setting up for the meal (opening milk, condiments, helping to select food).

All the listed sensory interventions may be considered when addressing the needs of the student, but it is also important to understand how these strategies can double as supports in the areas of structure/modifications, reinforcement, and social/communication.

Summary

Successful participation in school, family, and community is important to learning, socialization, and self-esteem, to name a few. Sensory/regulation strategies and supports used alone or alongside other supports offer a dynamic approach to creating an environment that meets the needs of autistic students.

Bibliography

American Psychiatric Association. *The Diagnostic and Statistical Manual of Mental Disorders* (5th ed.), Authors. (2013).

Bodison, S. C., & Parham, L. D. (2018). Specific Sensory Techniques and Sensory Environmental Modifications for Children and Youth With Sensory Integration Difficulties: A Systematic Review. *American Journal of Occupational Therapy*, 72, 7201190040.

Cai, Ru Ying, Amanda L. Richdale, Mirko Uljarević, Cheryl Dissanayake, and Andrea C. Samson. Emotion Regulation in Autism Spectrum Disorder: Where We Are and Where We Need to Go. *Autism Research*, 11, no. 7 (2018). pp. 962-978.

Mallory, Courtney, and Brandon Keehn. "Implications of Sensory Processing and Attentional Differences Associated With Autism in Academic Settings: An Integrative Review." *Frontiers in Psychiatry* 12 (2021): 695825.

Mazefsky, Carla A., Xenia Borue, Taylor N. Day, and Nancy J. Minshew. "Emotion Regulation Patterns in Adolescents With High-Functioning Autism Spectrum Disorder: Comparison to Typically Developing Adolescents and Association With Psychiatric Symptoms." *Autism Research* 7, no. 3 (2014): 344-354.

Narvekar, Nisha, Virginia Carter Leno, Greg Pasco, Jannath Begum Ali, Mark H. Johnson, Tony Charman, Emily JH Jones et al. "The Roles of Sensory Hyperreactivity and Hyporeactivity in Understanding infant Fearfulness and Emerging Autistic Traits." *Journal of Child Psychology and Psychiatry* (2024).

National Clearinghouse on Autism Evidence and Practice. Why a Clearinghouse? Frank Porter Graham Child Development Institute, The University of North Carolina. (2021). Accessed December 22, 2023 from https://ncaep.fpg.unc.edu.

Neufeld, Janina, Lisa Hederos Eriksson, Richard Hammarsten, Karl Lundin Remnelius, Julian Tillmann, Johan Isaksson, and Sven Bölte. "The Impact of Atypical Sensory Processing on Adaptive Functioning Within and Beyond Autism: The Role of Familial Factors." *Autism* 25, no. 8 (2021): 2341-2355.

Ni, Hsing-Chang, Hsiang-Yuan Lin, Yu-Chieh Chen, Wen-Yih Isaac Tseng, and Susan Shur-Fen Gau. "Boys with Autism Spectrum Disorder Have Distinct Cortical Folding Patterns Underpinning Impaired Self-Regulation: A Surface-Based Morphometry Study." *Brain Imaging and Behavior* 14, no. 6 (2019): 2464-76.

Phung, Jasmine, Melanie Penner, Clémentine Pirlot, and Christie Welch. "What I Wish You Knew: Insights on Burnout, Inertia, Meltdown, and Shutdown from Autistic Youth." *Frontiers in Psychology* 12 (2021).

Richey, J. Anthony, Cara R. Damiano, Antoinette Sabatino, Alison Rittenberg, Chris Petty, Josh Bizzell, James Voyvodic, et al. "Neural Mechanisms of Emotion Regulation in Autism Spectrum Disorder." *Journal of Autism and Developmental Disorders* 45, no. 11 (2015): 3409-23.

Sibeoni, Jordan, Laura Massoutier, Marie Valette, Emilie Manolios, Laurence Verneuil, Mario Speranza, and Anne Revah-Levy. "The Sensory Experiences of Autistic People: A Metasynthesis." *Autism* 26, no. 5 (2022): 1032-1045.

Steinbrenner, Jessica R., Kara Hume, Samuel L. Odom, Kristi L. Morin, Sallie W. Nowell, Brianne Tomaszewski, Susan Szendrey, Nancy S. McIntyre, Serife Yücesoy-Özkan, and Melissa N. Savage. "Evidence-Based Practices for Children, Youth, and Young Adults with Autism." Frank Porter Graham Child Development Institute (2020).

Tomchek, Scott D., Alissa Baker, Lauren M. Little, Anna Wallisch, and Evan Dean. "Interventions to Support Participation in Sleep for Autistic Children and Adolescents (2013–2021)." *The American Journal of Occupational Therapy* 77, no. Supplement 1 (2023).

Watling, Renee & Susan L. Spitzer. *Autism Across the Lifespan A Comprehensive Occupational Therapy Approach* (4th ed.). AOTA Press. (2018).

CHAPTER 8

Communication/Social Skills

Kathleen Taylor, OTR/L, and Kathleen A. Quill, EdD, BCBA-D with Marci Laurel CCC/SLP

According to the *Diagnostic and Statistical Manual of Mental Disorders* (5th ed.; DSM-5; American Psychiatric Association [APA], 2013), autistic individuals exhibit qualitative impairments in communication and social interaction. Indeed, communication and social skills are deeply intertwined, given that all human communication is social. When two or more people are together, this is a social situation—one in which it is important to know how to communicate. While children may learn to talk or use alternative forms of communication, this is of little value if they don't also develop the social skills necessary to use communication for meaningful interaction (Kang et al., 2020; Moody & Laugeson, 2020).

This chapter focuses on the communication and social skills challenges encountered by many autistic individuals. We will also introduce the STEPS model, a unique visual task analysis of the development of social skills (Laurel & Taylor, 2016) that allows professionals to be specific when teaching social skills that build on one another. Finally, the chapter will introduce a variety of strategies for use in individual and group instruction that may be beneficial to autistics and, therefore, need to be considered when completing a CAPS.

Challenges in communication and social skills that are part of the diagnostic criteria for autism include social-emotional reciprocity, nonverbal communication behaviors, and developing, maintaining, and understanding relationships (APA, 2013). As such, the following are key to understanding the communication and social skills characteristics of individuals with autism:

- They want to communicate, but don't understand how.
- They may use challenging behaviors to express frustration.
- They generally use communication to achieve a specific outcome and less for social pleasure.
- Their communication interactions may look very different from those of others.
- Their repetitive behaviors may be a means of communicating a variety of emotions, including social confusion.
- They struggle to understand the meaning of many nonverbal signals used by others.
- They rarely share experiences, understand the social perspectives of others, and engage in fluid and flexible reciprocal conversation unless they are provided instruction and support.

To further complicate matters, research has revealed that autistics' ability to understand and communicate greatly exceeded their conversation skills.

Figure 8.1. The Ability to Converse Compared to the Ability to Understand and Communicate of Young Autistic Adults (Roux, 2015).

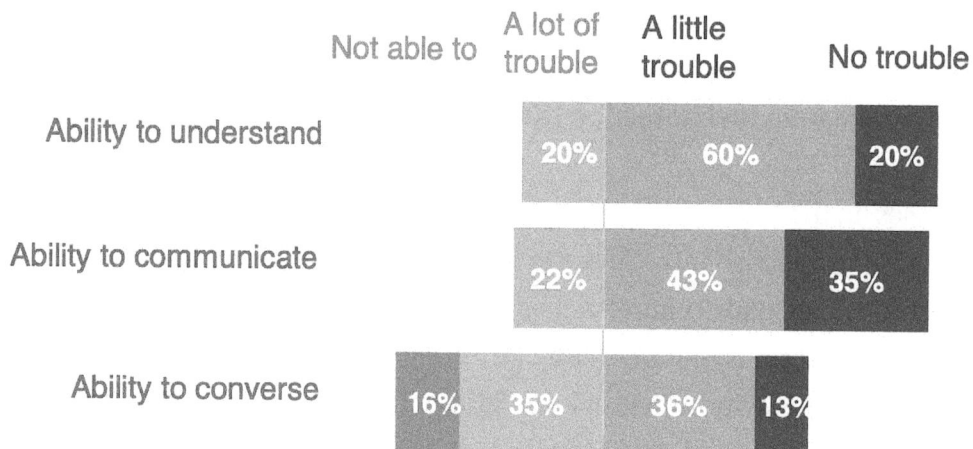

	Not able to	A lot of trouble	A little trouble	No trouble
Ability to understand		20%	60%	20%
Ability to communicate		22%	43%	35%
Ability to converse	16%	35%	36%	13%

Never assume that the individual with autism understands what you say! You are the competent communicator. Adjust your interaction style to the level of the person with autism.

What Are Communication and Social Skills?

Approximately 70-75% of autistic children are verbal. The remaining are minimally verbal, using fewer than approximately 30 words (Holland, 2023). But even if an autistic person is nonverbal, they can still use words in other ways (e.g., language board) (Koegel et al., 2020). Autistic individuals may have difficulties with several aspects of communication, including expressive, receptive, and pragmatic. To successfully communicate, a person must have a method to express themselves, a partner to receive the communication, and the ability to comprehend the information that is communicated back (Koegel et al., 2019). In addition, they must understand the set of social rules that govern the conversational use of language—pragmatics.

Expressive communication can be verbal or nonverbal. Challenges in this area often include (a) difficulty producing speech; (b) difficulty initiating requests, either verbally or nonverbally, to a communication partner; (c) use of echolalic or repeated speech patterns whose meaning is often not understood; (d) difficulty knowing the underlying ideas or desires that they want to express (Febriantini et al., 2021; Koegel et al., 2020).

Receptive communication involves understanding or comprehending communication. While some autistics may understand more than they are able to communicate, many are challenged by understanding verbal input and, despite responding to questions, often have little idea what was said to them. In contrast, they process and respond with greater accuracy to visually presented information.

Pragmatics refers to the social rules that govern the use of language in interactions, such as actively participating in dialogues, producing relevant comments, telling stories, and transitioning between topics. In addition, pragmatics also refers to using language subtleties, humor, irony, and interpreting nonverbal aspects of communication. These are all skills that generally must directly be taught to autistics (Hage et al., 2021).

While a communication impairment is often thought of as a lack of verbal speech, it may also be found in individuals with adequate verbal capabilities who struggle to initiate and sustain conversations with others. Indeed, communication and social skills are much like a game of catch, and although many of us can perform them with little thought, they do happen in a certain sequence. The passing of a message to another person and waiting for them to catch the message and then returning the message on a similar topic takes technique and patience, and one needs to be aware of the context, including the environment, as well as the people around them to make it meaningful (Vermeulen, 2012, 2022).

Why Communication and Social Skills Are Important— Bridging Communication and Social Skills

Although social skills come intuitively to some, many individuals are challenged by interacting socially (Kapp, 2023). The complexity of meeting people, carrying on a conversation, knowing how long and what to talk about, and building lasting relationships and the ease of these moments, can mask the dynamic interplay of the subtle yet complex skills required.

Clearly, social skills, which allow people to share space and experiences with others, are not just for making friends. Social skills are needed to function well in everyday life (Aspy & Grossman, 2022). Indeed, communication and social skills are the context for all learning, a prerequisite for positive adult outcomes, a predictor of the choices people make into adulthood (Keifer, 2020; Roux, 2015), and a deeply important part of being a person (Vermeulen, 2022).

In school, good communication and social skills (a) boost academic performance; (b) increase students' interest in learning; (c) improve learner behavior; (d) prevent and reduce bullying; and (e) improve school climate (Laurel & Taylor, 2016).

At work, communication and social skills are essential to employment success—recent trends reveal that requirements for social competence in the workplace have increased dramatically (Fajaryati et al., 2020). According to the *National Autism Indicators Report: Transition into Young Adulthood* (Roux, 2015), the biggest predictor of employment, being socially connected, and not experiencing social isolation is social skills. Moreover, employment and wage growth are strongest in jobs that require high levels of both cognitive and social skills (Hoffman & Tedalis, 2021).

As illustrated in the following graph, as their conversation ability increased, so did the percent of young adults who (a) attended postsecondary education, (b) lived independently, or

(c) were employed. Being disconnected socially decreased. Similar social isolation decreases as conversation skills increase. It should be noted that nonverbal autistics can converse when taught to do so. In addition, multiple practice opportunities should be provided to all learning the skill of conversation (Roux, 2015).

Figure 8.2. Relationship Between Conversation Skills and Postsecondary Education, Independent Living, Employment and Social Isolation.

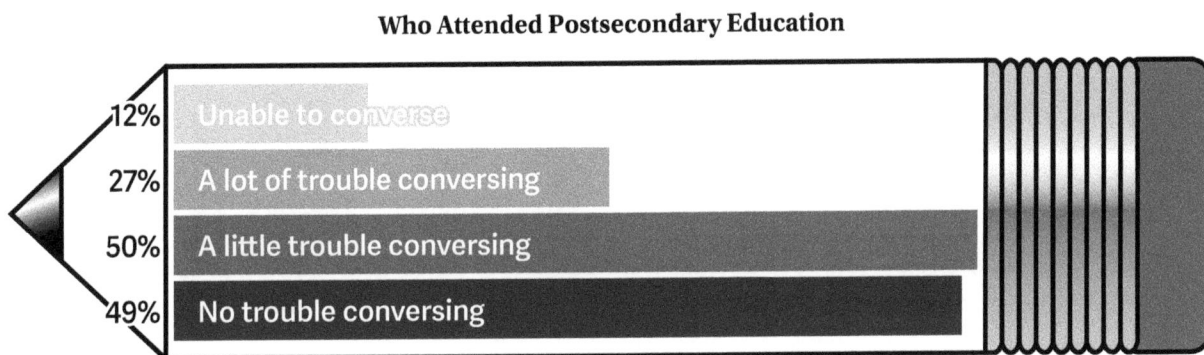

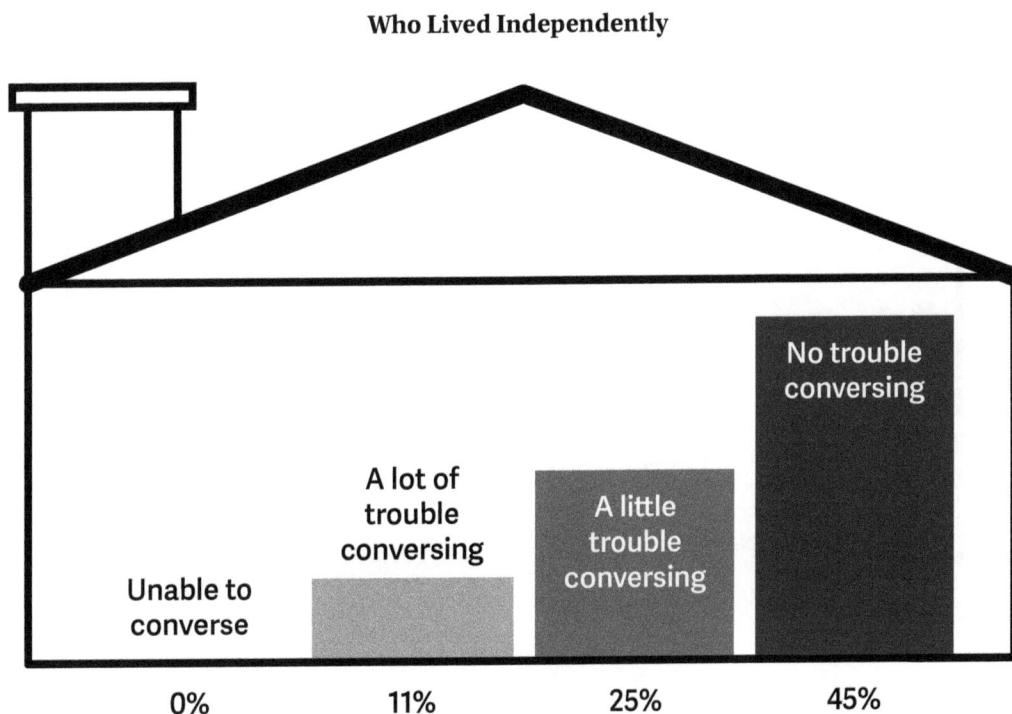

Who Attended Postsecondary Education

Percentage	Category
12%	Unable to converse
27%	A lot of trouble conversing
50%	A little trouble conversing
49%	No trouble conversing

Who Lived Independently

Unable to converse	A lot of trouble conversing	A little trouble conversing	No trouble conversing
0%	11%	25%	45%

CAPS

Who Were Employed

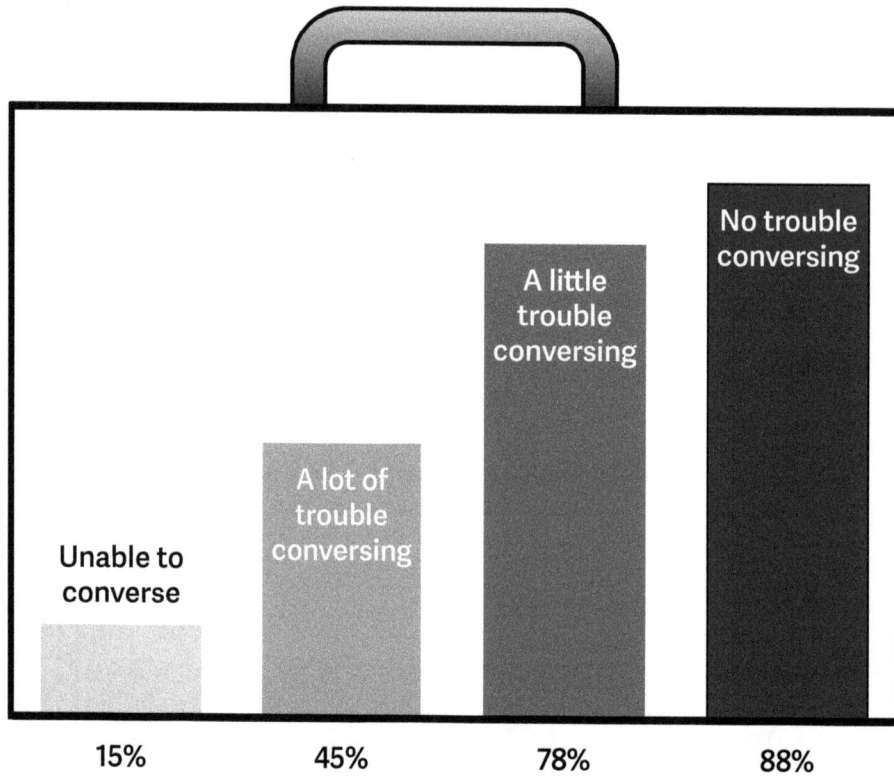

Unable to converse	A lot of trouble conversing	A little trouble conversing	No trouble conversing
15%	45%	78%	88%

Who Were Socially Isolated

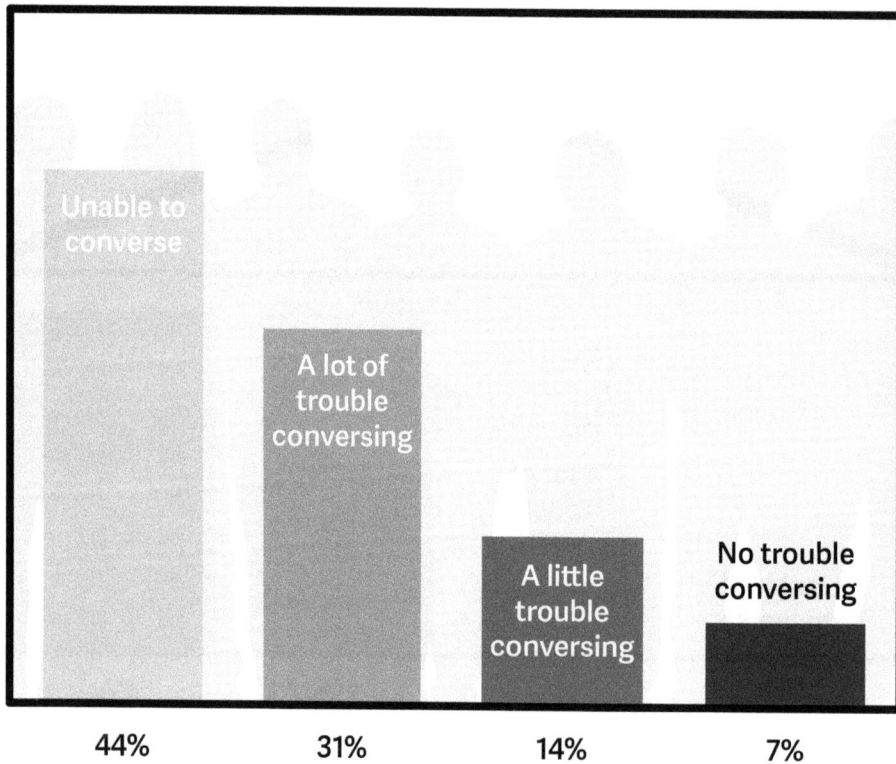

Unable to converse	A lot of trouble conversing	A little trouble conversing	No trouble conversing
44%	31%	14%	7%

Communication and social skills, often limited by a lack of instruction and support rather than the potential to learn, have traditionally been roadblocks for autistics across most facets of life (cf. Roux, 2015). Clearly, the development of academic skills, while obviously important, does not ensure success for autistics in postsecondary school settings or in the workplace. Rather, communication and social skills (such as the ability to maintain calm, exchange important pieces of information, understand a common goal, be flexible and collaborative, understand hierarchy, and consistently follow the myriad of social rules that govern behavior) are essential (Myles, 2024). Undoubtedly, any director of human resources working with people with or without disabilities would agree.

Equally important to the development of school and workplace skills is the ability to develop satisfying personal relationships that enrich a person's quality of life. Many have made the mistake of misinterpreting a lack of communication and social skills as a lack of interest when trying to understand the lives of autistics. Everyone, including those who struggle to learn communication and social skills, desire connection with other people and seek comfort, safety, and a sense of belonging as part of a social community (Yang et al., 2020).

Communication/Social Characteristics and Interventions

Early Childhood

In the first two years of life, a child reaches pivotal milestones to communicate and socially interact by watching and imitating others. These core milestones include the ability to (a) share joint attention, (b) use gestural communication, (c) engage in reciprocal interactions, and (d) demonstrate motor and vocal imitation. The emergence of these core skills is linked to a child's inherent comfort level and reaction to physical (e.g., the structure of the classroom, the loudness in an area) and social stimuli (e.g., the number of people present, whether unstated rules are understood), which then impacts their social motivation—their desire to interact with others.

In young autistic children, differences are observed in the development of these core communication and social skills.

Joint Attention and Gestural Communication

For example, they often struggle to alternate eye gaze between an interesting object and another person in a fluid manner (i.e., shared joint attention). Over-reliance on one joint attention skill to the exclusion of all others may be linked to the child's difficulty understanding the nonverbal emotional expressions of others, such as facial expression and tone of voice (Gomes et al., 2020). For example, autistic children may use gestures to regulate the behavior of others (e.g., request, protest, and attempt to get their needs met), but not use the same gestures to show or point to objects for the purpose of sharing their interest (i.e., gestural communication). As a result of differences in joint attention and gestural communication, reciprocal interactions are less spontaneous and flexible, and the child often insists on repeating specific routinized interaction patterns with others (Adamson et al., 2009; Cerullo et al., 2021).

Reciprocity and Modeling

Young autistic children also show considerable variability in spontaneous motor and vocal imitation and the ability to use imitation in novel contexts. Imitation challenges are associated with difficulties with joint attention and social-emotional understanding (cf. Cerullo et al., 2021). When they do imitate demonstrated actions or words, autistics are generally less focused on faces and, thus, may not understand all the social information that provides meaning to the action (cf. Griffin & Scherf, 2020).

The ability to imitate what others do or say without understanding the meaning of those actions or words distinguishes autistic children from other children of similar developmental levels. Imitation differences paired with limited levels of reciprocity have a cascading effect on all social learning. For example, the ability to watch and imitate what others are doing lays the foundation for most social and cognitive skills (Heimann et al., 2016; Posar & Visconti, 2019), so it is important never to give up on supporting autistic individuals to imitate.

Communication Development in Young Children

Communication is a verbal and/or nonverbal interactive exchange between two or more people to express needs, feelings, and ideas. It is a fundamental social skill. An effective communicator is constantly thinking about context, language, social and emotional aspects of the situation and making ongoing adjustments in response to the behavior of others.

Language can be expressed verbally (by means of spoken, signed, voice-output communication device, or written language) and nonverbally (by using pictures, gestures, emotion, and other behaviors). It is a formal symbol system that has the following structural qualities:

- *Morphology* – rules for how words are structured in a sentence (e.g., word endings to mark plural [book/books])
- *Semantics* – rules for how meaning is created by words and sentences (i.e., word and sentence meaning)
- *Syntax* – rules for the ordering of words in a sentence (i.e., sentence grammar).

Tips to Remember the Differences Between Language, Speech, and Communication:
1. ***You can communicate without language.*** You can communicate nonverbally through facial expressions, gestures, and other behaviors.
2. ***You can use language without communicating.*** You can talk to yourself without communicating to others. You can write information to yourself without communicating with others.
3. ***You can use speech without communicating.*** You can talk to yourself without communicating to others
4. ***You can use language without speech.*** You can use written language, sign language and technology-based voice-output communication aids (VOCA).
5. ***You can communicate without speech.*** You can communicate with others through written language, sign language, VOCA, and nonverbal means, such as facial expression, gestures, and behavior.

Successful communication requires an individual to focus and understand the meaning of rapidly changing language, social, and emotional information. Communication entails back-and-forth interaction and sharing experiences. Whenever two or more people are communicating, they take turns initiating a new idea and responding to what another says or does. This "interaction dance" seems to happen effortlessly.

> Communicative interactions require moment-to-moment attention to multiple contextual, language, social, and emotional information, an understanding of verbal and nonverbal messages, and an ability to make ongoing adjustments in response to the behaviors of others.

In contrast, when interacting with an autistic, you may feel that you are working very hard to gain their attention, get a response, and maintain the interaction. Sometimes, you may find that the autistic seems to have a single agenda when interacting with you (having their needs met) and is not responsive to what you say or do. At other times, they may respond, but the interaction never seems to go beyond the first question and answer. Often this "interaction dance" between a neuromajority person and an autistic can feel out-of-sync or different. In fact, the autistic person may be overwhelmed by the process of reciprocal interaction and either melt down or withdraw.

From a young age, children communicate for a wide variety of reasons. The "function of communication" is a term used to describe these many reasons to communicate a single message.

Table 8.1. Communicative Functions and Autism.

Functions Often Observed	Functions Often Not Observed
Request for personal needs • "I want ...	Commenting to share interests • "That butterfly is pretty."
Respond to questions/routine phrases • "What do you want to eat?"	Expressing feelings • "I feel overwhelmed."
Reject person, object, or activity • "I don't want"	Using prosocial statements • "Let me help you reach the book."
	Requesting new information • Can you tell me where the bathroom is?"

Single Verbal Messages

The reasons or purposes for communication are organized into several categories that include, but are not limited to:

- Requesting to satisfy personal needs (e.g., asking for a preferred item/activity)
- Responding to others (e.g., answering a simple question)
- Rejecting to satisfy personal needs (e.g., indicating "no" or a desire to be finished)
- Commenting (e.g., describing what he is doing)
- Requesting information (e.g., asking who, what, when, where, and why questions to obtain new information)
- Expressing feelings (e.g., saying "I feel sick")
- Use prosocial statements (e.g., saying "thank you" or giving a compliment)

The term "single verbal messages" is used to understand communication differences in autism. It is more common for autistic children to use language to request objects, food, or assistance, and less likely for them to spontaneously comment, express feelings, or use other prosocial statements (e.g., "thank you," "I like you"). Both can be strengthened by instruction and multiple practice opportunities.

Reciprocal Conversation

- The following skills are important in maintaining a conversation:
- Understanding the nonverbal rules for how to begin and end a conversation
- Comprehending the meaning of the other person's spoken message
- Understanding the meaning of another's nonverbal message (such as facial expression and emotion conveyed in the words)
- Interpreting the meaning of another person's spoken and nonverbal message in relation to the social situation
- Understanding the perspective of the other person (what they know or feel) to keep the conversation relevant
- Expressing ideas related to the topic of conversation
- Taking turns
- Adjusting to the changing language, social, communicative, and emotional messages of the other person (Abbot-Smith et al., 2023)

Autistics generally find these skills challenging; most require ongoing instruction and multiple practice opportunities to learn and generalize these skills (Abbot-Smith, 2023; Mataya et al., 2017).

In addition, autistics have reported difficulties in disregarding competing distractions (e.g., other people talking in the background, air conditioner running) to focus on a conversation. They emphasized that these listening difficulties are distinct from challenges, though the two, together, can make reciprocal conversation even more challenging (Sturrock et al., 2022).

Central to successful conversation is the ability to consider the nonverbal cues and perspective of the other person; that is, to continually monitor and adapt what to say and how to talk based on the needs of others and understand that their feelings differ from their own (i.e., theory of mind [ToM]). Only with this social perspective can a child interpret the meaning and intent of what others are saying. Social perspective taking also allows children to continually adjust their own language and communication with others and have a conversation about present, past, and future events (Rosello et al., 2020).

Difficulty understanding the meaning behind nonverbal social and emotional communication cues impacts reciprocal interactions in autistics (Abbot-Smith et al., 2023). Some only notice extreme expressions of emotion and miss more subtle social and emotional messages. Many misinterpret the meaning of these messages, making incorrect associations between a person's nonverbal message and the context (Vermeulen, 2012, 2022). For example, understanding the emotions of a person in tears depends on context—at a funeral, they mean sadness and at an awards ceremony, the same behavior may mean something completely different—overjoyed, overwhelmed, or humbled.

> People who see a frightened face in an angry situation describe the facial expression as angry, not frightened. In some cases, contextual information seems to be stronger than information coming from a facial expression, even with clear facial expressions if basic emotions like aversion, fear, happiness, anger, and sadness. That is, we often judge facial expressions based on the context, much more than on the basis of the emotion that is shown in the facial expression. (Vermeulen, 2012)

Although able to identify elements of affect in isolation (e.g., emotion, facial expression, gestural meaning, tone of voice), many autistics appear have difficulty integrating and acting on these multiple nonverbal features of conversation (pitch, loudness, rate, fluency) that occur simultaneously in natural contexts (cf. Silver & Parsons, 2022; Vermeulen, 2012).

Due to difficulties with social perspective taking (cf. Silver & Parsons, 2022), even autistic children with proficient complex language continue to show significant differences in reciprocal conversation. Their conversations are less fluid and more routinized. Some appear only to understand the turn-taking quality of conversation and engage in repetitive questions or statements to maintain a predictable interaction and response from the partner. Use of situation-specific statements, repetitive questions, and focus on a narrow range of topics often typify their conversations.

Some autistic children use pedantic (i.e., formal and literal) speech and can persistently talk about a topic of interest to them with no apparent recognition of cues from the listener (Ying et al., 2018). Communicative flexibility poses the biggest challenge (Thomas & Bambara, 2020). Their communication patterns appear to be the primary means to create meaningful interactions amid perceived social chaos. Ultimately, autistic children do their best to interact with others, applying their own understanding of the situation (Sturrock et al., 2022).

Behavior Is Communication

In the absence of understanding how to communicate in conventional ways, individuals with autism use a range of behaviors to express their needs and feelings. All behaviors, whether viewed as positive or negative, are communication.

Laughter is communication; a temper tantrum is communication; squealing is communication; running away is communication. Saying the same word repeatedly can be communication; asking the same question, even when the answer has been given a hundred times, can be an attempt to communicate.

The challenge is to figure out what the autistic individual is trying to communicate.

Because of a lack of instruction on how to communicate in conventional ways, autistic individuals often communicate with others in routine, predictable ways. Easily confused by complex social interactions, they try to minimize change and maximize routines. Comfort appears to exist in the use of familiar routines and rituals when interacting with others. This differs significantly from natural interactions that constantly change and are not predictable (e.g., do you know what I will say next?). In life, few conversations are routine (except for the beginning of a telephone conversation or a greeting), and most conversations require us to be "flexible" moment to moment. The ability to communicate in a flexible way is severely impacted in autism.

Examples of Communication Routines and Rituals:

- Making repetitive communicative vocalizations
- Engaging in repetitive movement while communicating (e.g., repetitively tapping a person, moving too close to a person's face)
- Using echolalia. This is the most common form of communication rituals observed in autism. There are two basic forms of echolalia:
    - *Immediate echolalia:* Repeating the last word/phrase/sentence that someone has just said.
    - *Delayed echolalia:* Saying the same word/phrase/ monologue from a song, book, TV/media repeatedly
- Asking the same questions repeatedly (spoken or on a communication device)
- Talking about the same topic repeatedly

All of these examples can be attempts to communicate and interact. They can also be used for nonsocial reasons; that is, the individual may repeat things without any intent to interact with others.

Communication Interventions

Approximately at least 30% of autistic individuals remain nonspeaking; however, this statistic is continuously changing due to advances in early diagnosis and treatment. A nonspeaking individual is either mute or, in some instances, says an occasional word inconsistently (Holland, 2024). Some nonspeaking individuals can learn to use an alternative language, such as sign language or written language. Others learn to use more basic symbols as a means of communication, such as photographs or graphic icons. Both complex language and basic picture-based symbols serve as alternatives to speech, called augmentative and alternative communication (AAC) systems. These alternatives can be generated by the individual using "low-tech" and "high-tech" AAC systems that include voice-output communication devices.

Many autistics are verbal but are challenged with issues of fluency, especially when dysregulated. Some of them are highly verbal with advanced vocabularies that are readily used when the individual is calm. An individual with these characteristics might also benefit from an alternative source of communication to engage with others more fluently.

There are obvious benefits of using AAC systems with nonspeaking individuals as well as those who have challenges with being verbally fluent, specifically,

1. Increased communication competence and functional communication
2. Increased rate of developing speech in comparison to those who do not use AAC systems
3. Decreased rate of problem behaviors associated with poor communication skills and associated communication frustration.

While speech is always the ultimate goal, AAC must be considered for any autistic who requires functional means to communicate more effectively. AAC is a broad field of study, and this section is limited to a discussion of the most common AAC supports, including:

- Sign language
- Low-tech systems, such as the Picture Exchange Communication System (Frost et al., 2002) and interactive communication boards
- High-tech systems, including voice output communication aids (VOCA)/speech generating devices (SGD)

There are different attributes and requirements for each augmentative system, as summarized on the next page.

Table 8.2. Attributes and Requirements for Specific AAC Systems.

AAC Attributes	Sign Language	Low-Tech Systems	High-Tech Systems
	Face-to-face	Exchange	Exchange
Interaction	Fluid	Slow	Slow
Grammar	Varies	Not required	Varies
Messages	Unlimited	Limited	Varies
Motor	Complex	Simple	Simple
Portability	n/a Unaided	Aided* Some limitations	Aided* Some limitations
Partners	Limited	Unlimited	Unlimited

* Aided" refers to AAC systems that require materials to communicate, ranging from paper and pencil to communication boards to high-tech devices that produce voice and/or written output.

Sign language is a formal language system with a complete grammar. Like speech, it requires face-to-face interaction and attention to fluid social interaction. Attention to others' signed messages requires rapid and immediate processing of the symbols. An individual must be able to remember the symbol from memory without any external cues. In addition, motor planning skills, motor imitation skills, and fine-motor abilities are necessary for sign language. Even if all these skills are present, it is important to remember that the individual's signed messages will only be understood by limited partners.

Some autistic individuals benefit from sign language because it is unaided and can be used across all environments. However, sign language requires face-to-face interaction and motor skills that may be a challenge for some. Furthermore, the use of sign language is restricted to those people in the person's life who understand the language.

Low-tech AAC system examples include the Picture Exchange Communication System (PECS) and communication boards. These types of systems place fewer social demands on the communicator. The communication is a simple, concrete exchange that is slow paced.

Low-tech systems typically use photographs, pictographs, or printed words. This allows the individual to focus a symbol for as long as necessary to understand the meaning. The symbols serve as reminders of what to say. Low-tech systems include messages that are generally understood by everyone; however, low-tech systems may limit the number of communication messages that an individual can generate.

One low-tech picture-based communication system, PECS (Frost et al., 2002), is a respected EBP with strong research support (Hume et al., 2022). The primary objective of PECS is to teach autistic children that communication is an "exchange." The child is taught to initiate communication by handing a picture to another person. The child then exchanges the picture symbol for a desired item or activity. PECS teaches children to gain a person's attention, deliver a (picture) message, and wait for a response—the core principles of reciprocal communication. With these core skills and the ability to discriminate among different photos and pictures, the child can develop a repertoire of symbols to convey various communicative functions (e.g., requests, comments, prosocial messages, feelings and more).

High-tech systems have gained enormous support in recent years due to the popularity and availability of portable phones and tablets. Tech devices allow the person to use photographs, pictures, graphic symbols, letters, words, and/or phrases to create messages. Speech-generating devices (GDs), also known as voice-output communication aids (VOCA), are electronic AAC systems with speech that may be a digitized recorded human voice or a synthesized computer-generated voice.

The advantage of speech-output devices is that they give nonspeaking individuals a "voice." High-tech systems can be intrinsically motivating and are available in a wide variety for users with a range of cognitive and language skills. For example, there are simple devices for children who do not discriminate pictures, although one must understand cause and effect to use them. The child learns to press a switch or button to activate a prerecorded message. A single-message device helps the child gain an adult's attention, such as a device that says, "Please come here." A preprogrammed voice message can also be used in a specific social setting, such as a device that says, "Happy birthday!"

For children who understand visual symbols, whether pictograph or printed words, and/or show an interest in technology, there is a growing number of programmable devices with speech output. Devices range from those that contain four messages to fully featured, computerized systems that contain an unlimited number of messages and allow for keyboarding.

When choosing an AAC system, it is important to consider a child's abilities and interests. As with all other AAC systems, the child's use of the device as a means of functional communication is the primary consideration.

Despite their many advantages, there are potential problems when some autistic children and teens use voice output systems.

1. The durability of the device must be considered for those with challenging and unsafe behaviors as many devices are not durable and expensive.
2. A person always needs access to a communication system; and some tablets may not be useful in all settings (e.g., swimming).
3. Some autistics enjoy exploring the device to hear a voice repeatedly or prefer to use the device to "play," and, thus, may use the device without communicative intent.

Multiple variables, particularly family preferences, go into the selection of a communication system. The appropriate selection of one or more communication tools can enhance the individual's abilities to build competency. Conversely, a mismatch between the individual's needs and the selected communication system can inhibit motivation and communication.

Ginny's CAPS in Chapter 3 reveals her communication supports—a language board and PECS. Her communication systems have been matched to her environment to ensure that she has access to information that is important for expanding her social circle, making choices, and accessing the curriculum.

Social Development

Social development involves engaging in play and leisure activities, interacting socially with adults and peers, and acquiring prosocial communication skills. Social skills encompass virtually every aspect of daily living, and social competence—the ability to continually monitor and flexibly accommodate, adapt, and adjust to ongoing social interactions—is necessary to be able to function in all home, school, and community environments.

Autistic children and youth require direct instruction and multiple practice opportunities to benefit from and contribute to social moments, with emphasis placed on (a) social interaction, (b) play, (c) group activities, and (d) social perspective taking.

Social Interaction

Unlike language development, which is rule-based, social development is dynamic and constantly changing. Social interactions demand moment-to-moment interpretation and integration of multiple contextual factors, such as socioemotional understanding, language, and prior experiences. Social interaction is complex. Every moment demands flexible attention, an understanding of what is socially relevant, and the ability to disregard what is not pertinent.

Social interaction requires fluid processing of multiple contextual language, social, and emotional messages. When we interact with others, we simultaneously observe and process the words, emotional expression, tone of voice, and body gestures of our social partners, as well as link these social messages to all the relevant features of the setting to understand the whole meaning of a situation.

Play

The play and leisure skills of autistics are a window into what they may and may not understand. The play and leisure behaviors of autistic children are particularly striking when compared with the richness of typical play development. Despite variability, certain qualitative characteristics appear consistently. Although these resemble mature forms of pretend play, flexibility and imagination are qualitatively different.

- Play patterns can be intensely ritualized and fall under restricted, repetitive patterns of behavior, interests, or activities. Children may fixate on a limited number of activities that are repeated and carried out alone for long periods of time, such as lining up

- Toy play ranges from simple, repetitive play sequences (e.g., adult builds block tower, student knocks it down) to elaborate but exact play routines (e.g., reenacting segments from a book or video from memory verbatim) (cf. Kent et al., 2020). For example, the child with autism may reenact the precise lines from a favorite movie during play, which differs from other children who invent their own characters, dialogue, and stories in play.

Nowhere is the need for social flexibility as urgent as during social activities with peers. The rapid, transient nature of social interaction places demands that pose great challenges for autistic children. During peer play, autistics are more socially responsive when they can predict the sequence of events; however, their social behavior becomes disorganized when play is not predictable (cf. Cannon et al., 2021; Quill, 2017; Vermeulen, 2022).

Group Activities

All group activities at home, in school, and in the community pose the same challenges for autistic children as found in play and leisure activities. Group activities require an individual to demonstrate skills, such as staying with the group, self-regulating, reading the social scene, sharing, staying on topic, and adjusting according to perspectives. Like play and leisure activities, groups vary in level of predictability. Group activities that are predictable—in which "everyone is doing the same thing at the same time"—are easier for the autistic to join and imitate (Quill, 2017). Parallel participation, and less social decision-making is required when a group activity occurs in unison (i.e., at the same time).

Group situations in which conversation is optional increases the likelihood that an autistic child will fully participate (Quill, 2017). In addition, autistic children are often more successful with group activities that have a closed-ended, predictable sequence of events (e.g., activities and games with rules and a clear beginning and end). In contrast, activities including random conversation and/or group activities that are open-ended are the most challenging situations.

Social Perspective Taking

Relationships are built on mutually enjoyable, meaningful interactions. To experience ongoing social connections requires such skills as noticing that someone else has similar interests, understanding the needs and feelings of others, and finding mutually reinforcing ways to be together.

We compare our perceptions, experiences, thoughts, and feelings to others' during shared social experiences. Theory of mind (ToM) refers a person's capacity to read the thoughts and feelings of others and understand that other people have intentions, thoughts, desires, and feelings that differ from their own. ToM can be described by the expression "put oneself into someone else's shoes" (i.e., to imagine another's thoughts and feelings). To understand the mind of another, it is necessary to (a) make sense of the inner mental states of self and others; (b) understand that others may have perspectives that differ from one's own; and (c) use this understanding to predict what they are going to do next. It is about recognizing, understanding, and predicting the social behaviors or mental states of others (Greenberg et al., 2023; Lecheler et al., 2020).

ToM blindness is proposed to explain the social and communication difficulties in autism (cf. Baron-Cohen, 1997; Berenguer et al., 2018). That is, with ToM impacted, autistic children are challenged to describe, explain, or infer mental states during social situations. Without instruction in social perspective taking, autistic children find it difficult to predict the behavior of others and, therefore, seek social interactions that are predictable. Lacking an understanding of social concepts such as others' mental states, they find it difficult to monitor, predict, and adjust to ongoing social and communicative interactions (Vermeulen, 2022).

Social Skills Interventions: The STEPS to Being Social Model

The STEPS of Being Social is a unique, visual, and easy-to-use model that every classroom, job development site, or any instructional arena can use to understand what social skills to teach and when to teach them. Based on research on the development of social skills, EBP, and the autistic neurology, the model guides social skills assessment and intervention, assisting educators in determining where to "step-on" and what interventions might be appropriate to teach identified skills (Laurel & Taylor, 2016).

A strong premise underlying this model is that social skills must be taught directly with deep respect to autistic individuals. Consequently, development of these skills is not supported by simply having the person who is struggling with "being social" spend time with others who have well-developed social skills. Rather, social skills need to be taught directly and purposely, and then practiced in various settings.

The four components of STEPS to Being Social are (a) Engagement: the Foundation, (b) Phase I: Being Together, (c) Phase II: Back & Forth Exchange, and (d) Phase III: Part of a Group and Beyond.

The three steps or phases sit atop Engagement—the foundation. After engagement is attained, the learner begins to move up the steps, learning skills that build on one another.

Figure 8.3. The STEPS to Being Social.

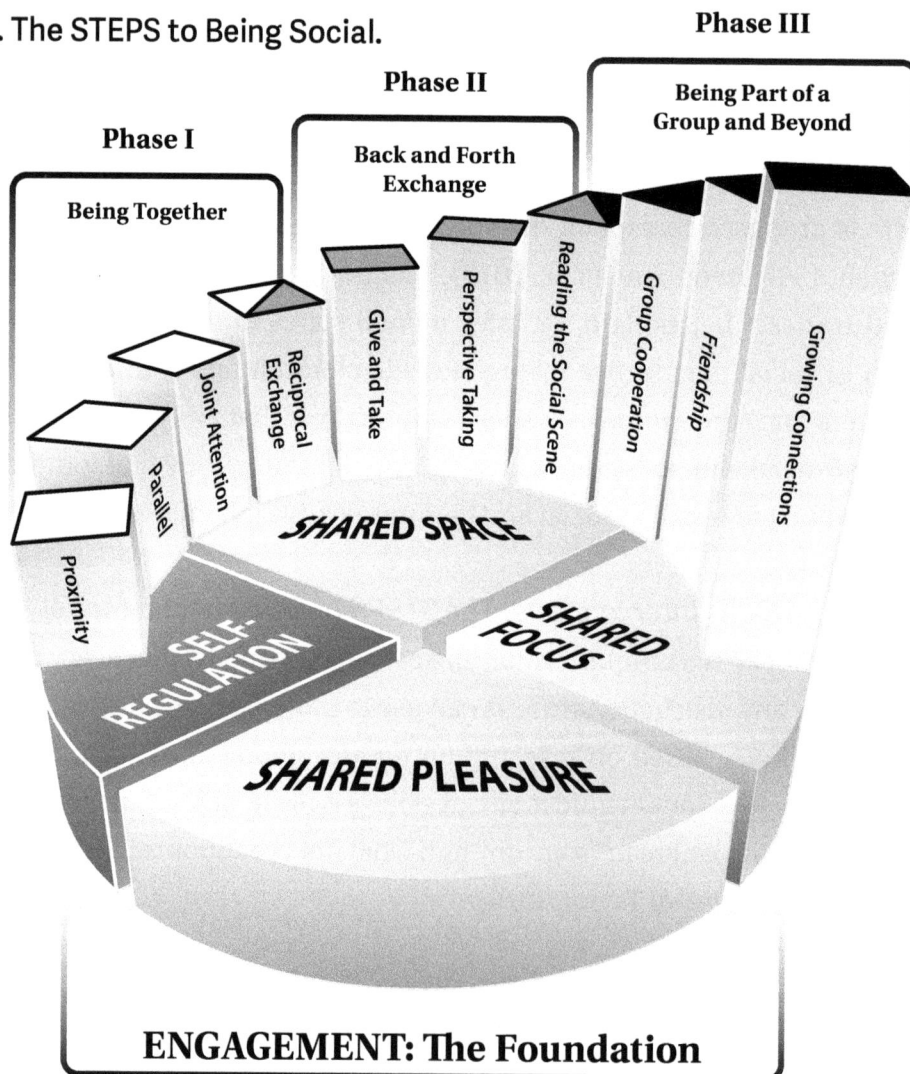

Engagement: The Foundation

Engagement is the foundation of being social. Although it is intuitive for many, engagement often does not "just happen" for autistics (Javad et al., 2020; Laurel & Taylor, 2106).

It is essential to understand what engagement looks like to set up the conditions for it to happen when it does not occur naturally. Engagement is the sense of being "with" another person and connected. Engagement has four elements:

- self-regulation
- shared space
- shared focus
- shared enjoyment

It is the synergy between these four elements that defines the special moments of engagement.

Figure 8.4. Engagement: The Foundation.

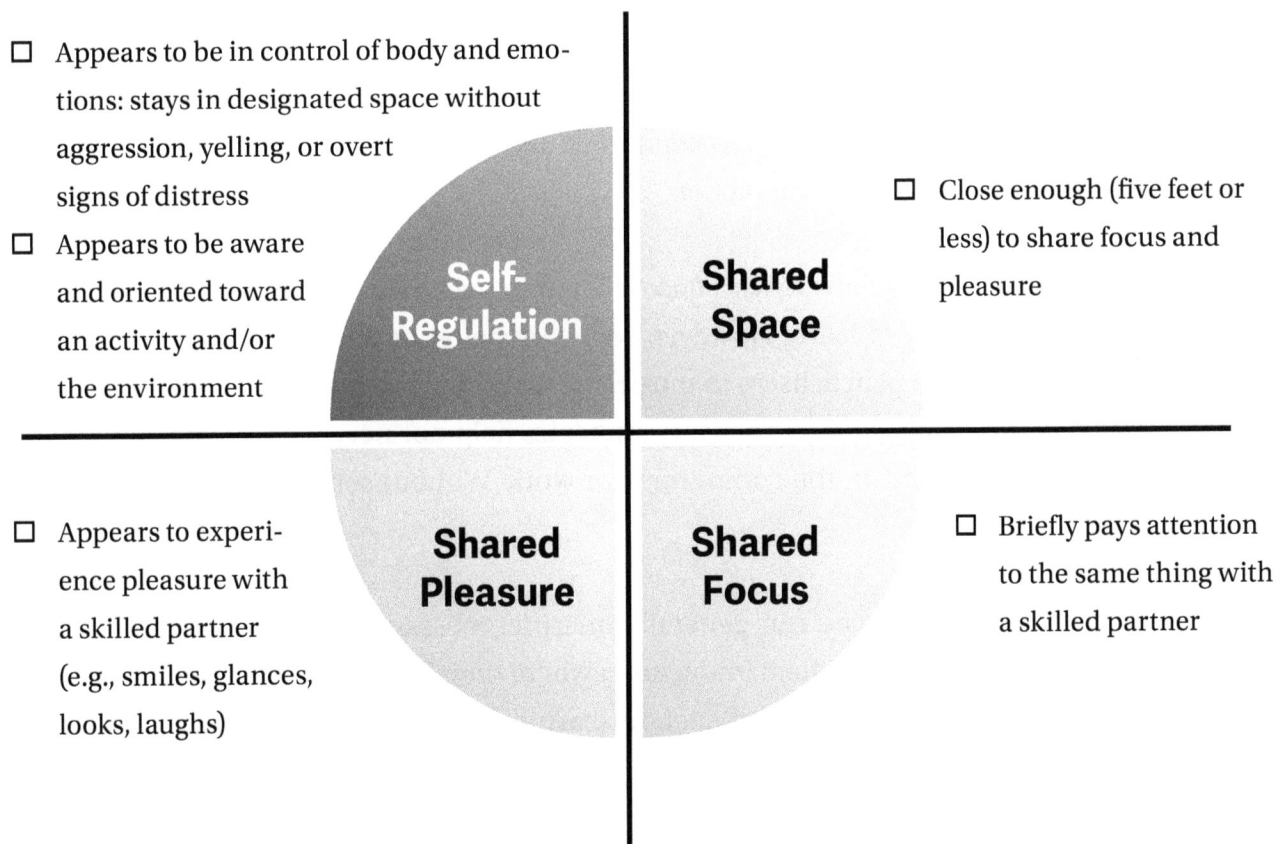

☐ Appears to be in control of body and emotions: stays in designated space without aggression, yelling, or overt signs of distress

☐ Appears to be aware and oriented toward an activity and/or the environment

Self-Regulation

Shared Space

☐ Close enough (five feet or less) to share focus and pleasure

Shared Pleasure

Shared Focus

☐ Appears to experience pleasure with a skilled partner (e.g., smiles, glances, looks, laughs)

☐ Briefly pays attention to the same thing with a skilled partner

Figure 8.4 (continued)

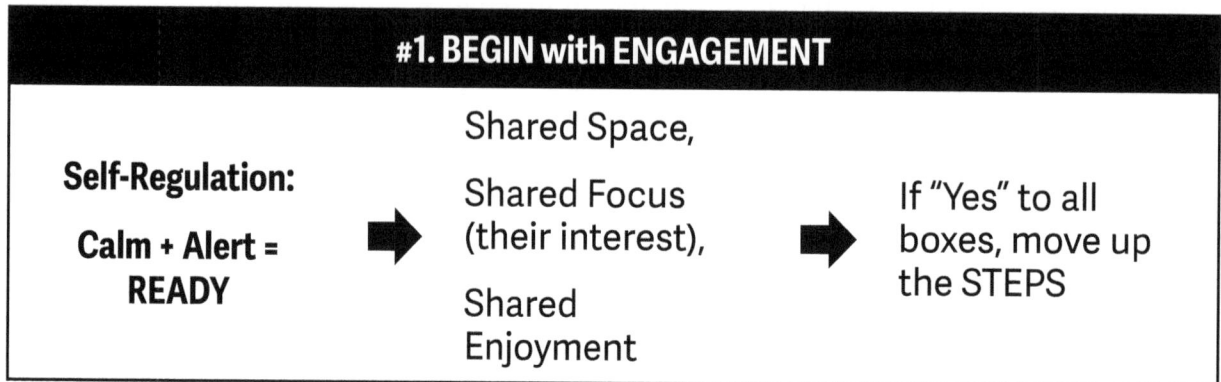

#1. BEGIN with ENGAGEMENT		
Self-Regulation: **Calm + Alert =** **READY** ➡️	Shared Space, Shared Focus (their interest), Shared Enjoyment ➡️	If "Yes" to all boxes, move up the STEPS

Take NOTE that this foundation will be visited over and over when the student becomes dysregulated.

Self-Regulation

In the Engagement graphic, the Self-Regulation section is shaded to show emphasis. Self-regulation is essential and must be in place before social skills can be taught. It is the element that we go back to time and again as we pursue social interactions. As discussed in Chapter 7: Sensory/Regulation, self-regulation is an emotional and physical state that supports learning and responding positively to an interaction.

Everyone learns to self-regulate, to use sensory input to help their bodies become calm and alert enough to be ready to learn. However, some are better at this skill than others. They might pace, fiddle with a pencil, listen to music, tap their foot, exercise, get out in nature, sip a drink, or bite their nails. All these sensory strategies help our nervous systems "get ready" to learn—at school, home, in the community, or work. Without self-regulation there is no engagement.

Learners who can self-regulate can generally interpret messages received from their proprioception system. This helps them understand where their body is in space and, therefore, brings a feeling of safety and ease. Challenges in learning self-regulation skills may be related to limitations in proprioceptive understanding (see Chapter 7: Sensory/ Regulation).

Self-Regulation: CALM + ALERT = READY

Engagement occurs when an educator can answer "YES" to the following questions:
1. Does the individual appear in control of their body and emotions?
2. Is the individual aware and oriented toward an activity and/or the environment?

This is when an individual is regulated and "READY" to learn. If the person is not regulated and needs support to get regulated, strategies from Chapter 7: Sensory/ Regulation as well as the common ideas below may be used to support self-regulation.

- Put something in your mouth (our mouths can help us self-soothe) gum, candy, something to drink
- Practice rhythmic movement like swinging, bouncing, or rocking
- Listen to music with a beat
- Exercise or engage in activities that use large muscle groups
- Get outside in nature
- Participate in a repetitive task or activity
- Find a quiet space to get away from stimuli.

Shared Space

Shared Space is the second element of engagement. Shared Space is being in proximity with another person. It is ONLY when regulated that one can begin to share space with another/ others to pursue a positive social interaction.

Distance often communicates whether someone is ready to socially engage. Often, and depending on the context, standing near someone indicates a readiness or willingness to engage. Moving away from a person generally indicates the opposite. It is important to intentionally take note of what space works for the student. This should occur in "real time," especially in the classroom or workspace.

Educators can ask themselves:

1. In what settings is this student comfortable?
2. What proximity to others does this student currently prefer?
3. How can the space be visually defined to help this student understand what is expected?
4. How can materials by limited or organized within the space to encourage engagement?

When an individual is close enough (typically within 5 feet) and able to share focus and enjoy they are in Shared Space and can continue to work on engagement. Within a Shared Space, individuals can begin to be attentive together.

Shared Space: A PLACE TO BE TOGETHER

Shared Focus

Once regulated and sharing space, learners move to the third element of Engagement, Shared Focus, in which at least two people attend to or are interested in the same thing. A simple, yet effective approach is to encourage shared focus by discussing the learner's special interest (see Chapter 6: Reinforcement). The benefits of incorporating a special interest are many, including:

- Focus and conversation are more likely to flow as the learner knows the content well
- Positive emotions are generated during discussions of a special interest; so, regulation challenges are often not apparent
- A sense of pride and general well-being are experienced when these discussion topics are introduced
- While socialization, in and of itself, may not be motivating, incorporating a special interest into an interaction can be

As educators, we might get tired of hearing all about the car dealerships in their community, water heaters, pipe cleaners, Minecraft, terminal diseases, or Anime. We might not see the interest in scribbling with a blue marker, flicking a straw, or rocking in a particular pattern.

While these topics or movements might not bring us as much joy as they bring to autistics, it is important to respect and acknowledge these interests and use them to support engagement.

Guiding questions as we begin to share focus can include:

1. What is the student most interested in doing? (e.g., objects, topics, movement)
2. Does the student try to bring your attention to something they like and, if so, what action is taken to accomplish this?
3. Are you able to bring the student's attention to something you select?
4. How long can you share focus together?

When an individual pays attention briefly with another person to a topic of interest or action of interest, they have Shared Focus.

Shared Focus: A REASON TO BE TOGETHER

Shared Enjoyment

When an individual is regulated, sharing space, and sharing focus, they are ready to move to the final element Engagement—Shared Enjoyment.

Having a pleasant experience together can look different for everyone—perhaps a belly laugh, a smile with one's eyes, or even a glance. With an autistic person, it might be a bit more subtle; it may take you a moment to discover the signs of Shared Enjoyment, but by no means is it any less important or gratifying. For some autistic people, their Shared Enjoyment is very evident and may include evidence of full body delight.

As you identify moments of enjoyment for the people you work and live with, consider:

1. Who knows the individual best and can help you to understand their unique cues?
2. What nonverbal cues are associated with enjoyment for this person?
3. How and where can you observe the individual to better understand how they show happiness?

It is the synergy of Shared Space, Shared Focus, and Shared Enjoyment within the context of a calm, alert state that defines the very special moment of Engagement.

Shared Enjoyment: ENJOYING THE MOMENT TOGETHER.

Summary of Engagement: The Foundation

Engagement is the foundation for interacting with others. When we know how to recognize engagement, we can see it. When we see it, we can make it happen more often and with more people. When engagement takes place, we find the magic of connection, and meaningful relationships are formed.

Figure 8.5. Engagement: The Foundation.

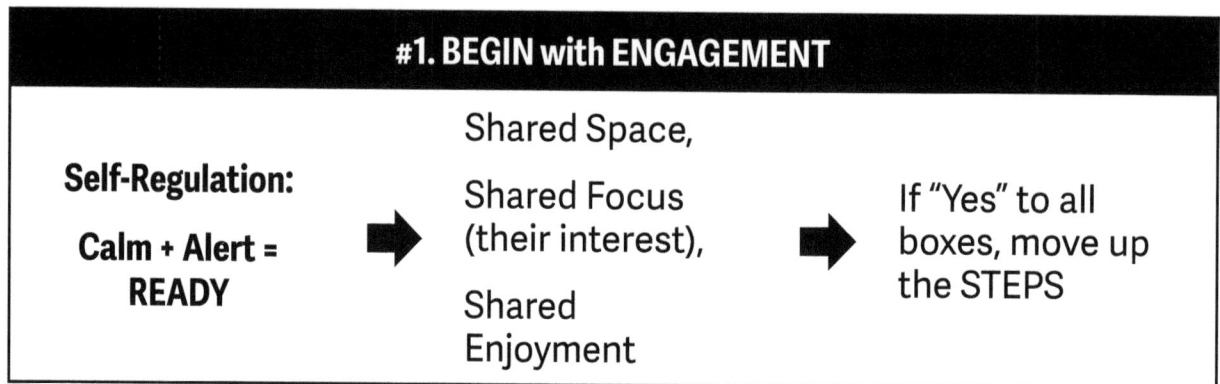

#1. BEGIN with ENGAGEMENT		
Self-Regulation: **Calm + Alert =** **READY** ➡	Shared Space, Shared Focus (their interest), Shared Enjoyment ➡	If "Yes" to all boxes, move up the STEPS

Engagement Interventions

Engagement is crucial to any consideration of learning to "be social." It is important to define in observable terms what "be social" means as this term is open to interpretation. When professionals talk about teaching social skills to autistics, there is often no shared definition of what skills are meant to be taught.

Consider an individualized education program (IEP) objective that might contain the objective, "improve social skills with 80% accuracy."

- What skills will be addressed and toward what end?
- What does it mean to take turns in conversation in four of five opportunities?
- How does "making friends," a parent priority, relate to developing social skills?

Engagement interventions described here are evidence-based and represent the following categories: (a) antecedent-based interventions, (b) parent-implemented interventions, (c) prompting, (d) reinforcement, (e) task analysis, and (f) visual supports (see Chapter 4 for a discussion of EBP).

The following describes how EBPs can be used at the engagement level:

- **Use visual supports.** Creating comfortable boundaries often helps the learner feel comfortable, focus on the task at hand, and understand that they are with a social partner. For example, you can:
  - Use a visual support to prime the learner so they understand their daily activities
  - Visually highlight boundaries using tape, carpet squares, etc. (see Chapter 5: Structure/Modifications).
- **Incorporate learner interests.** Using the student's special interests or motivating items have many benefits. Interests can be identified through observation, asking the student and/or family, or by a structured assessment. Remember that these items are generally highly reinforcing (see Chapter 6: Reinforcement).
- **Limit materials.** It is important that the teacher has control of materials and can make them available when the student is ready to attend. Having more than one motivating item to share is advisable to ensure that learners do not become inattentive.
- **Select effective reinforcement.** The activity and adult are powerful reinforcers as are special interests. All can be incorporated to increase engagement.
- **Use antecedent-based interventions.** Arranging the environment for success supports engagement, including moving to a corner of a room instead of the middle, sitting as opposed to standing, and using peers as a safe space. This includes having peers sit on each side of the learner and use their bodies to build a "container" to help the learner better understand space. Priming and visual supports are also antecedent-based interventions.

Phase I: Being Together

As the student becomes more frequently engaged for longer periods of time, the Phase I: Begin Together steps are addressed. Essentially, the steps involve learning to be together with a social partner—a person who is proficient and understands these skills—and beginning to participate in a back-and-forth interaction. Skills in Phase I: Being Together include: (a) proximity, (b) parallel, (c) joint attention, and (d) reciprocal exchange.

Proximity

Step one is **Proximity:** the ability to share the same space as another person, within at least five feet, though perhaps not interacting or engaging in the same activity. A quote from an somebody working on this skill set might be: "Oh, you are here?" This is just one small step above the foundation of engagement. The goal for proximity is to share the same space (< 5 ft) without aggression or excessive physical contact/ vocalizations for at least 5 minutes.

Parallel

The next step is **Parallel:** being with someone and using the same materials (though not necessary for the same purpose). A quote from somebody working on this skill set might be: "You are doing this, too." Skills to be learned here include:

- Tolerates a skilled partner (SP) using the same materials at 5 feet or less
- Indicates that the SP is using the same material or engaging in the same activity
- Indicates enjoyment by expression
- Attends briefly to SP's actions

As we teach the objectives of parallel play, we encourage the learner to notice the other person, by glancing or smiling or changing their expression, indicating awareness that a moment is being shared in a new way.

Joint Attention

The next step is **Joint Attention:** following, initiating, and visually attending to the same object or activity as another person. A quote from somebody working on this skill set might be: "We are looking at this."

Figure 8.6. Phase I Skills: Being Together.

Phase I, is the student able to share space and materials with others?

Observe the student in 2-3 environments on EACH subskill to determine their skill level:

0 = Not yet (not present at all)   2 = Practicing (practicing some places with some people)

1 = Beginning (emerging or seen once and a while)   3 = Got it (proficient across places and people)

NOTE: SP means a *Skilled Partner*, one who understand the steps and supports to achieve the social outcomes.

If not regulated return to *ENGAGEMENT*.

Subskills with scores of 1s and 2s are where to begin to teach.

Proximity
☐ Able to share space (no more than five feet) without aggression or excessive physical contact or vocalizations for at least five minutes

Parallel
☐ Tolerates skilled partner using the same material within five feet
☐ Indicates by vocalization, gesture, or glance that an SP is using the same material or doing the same activity
☐ Indicates pleasure by smiling or other change in expression
☐ Attends (e.g., looks at action or person) briefly to what the SP is doing

Joint Attention
☐ Attends to the same object or activity for at least three seconds
☐ Follows SP's direction to attend to an object of the learner's interest
☐ Initiates attention to an object of the learner's interest
☐ Alternates visual attention between object of interest and the SP

Reciprocal Exchange
☐ Orients body/attends to the SP
☐ Maintains a brief shared focus with the SP
☐ Imitates a sound or action
☐ Takes an offered object
☐ Gives an object and/or directs a sound or action to the SP
☐ Waits with expectation (e.g., maintains body orientation) for a response
☐ Engages in back-and-forth interaction for more than one exchange

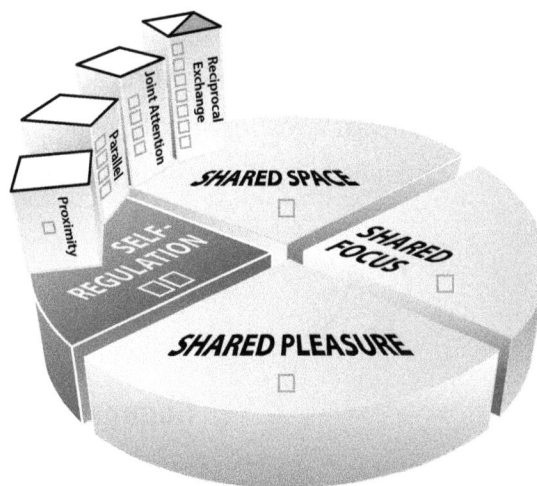

Taylor, K. M., & Laurel, M. (2016). *Social Engagement and the STEPS to Being Social.* Arlington, TX: Future Horizons.

When addressing joint attention, learners acquire the following skills:
- Attending to same object/activity for at least 3 seconds
- Following SP's direction to attend to object of interest
- Initiating attention to an object of interest
- Alternating visual attention between object of interest and SP

As the research indicates that joint attention is an absolute prerequisite for language development (Schaeffer, 2022), teaching these skills is imperative.

Reciprocal Exchange

The final step of Phase I: Being Together is **Reciprocal Exchange:** a back-and-forth interaction. This is a key component of any meaningful social communication; a quote from somebody working on this skill set might be: "Me, then you."

Reciprocal exchange contains the following skills:
- Orients body/attends to the SP
- Maintains a brief shared focus with SP
- Imitates a sound or action
- Takes an offered object
- Gives an object and/or directs a sound/action to the SP
- Waits for a response with expectation (i.e., maintains body orientation)
- Engages in back-and-forth interaction with more than one exchange

Summary of Phase I: Being Together

As illustrated, there is a marked step-by-step development in the Phase I: Being Together skills as the learner progresses from simply noticing that someone is with them in their space (proximity) to participating in a back-and-forth exchange, including a balance of starting an interaction and responding to someone else (reciprocal exchange).

Phase I: Being Together Interventions

Interventions to support Phase I include (a) antecedent-based interventions, (b) parent-implemented interventions, (c) prompting, (d) reinforcement, (e) task analysis, and (f) visual supports (Laurel & Taylor, 2016) (see Chapter 4 for a discussion of EBP).

Table 8.3. Phase I: Being Together Interventions.

STEPS Phase I Summary	Sample Interventions	Purpose	illustration
Learning to be with and participate in a back-and-forth interaction with a social partner	*Proximity* *Visual Timer:* Allows the student to see time passing. Time can be number of rotations, actual minutes, or estimated amounts. *Space Shapes:* Provide a 2D area for students to place their body in while in a group.	• Make time more concrete • Increase independence by reliance on a "thing" not a "person" • Support transitions and generalization • Assist student in understanding personal boundaries • Allow student to practice different sizes of boundaries • Provide feedback for staying in or moving out of a boundary.	
	Parallel *Card Games:* Each student has their own cards and plays in their own way but notices (visually, facial expressions) that others are playing with cards, too. *Bubble Play:* (age appropriate) Position the group in a circle, facing each other, and have them blow bubbles into the center.	• Notice others are doing a similar activity • Control own materials • Experience moments of enjoyment • Take notice when others smile, blow the bubbles, or try to pop the bubbles. • Notice enjoyment of the same thing as others are	

Table 8.3 (continued)

STEPS Phase I Summary	Sample Interventions	Purpose	illustration
Learning to be with and participate in a back-and-forth interaction with a social partner	***Joint Attention:*** *What's in the Grocery Bag?* Encourage the student to follow the exaggerated gestures and facial expressions of the teacher and look in the bag to see the motivating item.	• Practice connecting a motivating item with the teacher • Share in the enjoyment of a liked item • Follow the gesture or facial expression of another person	
	Reciprocal Exchange: *Logo Pass:* Create "logo cards" of restaurants or know items. Encourage the student to take a "logo" card from another person and pass it to the next person. The number of cards increases as the student's attention increases. The student examines the card and then passes it on to ultimately be placed in a box (there is a clear ending). NOTE. The teacher can substitute any motivating item for "logo."	• Practice taking an object and receiving an object (ideally of interest) from another • Begin to orient body toward another • Wait with expectation for the motivating item	

Phase II: Back & Forth Exchange

Phase II: Back & Forth Exchange also represents a significant leap in the journey toward "being social." These skills involve learning to use directed back-and-forth communication and understand that others have different ideas, and that social activity is happening everywhere.

It is during this phase that the learner also begins to understand why they are learning new social behaviors; that is, that their own actions affect their relationships with others. They learn why specific social skills will help them along their way to "being social."

There are four steps in this skill set: (a) reciprocal exchange, (b) give-and-take of conversation, (c) perspective taking, and (d) reading the social scene.

Reciprocal Exchange

Reciprocal Exchange is the first step of Phase II and the last step of Phase I. It is repeated because it is pivotal to all interactions. During Phase II, reciprocal exchange skills are further developed. Expectations for the skills at this level include (a) learning to wait for a response and (b) engaging in more fluid interactions. Thus, reciprocal exchange, a back-and-forth interaction, is the first step of the Phase II: Back and Forth Exchange. A quote from somebody working on this skill set might be: "Me, then you."

Again, reciprocal exchange includes:

- Orients body/attends to the SP
- Maintains a brief shared focus with SP
- Imitates a sound or action
- Takes an offered object
- Gives an object and/or directs a sound/action to the SP
- Waits for a response with expectation (i.e., maintains body orientation)
- Engages in back-and-forth interaction with more than one exchange

Give and Take of Conversation

The next step is **Give and Take of Conversation**. This entails sending and receiving messages on the same topic—verbally or nonverbally. A quote from somebody working on this skill set might be: "I got it and am coming right back at you."

CAPS

Figure 8.7. Phase II: Being Together Atop Engagement.

Phase II, is the student participating in a give and take situation with consideration for others?

Observe the student in 2-3 environments on EACH subskill to determine their skill level:

0 = Not yet (not present at all)

1 = Beginning (emerging or seen once and a while)

2 = Practicing (practicing some places with some people)

3 = Got it (proficient across places and people)

NOTE: SP means a *Skilled Partner*, one who understand the steps and supports to achieve the social outcomes.

If not regulated return to *ENGAGEMENT*.

Subskills with scores of 1s and 2s are where to begin to teach.

Reciprocal Exchange
- ☐ Orients body/attends to the SP/TP
- ☐ Maintains a brief shared focus with the SP/TP
- ☐ Imitates a sound or action
- ☐ Takes an offered object
- ☐ Gives an object and/or directs a sound or action to the SP/TP
- ☐ Waits with expectation (maintains body orientation) for a response
- ☐ Engages in back-and-forth interaction for more than one exchange

Give and Take of Conversation
- ☐ Verbally or nonverbally responds to a message
- ☐ Intentionally directs a message (nonverbal or verbal)
- ☐ Matches facial expression to verbal communication or intended meaning
- ☐ Engages in back-and-forth conversation on a topic (at least three full exchanges)

Perspective Taking
- ☐ Indicates by a word or action an understanding that others can have different thoughts (e.g., questions, comments, or facial expressions related to someone else's feelings)
- ☐ Response or lack of response that indicates an acceptance that others can have different thoughts

- ☐ Identifies ways to figure out what others are thinking by reading nonverbal cues (e.g., tone, facial expressions, body language)
- ☐ Communicates that what others think has an impact on personal feelings

Reading the Social Scene
- ☐ Labels the social interactions within a given environment
- ☐ Attends to social situations for enough time to choose whether to join
- ☐ Joins a social interaction
- ☐ Demonstrates methods to cope with nervousness and/or distress related to social performance (e.g., takes deep breaths, walks away, asks for help)
- ☐ Adjusts social communication based on social situation and partners

186

Individuals learn the following skills to master the give and take of conversation:
- Verbally or nonverbally responding to a message
- Intentionally directing a message (nonverbal or verbal)
- Matching facial expression to verbal communication or intended meaning
- Engaging in back-and-forth conversation on a topic (at least three full exchanges)

A message from somebody who is learning the give and take of conversation is considered an intentional direction, request, question, or comment that is clearly directed to another person. This step involves listening to another person and using facial expressions to communicate a message (Mataya et al., 2017).

Perspective Taking

Following Give and Take of Conversation is **Perspective Taking**—being aware that others have thoughts that may be different from one's own. A quote from somebody working on this skill set might be: "Wow, you're thinking about something else."

Perspective taking requires abilities related to ToM and executive functioning (EF) (Berenguer, 2018). These skills help conversational partners to understand what the people around them are thinking and feeling and, therefore, facilitate understanding of the social scene. When one understands a situation, they have more choice as to how to react or respond.

The following are addressed under perspective taking:
- Indicating by a word or action an understanding that others can have different thoughts (i.e., questions, comments, or facial expressions related to someone else's feelings)
- Identifying ways to figure out what others are thinking by reading nonverbal cues (e.g., tone, facial expressions, body language)
- Communicating that what others think has an impact on personal feelings

Reading the Social Scene

The final step in Phase II is Reading the Social Scene—noticing what is happening in the social environment, attending to what is relevant and finding a way to be part of the social situation. A quote from somebody working on this skill set might be: "Hey, there's a lot going on here."

The person who knows how to read the social scene:

- Labels the social interactions within a given environment
- Attends to social situations for enough time to choose whether to join in
- Joins the social interaction
- Demonstrates methods to cope with nervousness and/or distress related to social performance (e.g., deep breaths, walks away, asks for help)
- Adjusts social communication based on social situation and partners

Reading the Social Scene skills help conversational partners to look and understand the people around them and what is really happening. These skills not only keep people safe, they also help them feel less overwhelmed about the social environment (Laurel & Taylor, 2016). Developing and practicing these skills allows an individual to notice and make sense of the social world and, therefore, interact with more confidence.

Summary of Phase II: Back & Forth Exchange

During Phase II learners progress from beginning to interact and responding to each other (reciprocal exchange) to attending to a social situation with sufficient time to make a choice and demonstrate effective means of reacting to others.

Interventions for Phase II: Back & Forth Exchange

The authors of the model (Laurel & Taylor, 2016) recommend the following interventions to support Phase II: (a) antecedent-based interventions, (b) parent-implemented interventions, (c) prompting, (d) reinforcement, (e) task analysis, (f) visual supports, (g) social narratives, (h) social skills training, (i) video modeling, and (j) peer-mediated intervention and instruction (see Chapter 4 for a discussion of EBP).

Table 8.4. Phase II: Back & Forth Exchange Interventions.

STEPS Phase II Summary	Sample Interventions	Purpose	illustration
Using back-and-forth communication and understanding that others have different ideas, and that social activity happens everywhere	***Reciprocal Exchange*** *Group 3D "Put-in":* Encourage a small group of 3-4 students to sit down and pass an object to one another. The number of objects will increase as attention to task increases. Students can examine the objects and then pass them on to the last person, who puts them into a container with a lid ("put-in").	• Practice taking an object and receiving an object (ideally of interest) from another person • Begin to orientate one's body to another person • Wait with expectation of a motivating item	
	Give & Take of Conversation *A Colorful Conversation:* This activity involves three visual items: a stick figure visual card, 5-10 topic picture squares, and two different-colored poker chips (7-10 each). During a paired activity, students sit across from each other and have an equal number of poker chips, one color for each student. A topic picture card is selected and put on the "Bubble thought" stick figure card, indicating what the topic of conversation will be. As each student says something to the other about the topic, they place a poker chip between them, building a colorful conversation tower. The conversation can end when all the poker chips are used. Students can play again with a new topic card or be done.	• Increase length of verbal conversation • Increase opportunity to direct a message to another • Increase opportunity to talk about various subjects or topics • Increase depth of conversation • Increase opportunity to use facial expression with intended meaning	*conversation sheet* *topic photos* *thought bubble* *talk bubble talk token* *conversation sheet*

Table 8.4 (continued)

STEPS Phase II Summary	Sample Interventions	Purpose	illustration
Using back-and-forth communication and understanding that others have different ideas, and that social activity happens everywhere	*Perspective Taking* *Though Bubbles:* Sit in a group and select one picture scene and lay it in the middle of the group. Each group member has a thought bubble card and lays it near the person in the picture and indicates what that person might be thinking (not saying but thinking). Take turns discussing other thoughts.	• Practice reading nonverbal messages • Practice understanding that people can have different thoughts • Begin understanding that thoughts and feelings are connected • Practice waiting in a group • Practice listening to group members	
	Reading the Social Scene *What's Happening Here?* On the playground or in the community, ask students to "look around" and begin a group list of the social activities going on around them. Begin a discussion of what students have noted and how to join the groups if they would like to.	• Practice labeling social interactions within a given environment • Attending to a social situation for a given time • Discussing how to join a group • Beginning discussion on how it can be stressful to join groups	

Phase III: Part of a Group and Beyond

Phase III: **Being Part of a Group** contains the final steps to long-lasting, meaningful relationships that are the work of each person's lifetime. They are essential in learning to interact successfully as part of a group, create friendships, and move toward lasting meaningful relationships.

During this phase, learners begin to develop skills to be part of a group, including learning to adjust their own behavior in relation to the way others act around them. This skill set can be enjoyable, but because social interactions are filled with uncertainty, it can also evoke anxiety.

Learners will need prediction skills to be successful during this phase. There are four steps in this phase: (a) reading the social scene, (b) group cooperation, (c) friendship, and (d) growing connections.

Reading the Social Scene

The first step, **Reading the Social Scene**, is repeated from Phase II due to its complexity. Just as in Phase II, Reading the Social Scene, learners understand (a) what is happening, (b) what is relevant, and (c) how to be a part of an interaction. Yet in Phase III, a greater emphasis is placed on joining various social situations and using supports to minimize stress. Again, the quote somebody working on this skill set might be: "Hey, there's a lot going on here."

Again, reading the social scene entails:
- Labeling the social interactions within a given environment
- Attending to social situations for enough time to choose whether to join in
- Joins the social interaction
- Demonstrating methods to cope with nervousness and/or distress related to social performance (e.g., deep breaths, walks away, asks for help)
- Adjusting social communication based on social situation and partners

Group Cooperation

The next step is **Group Cooperation**—having one's brain and body in the group, while staying on topic and participating and becoming aware of the need to be flexible with ideas and thinking. A quote from somebody working on this skill set might be: "Okay, a little of my idea and a little of yours."

Group Cooperation contains eight objectives ranging from the desire to be in a group, to participating when a topic is chosen by someone else, to identifying social mistakes and taking the time to repair them. For some, learning these skills is second nature. Others work on these skills throughout their lives, and some are better at it than others:

- Expresses desire to be part of a group
- Physically stays with the group and in own personal space
- Agrees on a topic or activity
- Participates when a topic/activity is chosen by someone else
- Accepts winning and tolerates losing
- Appropriately breaks from or ends an interaction
- Recognizes that personal behavior affects the thoughts and feelings of others
- Identifies and repairs a social mistake
- Adjusts behavior based on the thoughts and feelings of others to be a part of the group

Friendship

The third step of Phase III: Part of a Group and Beyond is **Friendship**. This is the point that many autistic individuals and their families have longed for when first the term "social skills" was mentioned (Laurel & Taylor, 2016). Noticing that someone has similarities to you, accepting their differences, and finding reinforcing ways to be together are all a part of friendship. A quote from somebody working on this skill set might be: "I am interested in you, what can we do together?"

Skills under friendship include:
- Finding out what one has in common with another
- Accepting things that are not in common
- Accepting that people can have more than one friend
- Using social media safely
- Planning to be with a friend (e.g., time, place, activity)
- Spending time with another in more than one setting

Friendships are a key element in life, and many individuals can help us to develop our social and emotional skills (Quill, 2017). Building a friendship is an ongoing skill set that blends all the previous STEPS, including Engagement. Human beings have a desire to belong and developing these skills can support this longing for connection.

Figure 8.8. Phase III: Being Part of a Group Atop Engagement.

Phase III, is the student participating in a group and using flexible thinking?

Observe the student in 2-3 environments on EACH subskill to determine their skill level:

0 = Not yet (not present at all)

1 = Beginning (emerging or seen once and a while)

2 = Practicing (practicing some places with some people)

3 = Got it (proficient across places and people)

NOTE: SP means a *Skilled Partner*, one who understand the steps and supports to achieve the social outcomes.
   If not regulated return to *FOUNDATION*.
   Subskills with scores of 1s and 2s are where to begin to teach.

Reading the Social Scene
- ☐ Labels the social interactions within a given environment
- ☐ Attends to social situations for enough time to choose whether to join
- ☐ Joins the social interaction
- ☐ Demonstrates methods to cope with nervousness and/or distress related to social performance (e.g., deep breaths, walks away, asks for help)
- ☐ Adjusts social communication based on social situation and partners

Group Cooperation
- ☐ Expresses desire to be part of a group
- ☐ Physically stays with the group and in own personal space
- ☐ Agrees on a topic or activity (e.g., suggests, negotiates)
- ☐ Participates when a topic/activity is chosen by someone else
- ☐ Accepts winning and tolerates losing
- ☐ Appropriately breaks from or ends the interaction
- ☐ Recognizes that personal behavior affects the thoughts and feelings of others
- ☐ Identifies and repairs a social mistake
- ☐ Adjusts behavior based on the thoughts and feelings of others to be a part of the group

Friendship
- ☐ Finds out what he/she has in common with another person
- ☐ Accepts things that are not in common
- ☐ Accepts that people can have more than one friend
- ☐ Appropriately uses social media
- ☐ Makes a plan to be with a friend (e.g., time, place, activity)
- ☐ Spends time together in more than one setting

Growing Connections
- ☐ States differences in the types of friendship (e.g., best friend, girlfriend)
- ☐ States what information is typically shared in different types of relationships
- ☐ Maintains relationships over time
- ☐ Sustains relationships across distance
- ☐ States differences in various levels of intimacy
- ☐ States his/her own role in social relationships and conflicts
- ☐ Makes safe choices based on level of intimacy

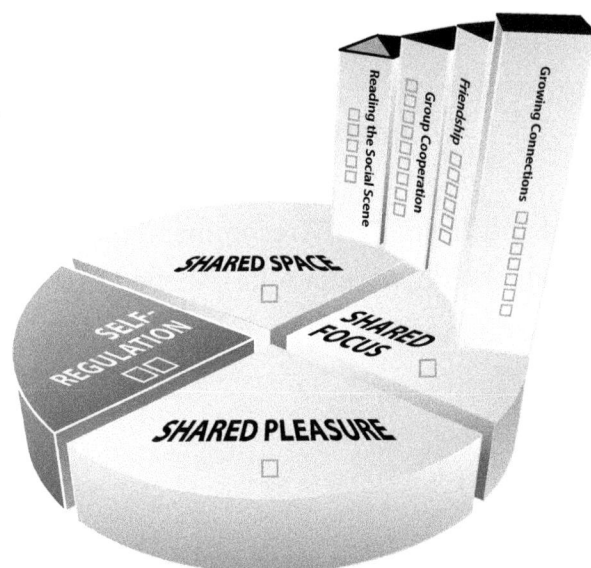

Growing Connections

Growing Connections is the final step of the STEPS model—maintaining a relationship over time and distance, with changing circumstances, and with varying levels of intimacy. A quote from somebody working on this skill set might be: "We are in it for the long haul."

Instruction in the skills below helps learners to understand the differences in types of relationships, to recognize the importance of maintaining and sustaining these connections, and to navigate conflicts and roles as they arise:

- Stating differences in types of friendship (i.e., best friend, girlfriend)
- Stating what information is typically shared in different types of relationships
- Maintaining relationships over time
- Sustaining relationships across distance
- Stating differences in various roles of intimacy
- Stating their own role in social relationships and conflicts
- Making safe choices based on level of intimacy

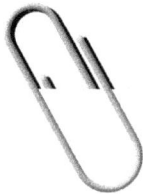

Summary of Phase III: Part of a Group and Beyond

During Phase III, learners progress from joining a social interaction and observing what is going on around them to understanding the subtle differences in types of relationships, understanding the work it takes to maintain a friendship, and making safe choices about various social situations.

Interventions for Phase III: Part of a Group and Beyond

Laurel and Taylor (2016) recommend the use of any of the EBP discussed in Chapter 4. Interventions should, of course, be matched to learner strengths and needs.

Table 8.5. Phase III: Part of a Group and Beyond Interventions.

STEPS Phase III Summary	Sample Interventions	Purpose	illustration
Learning to interact successfully as part of a group, create friendship, and move toward meaningful relationships	**Reading the Social Scene** *Calming Card:* With a facilitator, the student makes a list of at least 3-5 calming activities on an index card. This card is made accessible to the student. When stressful social situations arise, the students is prompted to use the card and practice their calming strategies. Begin this practice with situations that are the least stressful.	• Labeling social interactions within a given environment • Attending to a social situation for a given time • Discussing how to join a group • Beginning discussion on how it can be stressful to join groups	
	Group Cooperation *Who Goes First?* During a structured group with three or more students, a student picks a slip of paper that describes who would go first in a given activity of any game that requires an order of participation. The student reads it aloud to the group and determines who can line up in the order that is given. Examples: • The person with the biggest hands goes first. • *The person with the shortest hair goes first. The person with the most pets goes first.	• Desire to be in a group • Respecting personal space • Tolerance to change (flexible thinking) • Participating in an nonpreferred topic/game • Identifying and repairing social mistakes • Adjusting behavior based on others' thoughts and feelings	

Table 8.5 (continued)

STEPS Phase III Summary	Sample Interventions	Purpose	illustration
Learning to interact successfully as part of a group, create friendship, and move toward meaningful relationships	**Friendship** *"Plan to get together"*: Help a student develop a written plan (paper, phone or electronic) that indicates the executive functioning steps necessary to see a friend in the community. Have a pair of students or a small group work together talking and listening to compromise on the answers to the "plan" prompts.	• Practice understanding that people can have different thoughts and ideas • Practice listening to group members • Finding out what interests are in common with others • Accepting that people have more than one friend • Safe use of social media • Spending time in more than one setting	
	Growing Connections *Visual Organizer:* Use a visual organizer to help identify options to problem solve (e.g., for safety in various environments). Using a visual and the act of writing or typing items out can support long-term memory.	• Executive functioning skills • Recognizing different types of friendships • Understanding what to talk about and with whom • Making safe choices	

Summary of the STEPS Model

The STEPS Model provides a road map for moving thoughtfully toward the acquisition of meaningful social skills. Each step sits atop Engagement. As individuals advance from one step to the next, challenges in the autistic neurology periodically result in the need to "drop down" and spend some time in the foundation to become reconnected in their ability to regulate, share space, share focus, and share enjoyment.

This is similar to what is experienced by the neuromajority. Consider your own social world and the times when you might need to regroup to return to using your acquired skills in "being social."

Utilizing the STEPS Model can help professionals identify what social skills need support to assist a student in being comfortable and having access to social situations and relationships. Identifying what skills are needed to have more choice and "get along" in a variety of settings can bring a person more joy and feelings of belonging.

Ginny is in Phase II: Back and Forth Exchange: Give and Take in Conversation. She is working on directing and responding to a message intentionally and engaging in back-and-forth conversation with 3+ exchanges. Ginny is also focusing on proximity and orientation to peers and turn taking. Activities, such as cooperative learning games and reading with peers, allow for additional practice opportunities under supervision.

Summary

Given that social interaction is one of the core areas of concern in autism, it is imperative that comprehensive autism planning incorporate social skills instruction. However, autistic individuals do not exhibit social skills deficits in a uniform manner (Erhard et al., 2022; Neuhaus, 2021). As a result, communication and social skills instruction must be individualized to meet the needs of every learner.

Despite the recognition that communication and social skills contribute heavily to life success, few curricula have focused on the skills that are foundational. Even fewer have addressed the needs of individuals across the spectrum as a whole. It is essential that educators understand that the communication and social skills that come so intuitively to many is not that easy for autistics. If the student has trouble learning a skill, it helpful to teach it in "steps" just like in math, reading, jump rope, or soccer, so that skills can build on one another.

When educators can identify the communication and social skills that build on one another, they can then pinpoint where learners need support. At the same time, it is important for both the teacher and the learner to understand that communication and social skills are dynamic and that they change with age, the company they keep, and the situations they have access to.

Bibliography

Abbot-Smith, Kirsten, Julie Dockrell, Alexandra Sturrock, Danielle Matthews, and Charlotte Wilson. "Topic Maintenance in Social Conversation: What Children Need To Learn and Evidence This Can Be Taught." *First Language* 43, no. 6 (2023): 614-642.

Adamson, Lauren B., Roger Bakeman, Deborah F. Deckner, and MaryAnn Romski. "Joint Engagement and the Emergence of Language in Children with Autism and Down Syndrome." *Journal of Autism and Developmental Disorders* 39 (2009): 84-96.

American Psychiatric Association. *Diagnostic and Statistical Manual of Mental Disorders* (5th ed.) (2013). Washington, DC: Author.

Aspy, Ruth & Barry Grossman. *Designing Comprehensive Interventions for High-Functioning Individuals with Autism Spectrum Disorders: The Ziggurat Model* (Release 2.0). Ziggurat Group (2022).

Baron-Cohen, Simon. *Mindblindness: An Essay on Autism and Theory of Mind.* MIT Press (1997).

Berenguer, Carmen, Ana Miranda, Carla Colomer, Inmaculada Baixauli, and Belén Roselló. "Contribution of Theory of Mind, Executive Functioning, and Pragmatics to Socialization Behaviors of Children With High-Functioning Autism." *Journal of Autism and Developmental Disorders* 48 (2018): 430-441.

Cannon, Jonathan, Amanda M. O'Brien, Lindsay Bungert, and Pawan Sinha. "Prediction in Autism Spectrum Disorder: A Systematic Review of Empirical Evidence." *Autism Research* 14, no. 4 (2021): 604-630.

Cerullo, Sonia, Francesca Fulceri, Filippo Muratori, and Annarita Contaldo. "Acting With Shared Intentions: A Systematic Review on Joint Action Coordination in Autism Spectrum Disorder." *Brain and Cognition* 149 (2021): 105693.

Erhard, Patricio, Terry S. Falcomata, Molly Oshinski, and Austin Sekula. "The Effects of Multiple-Exemplar Training on Generalization of Social Skills with Adolescents and Young Adults With Autism: A Systematic Review." *Review Journal of Autism and Developmental Disorders* (2022): 1-20.

Fajaryati, Nuryake, Muhammad Akhyar Budiyono, and Wiranto. "The Employability Skills Needed To Face the Demands of Work in the Future: Systematic Literature Reviews" *Open Engineering* 10, no. 1 (2020): 595-603.

Febriantini, Weny Anita, Rahima Fitriati, and Lulud Oktaviani. "An Analysis of Verbal and Non-Verbal Communication in Autistic Children." *Journal of Research on Language Education* 2, no. 1 (2021): 53-56.

Frost, Lori, Andy Bondy, and Rayna Bondy. *The Picture Exchange Communication System: Training Manual.* (2002).

Gomes, Sandra R., Sharon A. Reeve, Kevin J. Brothers, Kenneth F. Reeve, and Tina M. Sidener. "Establishing a Generalized Repertoire of Initiating Bids for Joint Attention in Children with Autism." *Behavior Modification* 44, no. 3 (2020): 394-428.

Greenberg, David M., Varun Warrier, Ahmad Abu-Akel, Carrie Allison, Krzysztof Z. Gajos, Katharina Reinecke, P. Jason Rentfrow, Marcin A. Radecki, and Simon Baron-Cohen. "Sex and Age Differences in "Theory of Mind" Across 57 countries Using the English version of the "Reading the Mind in the Eyes" Test." *Proceedings of the National Academy of Sciences* 120, no. 1 (2023): e2022385119.

Griffin, J.W., Scherf, K.S. "Does Decreased Visual Attention to Faces Underlie Difficulties Interpreting Eye Gaze Cues in Autism?" *Molecular Autism* 11, 60 (2020).

Hage, Simone Vasconcelos Rocha, Lidiane Yumi Sawasaki, Yvette Hyter, and Fernanda Dreux Miranda Fernandes. "Social Communication and Pragmatic Skills of Children With Autism Spectrum Disorder and Developmental Language Disorder." In *CoDAS*, vol. 34, p. e20210075. Sociedade Brasileira de Fonoaudiologia, 2021.

Heimann, Mikael, Emelie Nordqvist, K. Strid, J. Connant Almrot, and T. Tjus. "Children With Autism Respond Differently to Spontaneous, Elicited and Deferred Imitation." *Journal of Intellectual Disability Research* 60, no. 5 (2016): 491-501.

Hoffman, Mitchell, and Steven Tadelis. "People Management Skills, Employee Attrition, and Manager Rewards: An Empirical Analysis." *Journal of Political Economy* 129, no. 1 (2021): 243-285.

Holland, K. Understanding Nonspeaking Autism. Healthline. (nd). Accessed January 10, 2024 from https://www.healthline.com/health/autism/nonverbal-autism.

Kang, Erin, Lee Ann Santore, James A. Rankin, and Matthew D. Lerner. "Self-Reported Social Skills Importance Ratings, Not Social Skills Themselves, Predict Sociometric Status Among Youth With Autism Spectrum Disorder." *Research in Autism Spectrum Disorders* 74 (2020): 101552.

Kapp, Steven K. "Profound Concerns About "Profound Autism": Dangers of Severity Scales and Functioning Labels for Support Needs." *Education Sciences* 13, no. 2 (2023): 106.

Keifer, Cara M., Amori Yee Mikami, James P. Morris, Erin J. Libsack, and Matthew D. Lerner. "Prediction of Social Behavior in Autism Spectrum Disorders: Explicit Versus Implicit Social Cognition." *Autism* 24, No. 7 (2020): 1758-1772.

Kent, Cally, Reinie Cordier, Annette Joosten, Sarah Wilkes-Gillan, Anita Bundy, and Renee Speyer. "A Systematic Review and Meta-Analysis of Interventions to Improve Play Skills in Children with Autism Spectrum Disorder." *Review Journal of Autism and Developmental Disorders* 7, no. 1 (2020): 91-118.

Koegel, Lynn Kern, Katherine M. Bryan, Pumpki L. Su, Mohini Vaidya, and Stephen Camarata. "Definitions of Nonverbal and Minimally Verbal in Research for Autism: A Systematic Review of the Literature." *Journal of Autism and Developmental Disorders* 50 (2020): 2957-2972.

Koegel, Lynn Kern, Katherine M. Bryan, P. Su, M. Vaidya, and S. Camarata. "Intervention for Non-Verbal and Minimally-Verbal Individuals With Autism: A Systematic Review." *International Journal of Pediatric Research* 5, no. 2 (2019): 1-16.

Laurel, Marci, and Kathleen Taylor. *Social Engagement and the Steps to Being: A Practical Guide for Teaching Social Skills to Individuals with Autism Spectrum Disorder*. Future Horizons (2016).

Lecheler, Mishon, Jon Lasser, Phillip W. Vaughan, Jesi Leal, Kirstina Ordetx, and Michelle Bischofberger. "A Matter of Perspective: An Exploratory Study of a Theory of Mind Autism Intervention for Adolescents." *Psychological Reports* 124, no. 1 (2021): 39-53.

Mataya, Kerry, Ruth, Aspy, & Hollis Shaffer. *Talk With Me: A Step-By-Step Conversation Framework for Teaching Conversational Balance and Fluency for High-Functioning Individuals With Autism Spectrum Disorder*. Future Horizons (2017).

Moody, Christine T., and Elizabeth A. Laugeson. "Social Skills Training in Autism Spectrum Disorder Across the Lifespan." *Psychiatric Clinics* 43, no. 4 (2020): 687-699.

Myles, Brenda Smith. *Autism and Difficult Moments, Revised Edition: Practical Solutions for Reducing Meltdowns*. Arlington, TX: Future Horizons, 2024.

Neuhaus, Emily, Raphael A. Bernier, See Wan Tham, and Sara J. Webb. "Gastrointestinal and Psychiatric Symptoms Among Children and Adolescents With Autism Spectrum Disorder." *Frontiers in Psychiatry* 9 (2018): 515.

Posar, Annio, and Paola Visconti. "Long-term outcome of autism spectrum disorder." Turkish Archives of Pediatrics/Türk Pediatri Arşivi 54, no. 4 (2019): 207.

Quill, Kathleen. Selecting evidence-based practices to enhance social and communication skills. In K. Quill, K. & L. Stansberry Brusnahan. *Do-Watch-Listen-Say: Social and communication intervention for autism spectrum disorder*. 2nd edition. (2017). Baltimore, MD: Paul H. Brookes Publishing Co.

Rosello, Belen, Carmen Berenguer, Inmaculada Baixauli, Rosa García, and Ana Miranda. "Theory of Mind Profiles in Children With Autism Spectrum Disorder: Adaptive/Social Skills and Pragmatic Competence." *Frontiers in Psychology* 11 (2020): 567401.

Roux, Anne M. *National Autism Indicators Report: Transition Into Young Adulthood*. AJ Drexel Autism Institute, 2015.

Silver, Kate, and Sarah Parsons. "Noticing the Unusual: A Self-Prompt Strategy for Adults With Autism." *Advances in Autism* 1, no. 2 (2015): 87-97.

Sturrock, Alexandra, Hannah Guest, Graham Hanks, George Bendo, Christopher J. Plack, and Emma Gowen. "Chasing the Conversation: Autistic Experiences of Speech Perception." *Autism & Developmental Language Impairments* 7, (2022): 1-12.

Thomas, Amanda, and Linda M. Bambara. "Using Peer-Mediation to Enhance Conversation and Reduce Inappropriate Communication Acts In Adolescents With Autism." *Education and Training in Autism and Developmental Disabilities* 55, no. 2 (2020): 185-200.

Vermeulen, Peter. *Autism as Context Blindness*. Future Horizons (2012).

Vermeulen, Peter. *Autism and the Predictive Brain: Absolute Thinking in a Relative World*. Taylor & Francis (2022).

Yang, Xiao-Lei, Shuang Liang, Ming-Yang Zou, Cai-Hong Sun, Pan-Pan Han, Xi-Tao Jiang, Wei Xia, and Li-Jie Wu. "Are Gastrointestinal and Sleep Problems Associated With Behavioral Symptoms ff Autism Spectrum Disorder?" *Psychiatry Research* 259 (2018): 229-235.

Ying Sng, Cheong, Mark Carter, and Jennifer Stephenson. "A Systematic Review of the Comparative Pragmatic Differences in Conversational Skills of Individuals with Autism." *Autism & Developmental Language Impairments* 3 (2018): 2396941518803806.

CHAPTER 9

Data Collection

Andi Babkie, PhD

One of the basics of the CAPS process—as is true of special education programming in general—is to have clearly defined IEP (individualized education program) goals and objectives that are readily accessible to all involved in working with the student. A next step is taking those goals and objectives, matching them with an intervention, and then determining both the efficacy of the intervention and the appropriateness of the goals and objectives.

This is where collecting data comes in. Based on what is discovered in the data, interventions may be altered or may be continued as is; objectives may be adjusted if it is found that they have been mastered or that they are inappropriate at the moment; and changes may occur in the process of encouraging generalization through increasing a student's self-monitoring. Whatever the case may be, the collection and sharing of data is vital to increasing success for students.

Briefly, data collection involves gathering information about how an individual is performing in terms of a specific social or academic behavior. This information is then used both to measure progress and to make decisions. To gain accurate information, the process must be systematic and ongoing. This chapter describes how to determine the behavior(s) to select, the methods for collecting data, and the overall procedures for effective use of the data collected.

The Data Collection Process

Data collection is a multistep process that begins with selecting the target behavior and ends with using the collected information in making decisions. This also includes deciding the who, what, where, when, why, and how of the process to achieve success for the student. The steps of this process are as follows:

1. Establishing the target behavior
2. Deciding on a system for collecting the data
3. Keeping track of data
4. Determining when and where data will be collected
5. Determining who will collect the data
6. Determining a system for sharing data
7. Using information collected for decision making

Establishing the Target Behavior

The first step in collecting data is to establish the target behavior. While the student's IEP includes goals and benchmarks, target behaviors are generally more discrete behaviors, representing a step on the way toward achieving the goal. Once the target behavior is selected, it is important to make sure it is described in terms that are specific, objective, and measurable. For example, if a social objective for a student is to "interact with peers," a target behavior might be to "respond when greeted by a peer." Data would then be collected on this specific target behavior rather than on the objective as a whole. Once the target behavior has been mastered, another behavior in the sequence to achieve the objective is selected and measured.

Figure 9.1. Target Behaviors: What They Are and What They Are Not.

Targeted behaviors must be:	Non-example:
• **Specific:** are clear enough so that two independent observers would count the same number of instances of behavior—define it • **Observable:** can be seen • **Measurable:** can be counted in some fashion • **Voluntary:** can be changed • **Replicable:** can be done again	• Be annoying • Act appropriately **Example:** • Touch others • Take others' possessions • Raise hand • Wait in line until called

Deciding on a System for Collecting the Data

Once the target behavior has been identified and defined, the next step is to select a system for data collection that matches the behavior. While many systems are available, systems that allow for observation and recording of behavior as it occurs are particularly useful in analyzing questions such as those that address student response to instruction, student engagement, and student behaviors.

Figure 9.2. Commonly Used Observational Data Recording Systems.

- **Event Recording -** an exact measure of behavior
  - Use for discrete behaviors (those having a definite beginning and end)
  - Count/tally how many times behavior occurs
    - Examples: raise hand, call out, ask question

- **Latency Recording -** an exact measure
  - Measure how long it takes to begin something
    - Examples: follow directions, begin work

- **Duration Recording -** an exact measure
  - Measure how long a behavior persists
    - Examples: temper tantrum, out of seat

- **Time Sampling -** an estimate of behaviors
  - Use for ongoing or high-frequency behaviors
  - Record whether behavior is or is not occurring at the end of every specific period of time (e.g., every 30 seconds) for a specific session (e.g., a session of 5 minutes at the beginning of class)
    - Examples: talk to peers (if high frequency), stay on task

The decision about which data collection method to use depends on the type of behavior that is targeted, including its frequency and intensity. For example, a low-incidence behavior with a definite beginning and end (such as "open book") may best be measured by event recording because it is easily counted. On the other hand, an ongoing or high-frequency behavior (such as a self-stimulatory behavior) may best be measured through use of time sampling. When working with high-frequency or ongoing behaviors, it is difficult to count each instance of the behavior. Therefore, checking periodically (time sampling) to see if these behaviors are being displayed gives a fairly accurate picture of the behavior and prevents the data collection process from becoming overwhelming.

Keeping Track of Data

Once a decision has been made about which method to use to collect data, the next decision involves how to keep track of the data so it is easy to analyze. This may take the form of a data collection sheet or some other means. For observational recording systems, educators may design their own data collection sheets or select one from a number of commercially packaged products. Each data collection system is specified in more detail below.

Event recording gives an exact measure of behavior because each instance is counted. Therefore, as noted above, it is used for behaviors that are easy to count and happen at a relatively low frequency.

For example, Ginny, the student in the example from Chapter 1, has a targeted skill to "Chart lunch count." For this behavior, the observer could collect data on a target behavior of "ask peers what lunch choice (they) want" by placing a tally mark in the box each time the behavior occurs and have a specific number at the end for day-to-day comparison.

Figure 9.3. Basic Event Recording Sheet.

Event Recording Form

School: Anywhere Elementary

Student: Ginny

Target Behavior: Ask peers what lunch choice (they) want

Day	Activity	Perform Target Behavior	Total
Monday	Lunch Count	𝍦 𝍦 𝍦 𝍦 𝍦	25
Tuesday	" "	𝍦 𝍦 𝍦 𝍦 ////	24
Wednesday	" "	𝍦 𝍦 𝍦 𝍦 𝍦	25
Thursday	" "	𝍦 𝍦 𝍦 𝍦 ///	23
Friday	" "	𝍦 𝍦 𝍦 𝍦 𝍦	25
Total for Week	_____	_____	122

Alternatively, when using event recording, the teacher may decide that a comparison or collecting information on the percentage of occasions when the behavior occurs is necessary. In this case, the data collection sheet would be slightly different; it would include a space for listing opportunities to perform a given behavior as well as a space for recording actual performance, leading to a percentage rather than a number for comparison purposes.

Again, in the case of Ginny, one of her target behaviors is to use her language board. Just having information on use would not tell the whole story. More information is gained from collecting data on both the opportunities to use the board and her actual usage. This percentage leads to a more appropriate picture of her behavior.

Figure 9.4. Event Recording Sheet With Comparison.

Event Recording Form

School: Anywhere Elementary   Date: 2-23-13

Student: Ginny

Target Behavior: Use interactive language board

Time	Activity	Opportunity to Perform Behavior	Performed Behavior	Percentage Achieved
7:30-7:55	Breakfast	卌 卌 卌	卌 ////	9/15 = 60%
8:05-8:20	Independent morning work	卌 卌	卌 ///	8/10 = 80%

Lastly, another type of event recording form may be used if the concern is the level of prompting necessary for the target behavior to occur. This type of data can be used to assist in planning for gradually decreasing the level of prompting needed. An example of this for Ginny is monitoring of transitions.

Figure 9.5. Prompt Level Event Recording Sheet.

Event Recording Form

School: Anywhere Elementary   Date: <u>2-23</u>|
Student: <u>Ginny</u>
Target Behavior: <u>Use transition</u>

Schedule Present: <u>Y</u>   N   **Schedule in Use:**   <u>Y</u>   N

Schedule Type: Stationary   **Mobile**

Schedule Steps: **"Check Schedule"**
                       1. Put picture in finished pocket
                       2. Pull next picture off
                       3. Put in the "work area"
                       4. Go to designated area
                       5. Complete activity

Activity 1:	Step	Status/Prompting				
_____	1	I	V	G	M	P
	2	I	V	G	M	P
	3	I	V	G	M	P
	4	I	V	G	M	P
	5	I	V	G	M	P

Activity 2:	Step	Status/Prompting				
_____	1	I	V	G	M	P
	2	I	V	G	M	P
	3	I	V	G	M	P
	4	I	V	G	M	P
	5	I	V	G	M	P

Activity 3:	Step	Status/Prompting				
_____	1	I	V	G	M	P
	2	I	V	G	M	P
	3	I	V	G	M	P
	4	I	V	G	M	P
	5	I	V	G	M	P

Note: I=Independent; V=Verbal; G=Gesture; M=Model; P=Put-through.

Latency recording is another observational system that is also an exact measure of the target behavior. It is used when the goal is to determine how long it takes for the target behavior to occur after the prompt. For example, if the purpose were to determine how quickly Ginny responded to others/questions by using her language board, one would use a latency recording sheet rather, as illustrated below.

Figure 9.6. Latency Recording Form.

Latency Recording Form

School: <u>Anywhere Elementary</u>   Date: <u>2-23</u>
Student: <u>Ginny</u>
Target Behavior: <u>Use interactive language board</u>

Time	Activity	Time of prompt	Time target behavior occurred	Latency
7:30-7:55	Transition from car to breakfast	7:31 7:35 7:45	7:33 7:36 7:47	2 minutes 1 minute 2 minutes
8:05-8:20	Independent morning work	8:06 8:10	8:07:30 8:11	1&1/2 minutes 1 minute

Duration recording, a third observational data collection system, is used to keep track of how long a behavior persists. For example, one of Ginny's target behaviors is to "stay next to assigned peer."

Time sampling, the last observational data collection system to be addressed here, provides an estimate of the occurrence of the target behavior in instances when the behavior is either ongoing or high-frequency and, therefore, cannot be reliably counted. In time sampling, the person collecting the data records whether the target behavior is or is not occurring at the end of a specific period of time (for example, every thirty seconds) for a specific session (for example, a session of five minutes at the beginning of class). While not an exact measure, time sampling is useful for giving an overall picture of a behavior.

In Ginny's case, she has been having difficulty completing work that must be done independently. The teacher decides to collect data on the target behavior of "work independently" for every fifteen minutes across activities, checking at the end of every three minutes of independent work time to see if Ginny is on task. While this will not give an exact accounting of how much time Ginny is actually working independently, it will give a general estimate of the behavior.

Figure 9.7. Duration Recording Form.

Duration Recording Form

School: <u>Anywhere Elementary</u>   Date: <u>2-23</u>
Student: <u>Ginny</u>
Target Behavior: <u>Stay next to assigned peer</u>

Time	Activity	Behavior began	Behavior ended	Duration	Total Duration of behavior for Activity
7:30-7:55	Transition from car to breakfast	7:31 7:43	7:33 7:48	2 minutes 5 minutes	7 minutes
8:05-8:20	Independent morning work	8:06 8:15	8:10 8:17	4 minutes 2 minutes	6 minutes

Duration for Day: ___13m_____

/

Determining When and Where Data Will Be Collected

Once the behavior has been defined and the method of data collection selected, a decision must be made about when and where to collect the data. This decision takes into account the potential influence on the behavior of different environments, different classes/subjects, different groups, different activities, and different teachers. In addition, to maximize the picture of the behavior and the quality of the data obtained, collecting data at different points in time during the day and week may be necessary.

In the CAPS system, data are routinely collected across time, activities, interventions, and environments, thus ensuring ongoing information on student progress, as well as encouraging generalization of the skills as a matter of everyday practice. This prevents failure to track a student's behavior because of missed opportunities. For example, a student might stay on task during morning activities but not during the afternoon. Evaluating what is different during those times (instructional content, time of day, groupings, instructional delivery) and collecting data during different activities assists in pinpointing why a given intervention is or is not effective (Kubiszyn & Borich, 2024).

Figure 9.8. Time Sampling Data Collection Sheet.

Time Sampling Recording Form

School: <u>Anywhere Elementary</u>   Date: <u>2-23</u>
Student: <u>Ginny</u>
Target Behavior: <u>Work independently</u>

Session: <u>15 minutes of each independent work period across activities during the day</u>
Interval: <u>End of every 3 minutes</u>

Activity: <u>Independent morning work 8:05-8:20</u>

3 mins.	6 mins.	9 mins.	12 mins.	15 mins.
O	X	X	O	X

Percent on task at observation point: <u>40%</u>

Activity: <u>Morning Activities 8:25-8:50</u>

3 mins.	6 mins.	9 mins.	12 mins.	15 mins.
X	X	X	O	X

Percent on task at observation point: <u>80%</u>

Activity: <u>Special: Computer 9:10-9:25</u>

3 mins.	6 mins.	9 mins.	12 mins.	15 mins.
O	X	O	O	O

Percent on task at observation point: <u>20%</u>

Activity: <u>Writing 9:45-10:00</u>

3 mins.	6 mins.	9 mins.	12 mins.	15 mins.
O	O	X	O	X

Percent on task at observation point: <u>40%</u>

X= target behavior occurring   O= target behavior not occurring

Determining Who Will Collect the Data

In a school setting, it is usually the teacher or paraeducator who collects information on the target behaviors of a given student. However, due to the comprehensive nature of CAPS, and the relative ease with which it is completed, anyone working with the student could collect data on various target behaviors as appropriate. Potentially, the lunchroom staff could check Ginny's use of a language board to communicate choices or the school secretary could note the latency between asking Ginny a question and her response. In addition, the student's family would certainly be included to ensure that behaviors are also addressed in out-of-school settings.

Generalization across people, activities, settings, and times remains essential to the student actually mastering a behavior. Additionally, for the student to assume control of their behavior, self-monitoring may be an appropriate choice for some or all target behaviors. These decisions would be made by the team.

Determining a System for Sharing Data

Charting or graphing data to have a visual representation is often the most effective approach to analyzing and sharing data. A visual representation makes it clear what is happening with the behavior, such as when it occurs most often, and that information may be used to assist in reviewing the efficacy of interventions. Anecdotal records accompanying the data can lead to additional reflections on the success of interventions.

A general rule of thumb is to collect data and chart them until a pattern emerges. If the data line is flat, there is no change. If the data line increases or decreases, there is change that may be tied to the intervention. Obviously, if it is a behavior you want more of, an increasing line is a positive, whereas a decreasing line suggests deterioration in the behavior and may indicate that the intervention approach is not effective and that another intervention is warranted. The following graph represents the duration data collection of Ginny's target behavior of "stay next to assigned peer" for one day across different activity periods.

Figure 9.9. Graph of Ginny's Target Behavior: "Stay Next to Assigned Peer."

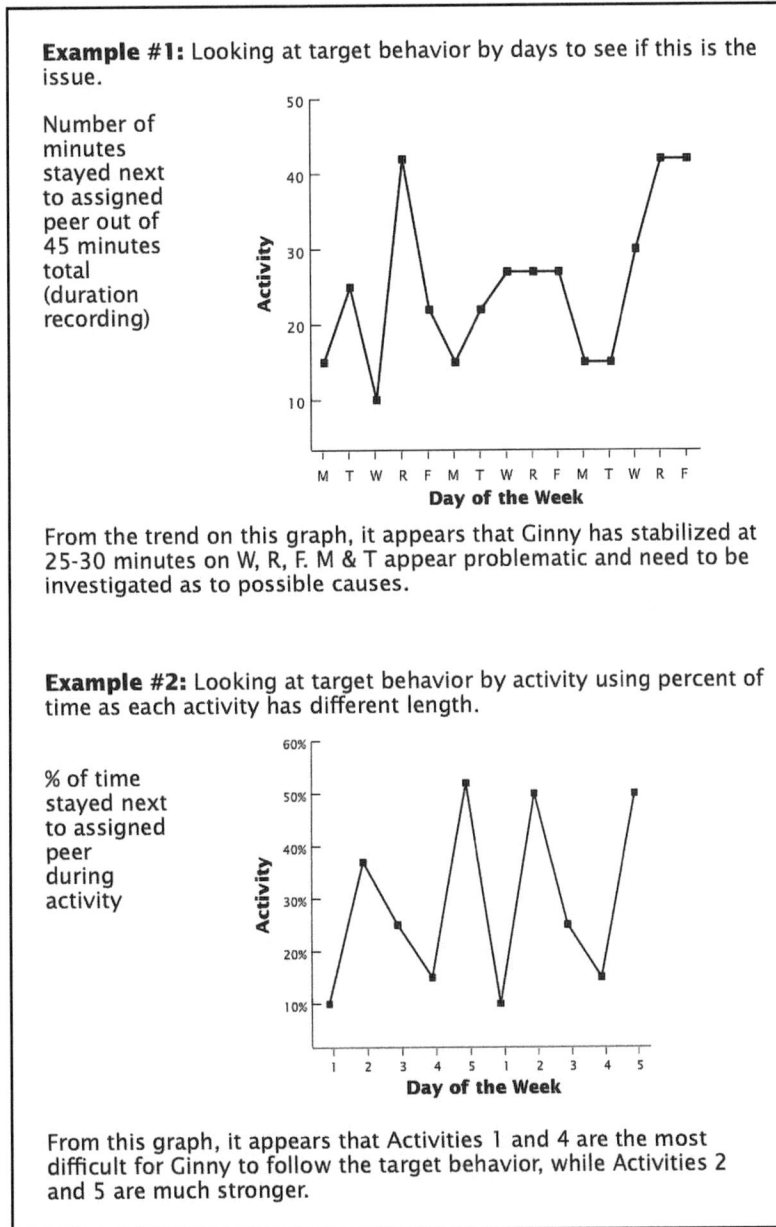

Example #1: Looking at target behavior by days to see if this is the issue.

Number of minutes stayed next to assigned peer out of 45 minutes total (duration recording)

From the trend on this graph, it appears that Ginny has stabilized at 25-30 minutes on W, R, F. M & T appear problematic and need to be investigated as to possible causes.

Example #2: Looking at target behavior by activity using percent of time as each activity has different length.

% of time stayed next to assigned peer during activity

From this graph, it appears that Activities 1 and 4 are the most difficult for Ginny to follow the target behavior, while Activities 2 and 5 are much stronger.

Using the Data for Decision Making

Based on an analysis after the data have been collected for a long enough time to identify a pattern, the next step is to develop a plan for future action. For example, the team sees that data collected on Ginny's lunch count indicate that she is consistently doing well on this behavior. Based on those findings, the school team can decide to collect data on another target behavior and just periodically check to see if Ginny's lunch count behavior remains strong. If Ginny was not consistently being successful at taking lunch count as shown by her data, a new intervention might be put in place to help her achieve the objective.

Summary

Collecting data on student behaviors, while sometimes time-consuming, is a necessary and efficient way for educators to effect change in their classrooms and increase student achievement. As part of the CAPS systematic approach to intervention, data collection allows the student and the team to measure student success in a routine and systematic fashion.

Bibliography

Kubiszyn, Tom, and Gary D. Borich. *Educational Testing and Measurement*. John Wiley & Sons, (2024).

Sprick, Randall S., and Lisa M. Howard. *The Teacher's Encyclopedia of Behavior Management: 100 Problems/500 Plans for Grades K-9*. Sopris West (1995).

CHAPTER 10

Generalization

Paul LaCava, PhD

Highlights of the Individuals with Disabilities Education Act (IDEA; 2004) emphasize high expectations, including learning skills that can be used across settings, for all students. The vehicle to guide this process is the individualized education program (IEP) created to help students become more self-sufficient and independent. Thus, the teaching and learning of knowledge and skills is the bottom line.

To ensure this goal is met, learning must be measured. There are several ways to measure student learning (accuracy of target skills, behavior, etc.). While acquisition is the first and most important step, fluency, generalization, and maintenance of skills is vital for success past initial learning and essential for good outcomes (Alberto et al., 2022). We might say that learning hasn't truly occurred if a student can't generalize a skill to other settings, people, and contexts.

Johnny, a 6-year-old autistic boy, learned to ask for food when he was hungry. Since he had no verbal language, his mother had taught him to use the sign "more" to request more of whatever he was eating or drinking while at home in their kitchen. Unfortunately, if Johnny was at his grandmother's house or at school, he did not use the "more" sign. Unless he was with his mother at home, he did not have a way to communicate his needs and, therefore, relied on his caregivers to anticipate them.

Johnny had not yet been taught to use his sign language skills in multiple settings. He needed instruction and support to use "more" at his grandmother's house, school, and other locations.

Like Johnny, many students may have learned to use a particular strategy/support but only in the presence of the adult who taught them or in one setting.

> Mr. Meira created a visual support to help Malcom, a 10-year-old boy with classic autism, learn to use a urinal independently. After several days of instruction, Malcom used the visual aid without help. Unfortunately, he only used it in the bathroom in Mr. Meira's classroom as he did not understand that the toileting routine applied to all bathrooms.

Malcom required additional instruction to use the toileting sequence throughout the school day and in the community. In addition, each of Malcolm's teachers, including those who taught music and art, needed assistance on how to help Malcom use his visual support.

Educators and families will recognize these vignettes as it is common that a student can do something in one setting (classroom) but not another (playground). A teacher may be proud when a student has mastered a skill within a small-group special education setting, but then be surprised when that student is unable to complete the same skill just down the hall in another classroom or at home. While the skill may have been taught, it was not taught to generalization.

What Is Generalization?

The vignette of Johnny above is an example of an issue with generalization of responses. "Generalization" in this context means being able to complete a skill or behavior after instruction has taken place with people, places, materials, and so on, that are different from the dimensions of the original learning environment (Alberto et al., 2022). Families and educators, alike, have found that autistic people often have difficulty with generalizing skills and behaviors to other contexts (Erhard et al., 2022; MacFarland & Fisher, 2021; Vermeulen, 2012). Students similar to Johnny and Malcolm require instruction in other contexts. Johnny needed additional instruction at home and school. Malcolm needed to understand that his urinal routine could be used in all urinal-related environments.

Alberto et al. (2019) noted four dimensions of generalization: instruction, materials, persons, and settings.

Table 10.1. Dimensions of Generalization.

Dimension	Definition	Examples
Instruction	Responding to different types of stimuli	Verbal, text, sign language, pictures, icons, video, etc. This type of generalization includes knowing multiple ways to communicate the same idea. For example, the following are interchangeable: (a) give me the apple, (b) hand me the apple, and (c) please share that apple with me.
Material	Using a variety of materials to complete a skills	Real objects, pretend objects, models, etc. Perhaps a student is learning to write using a pen, pencil, marker, crayon, chalk, etc. Learners who can generalize across materials understand that items can be the same despite having different attributes. For example, an apple can be different colors, sizes, etc., but it is still an apple. Dogs can look very different, but they are all dogs.
People	Using a skill with different people	Parents, siblings, neighbors, teachers, community members, etc.
Setting	Using a skill across settings	Home, school, neighborhood, stores, community, athletics, religious institutions, etc.

Ginny's CAPS in Chapter 3 includes a number of generalization dimensions:
- **Material.** Ginny is to use her language board during mealtimes at home.
- **Setting/people.** Ginny is learning the names of peers in her classroom in order to greet and converse with them. She will learn to use the names of her peers throughout the day in the hallways, cafeteria, recess, and so forth to expand her interactions with others.
- **Instruction.** Ginny is to use self-monitoring in different academic areas.

We are still learning about the importance of generalization and how to support its occurrence. The results about generalization in the published literature are mixed, and many studies have not included an assessment of generalization (Carruthers et al., 2020; Wattawonagwan et al., 2022).

Barriers to Generalization

There are many reasons why a student might not generalize a skill.
- Perhaps they have not been taught to generalize.
- They may not be getting enough instruction and support through prompting and/or reinforcement.
- They may not have had enough opportunities to practice the skill.
- Perhaps generalization was not emphasized when teaching.

Some may assume that generalization of skills will just happen naturally after the skill has been taught. This flies in the face of what Gresham (1998, as cited in McIntosh & MacKay, 2008) called the most important part of teaching—generalization!

The neurology of autism contributes to generalization difficulties and is manifested as (a) insistence on sameness, (b) attention/distraction, (c) attention to details, (c) sensory needs, and so forth (American Psychiatric Association [APA], 2013). Understanding and addressing these needs will help students learn and generalize skills, ultimately leading to greater independence and success.

Teaching Generalization

To ensure that students generalize and maintain skills over time, people, settings, and so on, it is critical that these dimensions are considered in the teaching process. It is not enough to just teach a skill unless the goal is to have the student use that skill in one environment with one individual. Educators need to think about all the variability in how skills will be used and then teach with a variety of strategies to ensure generalization.

Generalization components can be written as part of goals and benchmarks or in positive behavior support plans. Including different people in the teaching and generalization process is also important as is using a variety of materials to augment learning. If generalization in school is to occur, collaboration among educational professionals is essential to ensure that the student is demonstrating the skill with different individuals, in different settings, and with different materials. If generalization to home is the goal, then collaboration among teachers and parents is important. Clearly, generalization requires strong communication and collaboration among the adults who support the student.

While consistency is a hallmark of teaching, Baer (1981) emphasized that "training loosely" is important with autistic learners to facilitate generalization of skills. This means varying the people, stimuli, verbal requests, materials, and so on, in the instruction phase. For example, if teaching a student to write their name, a variety of writing tools, types of paper, white boards, and so on, would be used. In addition, the learners would receive prompts and reinforcement from multiple teachers.

Using the CAPS to Support Generalization

True to its comprehensive nature, the CAPS addresses generalization by providing an organizing framework to support generalization of supports and skills. Thus, the Generalization to Community column on the CAPS serves to remind adults that supports used in one setting or with one adult are applicable to others. For example, Tomi's Circle of Friends group (cf. Gold, 1994; Kalyva & Avramidis, 2005) that occurs during lunch can also happen at recess. The PECS (The Picture Exchange Communication System; Frost & Bondy, 2002) that Ling uses in his general education reading class can also be used at recess and in music class.

It is important to consider generalization in planning a student's program, goals and benchmarks as well as in positive behavior support plans. Systematic programming is essential to ensure that a student generalizes newly acquired skills across settings, people, materials, and events. Without this step, the learner does not truly possess the skill. The following tables show examples of how supports and skills, respectively, may be generalized.

Table 10.2. Generalization of Supports.

CAPS Categories	Support	Is Used During ...	Can Also Be Used ...
Structure/ Modifications	• Circling problems to be completed on a worksheet • Using book on tape	• Math • Reading	• Science, reading, social studies, PE, music • Social studies, science
Sensory/ Regulation	• Slant board • Therapy ball	• Language arts • PE	• Math class, art • Reading, math, social studies
Social/ Communication	• Social script • Language board	• Attendance • Specials	• Academic times for taking surveys, asking a child to play at recess, initiating interactions with members of a cooperative group, • Any other setting

Figure 10.1. Michelle's CAPS.

Comprehensive Autism Planning System (CAPS)

Child/Student: **Michelle**   Date: **5/7**

Time	Activity	Skills to Teach	Structure/ Modifications
1:35 – 2:15	Physical Education Class	• Playing group games: kickball, tag, dodgeball, etc.	• Allow student to kick first • Peers assist with running bases • Use visual mini-schedule *Use prompting and fading to teach skills*

Table 10.3. Generalization of Skills.

Skills to Teach	Is Used During ...	Can Also Be Used ...
Asking for help	General education academic time	Recess, lunch, when completing daily living skills
Using a calculator	Math, science	Grocery store, bank, school store, on a computer or smart device
Interpreting facial expressions	Social skills group	Recess, lunch
Taking turns	Circle time	Game playing, PE, home

Even though the Generalization to the Community column is the last column in the CAPS model, it should never be thought of as last. Generalization is part of the planning and teaching process. Michelle's CAPS has a strong generalization component. Generalization of skills is also included as part of Data Collection and is further addressed under Structure/Modifications.

Figure 10.1 (continued)

Reinforcement	Sensory/ Regulation	Communication/ Social Skills	Data Collection	Generalization to Community
• Verbal praise from peers and teachers • Token economy with special interest: car hood ornaments • Tokens for participating in longer amounts of the game	• Wear a hat when it is windy • Weighted vest prior to class • Incredible 5-Point Scale	• Asking for help • Praising peers • Making comments during game • List of different phrases that can be used in games; added to as they occur	• Minutes playing game (TR/F, duration) • Tokens earned (#, daily) • Independence over time (# of prompts, T/W)	• Playing with different sports equipment and people in different settings (playground, gym, home and in the community • Use of diffferent phrases (i.e., your turn, time to kick, batter up, etc.)

CAPS

Summary

Applying skills learned in one environment or with one person to other settings and people or using one material in multiple ways and multiple places poses unique challenges for autistic students. A specific focus on generalization of supports and skills ensures that the student has what they need to be successful across the day in different contexts. As such, the Generalization column on the CAPS ensures that generalization is built into every phase of the student's program because it makes it explicit.

Besides inputting generalization activities into the CAPS, it is vital to actively plan how staff will prompt and reinforce skills and behaviors in different settings to ensure that the student has truly mastered a given skill across settings, people, and material. In other words, the student truly possesses the skill. As Mayerson noted in the *New York Law School Law Review* (2019), generalization is at the core of meaningful learning for students as outlined by the Endrew F. Supreme Court Decision of 2017.

Bibliography

Alberto, Paul, Anne C. Troutman, and Judah B. Axe. *Applied Behavior Analysis for Teachers*. Upper Saddle River, NJ: Pearson Merrill Prentice Hall, 2002.

American Psychiatric Association, and American Psychiatric Association. "Diagnostic and Statistical Manual of Mental Disorder." Washington, DC (2013).

Baer, Donald M. "A Flight of Behavior Analysis." *The Behavior Analyst* 4 (1981): 85-91.

Carruthers, Sophie, Andrew Pickles, Vicky Slonims, Patricia Howlin, and Tony Charman. "Beyond Intervention Into Daily Life: A Systematic Review of Generalization Following Social Communication Interventions for Young Children with Autism." *Autism Research* 13, no. 4 (2020): 506-522.

Erhard, Patricio, Terry S. Falcomata, Molly Oshinski, and Austin Sekula. "The Effects of Multiple-Exemplar Training on Generalization of Social Skills with Adolescents and Young Adults with Autism: A Systematic Review." *Review Journal of Autism and Developmental Disorders* (2022): 1-20.

Frost, Lori, Andy Bondy, and Rayna Bondy. *The Picture Exchange Communication System*: Training Manual. (2002).

Gold, Deborah. ""We Don't Call it a 'circle'": The Ethos of a Support Group." *Disability & Society* 9, no. 4 (1994): 435-452.

Individuals with Disabilities Education Act, 20 U.S.C. § 1400 (2004).

Kalyva, E., and E. Avramidis. (2005). "Improving Communication Between Children with Autism and Their Peers Through the 'Circle of Friends': A Small-Scale Intervention Study." *Journal of Applied Research in Intellectual Disabilities*, 18, 253-261.

MacFarland, Mari C. and Marisa H. Fisher. (2021). "Peer-Mediated Social Skill Generalization for Adolescents with Autism Spectrum Disorder and Intellectual Disability." *Exceptionality* 29 no. 4 (2021). 114-132.

Mayerson, Gary S. "Generalization After Endrew F.: Shrinking the Gap Between Access and Outcome for Students Diagnosed with Autism." *New York School Law Review* 63 (2018): 51.

McIntosh, K., & MacKay, L. D. (2008). "Enhancing Generalization of Social skills: Making Social Skills Curricula Effective After the Lesson." *Beyond Behavior*, 18, 18-25.

Vermeulen, P. (2012). *Autism as Context Blindness*. Arlington, TX: Future Horizons, Inc.

Wattawonagwan, S., Ganz, J. B., Pierson, L. M., Hong, E. R., Yllades, V., Dunn, C., & Foster, M. (2022). "Quality Review of Social-Communication Interventions for Adolescents and Adults With ASD: Maintenance, Generalization, and Social Validity." *Education and Training in Autism and Developmental Disabilities*, 57(1), 67–91.

CHAPTER 11

Instruction Often Occurring in Specialized Settings

Sheila M. Smith, PhD with Sherry Moyer, LMSW

Terms such as "least restrictive environment (LRE)," "inclusive practices," "specially designed instruction," "evidence-based practices (EBP)," and "access to the curriculum" are used when discussing instruction of students with disabilities (SWD), including autistic learners. Specifically, the Individuals with Disabilities Education Act (IDEA) mandates that SWD receive an individualized education program (IEP) that provides specially designed instruction matched to their unique needs using evidence-based practices in the LRE with as much inclusion as possible. Consequently, education professionals work collaboratively with families to address the needs of the whole child with their same-age peers, matching interventions to unique needs and preparing students to live their best lives.

Individual states have also been responsive to these evolving concepts and developed learning standards to assist educators with planning and instruction. Most state-level standards focus on academic subjects, the goal being to meet students' academic needs and assist educators in building student skills toward grade level expectations. Some examples include:

- Ohio's Extended Standards with Learning Progressions:
  https://education.ohio.gov/Topics/Special-Education/Ohios-Learning-Standards-Extended

- North Carolina's Extended Standards:
  https://www.dpi.nc.gov/districts-schools/classroom-resources/exceptional-children/resources-unique-needs/significant-cognitive-disabilities/nc-extended-content-standards

Both sets of standards task-analyze grade-level concepts and provide a place to begin the "instruction" conversation, breaking down the standards with prerequisite skills delineated, allowing for attainable goals and concrete steps towards achieving them.

Despite these efforts, the educational standards do not contain the breadth of skills needed to be successful. This is particularly evident when discussing autism. Neurological research has revealed differences in brain structure that point to the need for education and support beyond academics (cf., Cockerham & Malaia, 2016; Wilcox et al., 2021). As a result, in addition to academics, it is essential that the educational community identify standards in other areas, such as communication/social skills and sensory/regulation, and match them to EBPs (Anixt et al., 2024; Wong et al., 2015).

Online resources, strategies, and supports have emerged in recent years to support general and special educators in teaching autistic students and other SWD in the LRE, using EBP and inclusive practices. Examples include:

- The National Clearinghouse on Autism Evidence and Practice (NCAEP): **https://ncaep.fpg.unc.edu/**—a clearinghouse for current information on EBP for autistic students, online modules, step-by-step guides for implementation, and much more.

- The Autism Certification Center: **https://autismcertificationcenter.org**—provides video-based modules on EBP at the early-childhood, school-, and transition-age levels.

- Autism Internet Modules: **https://autisminternetmodules.org/**—offer a series of modules both EBP and promising practices across age levels from early childhood through adulthood.

While having abundant resources can be seen as positive, navigating through and matching resources to the unique needs of a student can be challenging given the competing priorities educators face today. Further, while many of these resources can be effectively implemented in an inclusive setting, instruction in a small group or one-on-one setting outside the general education setting is sometimes most effective for the student.

To make the job of educators simpler and as effective as possible, this chapter presents examples of EBPs and other promising practices for autistic students, including EBP implementation guides, instructional interventions, and interpretation strategies. This overview is followed by a discussion of the development of supports. That is, it is important that once appropriate strategies have been identified a process is in place to ensure that the materials are (a) developed in a timely manner and (b) taught to everybody who will be using them, (c) that a plan is established for evaluating their effectiveness.

Evidence-Based Practices Implementation Guides

As mentioned, instruction in a small group or one-on-one setting outside the general education setting is sometimes most effective for the student. Although some of these strategies can be time consuming to implement, they yield results that can ultimately improve the student's skills across multiple environments (Steinbrenner et al., 2020).

The National Clearinghouse on Autism Evidence and Practice (NCAEP) (https://ncaep.fpg. unfc.edu/) has developed multiple resources. In addition to modules, the site contains step-by-step implementation guides for each EBP, the research supporting the EBP, and much more.

Pamela Wolfberg's *Peer Play and the Autism Spectrum* (2003) is an excellent example of an implementation guide for integrated play groups. Briefly, play groups involve "expert" and "novice" players engaging in play with the support of a "play guide." As novice players, autistic individuals need opportunities to learn from "expert" peer players. Play groups occur in a natural setting and are facilitated by a trained play guide. Play groups work best when a play guide creates an action plan and prepares various supports ahead of time.

Table 11.1. Integrated Play Groups.

Steps for Setting up and Implementing Integrated Play Groups

1. Provide visual supports that state what the game plan is for the facilitated play session. Visuals can be pictures or written cues but should be used to guide the play and keep a clear focus. Turn-taking visual supports should be provided if a board game is being played or if children are struggling to take turns with blocks, cars, etc. Play guides should prepare visual supports before the group begins. A suggested visual schedule would include (a) play with toys (b) outside play; (c) play with toys, (d) snack, (e) art/craft time, (f) play with toys, and (g) goodbye activity.

2. Prepare the play setting and organize materials ahead of time. Limit the number and types of toys that are present so that children are encouraged to play together.

3. Create a list of Play Group Rules, such as: be nice to your friends; be nice to the toys; ask for help; and play together.

4. Provide support and facilitate the group.

A Play Guide's Role During Integrated Play Groups

1. Review the rules and the visual schedule for the play group before play begins.

2. Follow the children's lead but set the tone for how the players treat each other and include everyone.

3. Direct children to the visual supports to aid in transitions and support play.

4. Build in routines particularly at the beginning and end of the play group (sometimes a song or chant works great).

5. Direct the children to each other, not the adult.

6. Scaffold the play.

7. Set up arts/crafts activities as cooperative, whenever possible, so that children become accustomed to interacting with each other. For example, have one child in charge of the scissors, one child in charge of the paper, one child in charge of the glue sticks, etc. Then prompt the children to ask, "Who needs glue?" etc.

8. Even when play is going well, be nearby "just in case" to ensure the group stays successful.

Instructional Strategies

The foundation of any effective intervention involves identifying which skills are present and where skills break down in the face of daily demands. The following can be used to support skill acquisition in academics, daily living skills, communication/social skills, and sensory/regulation skills.

Direct Instruction

Direct instruction (DI) as a systematic approach to teaching that is often scripted with sequential lessons providing opportunities for one-on-one and small-group instruction. Opportunities are provided for teacher/student interactions that promote working to mastery of a skill while providing opportunities for reinforcement and correction along the way (Steinbrenner et al., 2020). NCAEP (https://ncaep.fpg.unc.edu/) provides a DI module that educators can view online or download using the DI Brief Packet (https://afirm.fpg.unc.edu/ sites/afirm.fpg.unc.edu/files/imce/resources/DI%20Brief%20Packet%202022.pdf). In addition, a DI implementation checklist supports educators who use this strategy (https://afirm. fpg.unc.edu/sites/afirm.fpg.unc.edu/files/imce/resources/DI%20Implementation%20 Checklist%202022.pdf). Finally, a Step-by-Step Guide for DI is available (https://afirm.fpg. unc.edu/sites/afirm.fpg.unc.edu/files/imce/resources/Step-by-Step%20Guide%20for%20 DI%202022.pdf).

Social Narratives

While most individuals intuitively understand social norms and conventions, autistics often need explicit instruction. Social narratives are simple stories that visually explain social situations and social behaviors. As such, they provide information to help the autistic student better understand the social context and their role in it. Social narratives are written to match individual abilities, attention span, and interests. They generally consist of the following elements.

Table 11.2. Elements and Content Outline of Social Narratives.

Elements	Describes
Title	Who
Tailored to student's needs	What
Uses "I" or "he/she/they"	When
Uses past, present, or future tense	Where
Communicates a positive and patient tone	Why

Table 11.2 (continued)

Elements	Describes
Is literally accurate	How
May provide guidance on what to do	Other's perspectives
Often contains "I will try to" statements	
Uses flexible words, such as "usually," "sometimes," or "often"	

Communication/social skills are a major challenge for autistic individuals, and a wide range of interventions, tools, and strategies are available to help support students in this area.

Power Card Strategy

Recognizing the impact of special interests, Gagnon created the Power Card Strategy (Gagnon, 2023). This strategy meets the criteria for EBP as an antecedent intervention (see Chapter 3: A Brief Review of Evidence-Based Practices in Autism). The Power Card Strategy can support the use of social skills, academic behaviors, self-calming strategies, and other behaviors that may be supported using an individual's special interest.

The first step is to identify a hero associated with the special interest because the student usually wants to emulate or be like their hero. For example, if the student likes dinosaurs, the hero could be Barney™ for a younger individual or a paleontologist for an older individual.

After identifying the hero, a short scenario is written in the first person at the individual's comprehension level to introduce the hero. The scenario consists of two parts. In the first paragraph, the hero (a) describes the problem, (b) uses a strategy to solve it, and (c) experiences success. The second paragraph encourages the individual to try the new strategy which is detailed in manageable steps. The scenario can be written on a single sheet or in booklet form.

The Power Card is then created. The size of a trading card or business card, the Power Card recaps how the learner can use the same strategy as the hero to solve a similar problem. Often a picture of the special interest is included. The Power Card can be carried in a purse, wallet, or pocket; it can be Velcroed™ inside a notebook or locker, placed on the corner of a student's desk, or presented on a smartphone or tablet.

A Power Card Example

Nine-year-old Gary was enthusiastic about answering every question the teacher asked whether it was directed at him or not. He often blurted a response or interrupted others who were trying to respond. Gary's special interest was Angry Birds.

The following scenario was developed based on Gary's special interest and the behavior: difficulty waiting his turn. In the first paragraph, Gary learns that for his heroes to be part of the team, they had to learn how to answer questions. The second paragraph encourages Gary to try to answer questions using the Angry Birds' four steps. Gary was encouraged to practice the new behavior several times and was verbally praised for "answering questions just like the Angry Birds Team."

Figure 11.1. Gary's Power Card Scenario.

The Angry Birds Learn to Wait Their Turn

Before they can join the Angry Birds, the birds had to attend school and learn how to be part of the team. The red bird had a particularly hard time learning to wait his turn. He wanted to answer all of the questions. When the teacher asked the group a question, he sometimes shouted out the answer without raising his hand. The blue bird, the white bird, and the black bird often became upset when the red bird was not following the classroom rule about waiting his turn.

The Angry Birds' teacher taught the red bird these four steps:

1. Listen to the question.
2. Think to yourself, "Do I have an answer?"
3. If you have an answer, raise your hand. Don't speak unless the teacher calls your name.
4. If the teacher calls on you, answer the question.

> Just like the red bird, you can be part of the Angry Birds' team. Being a part of the team will make all of the Angry Birds happy. They will be happy that you are on their team!

After Gary was introduced to the scenario, he was given the Power Card. The size of a business card, the Power Card consists of a picture related to the Angry Birds and the steps that Gary needs to remember when answering questions.

Figure 11.2. Gary's Power Card.

The Angry Birds follow these 4 steps to answer questions:

1. Listen to the question.
2. Think to yourself, "Do I have an answer?"
3. If you have an answer, raise your hand. Don't speak unless the teacher calls your name.
4. If the teacher calls on you, answer the question.

The Power Card strategy is a positive intervention that may help autistics learn more comfortably and effectively. By using a special interest, the individual is motivated to use Power Card Strategy. This relatively simple strategy can make a meaningful difference for autistic students.

Social Descriptions

A descriptive story explains a situation, usually from the point of view of the autistic individual. Descriptive stories are generally short and written at a level that the learner can easily understand. Many times, they include pictures that help explain the story. Undoubtedly, the most recognized social description is Carol Gray's Social Stories. Introduced in 1993 by Gray and Garand, the intervention has evolved over time from audio recorded to written stories;

from text only to including photos, icons, and drawings, and from being individualized to pre-created stories (Gray, 2016).

The following descriptive story provides information about schedule changes for an individual who finds them disconcerting.

When My Schedule Changes

Sometimes I get angry when the schedule changes. Teachers usually tell me before things change. Sometimes teachers cannot tell me before things change. I will try to ask a teacher what to do if I am confused about the new schedule. It will be easier for her to understand what I need if I am not crying or yelling. Schedules can be changed, and it is okay to follow a new schedule.

Social Scripts

Social scripts provide ready-to-use language for specific events. They may be structured as conversation starters, scripted responses, or cues to change topic (cf. Leaf et al., 2020). For instance, an autistic individual may practice a script that includes key questions that can be helpful in a given situation. For the autistic person who has trouble spontaneously generating language, for example, social scripts are effective because they help with language recall.

The following social script provides guidance for asking questions.

Asking Questions in Class

If you want to ask questions in class, here are some words that you can use with your teacher:
1. May I ask a question?
2. I have a question.
3. Would you please say that again?

Curricula That Support Conversation

Several traditional curricula (that is, curricula designed for autistic students for use by educational professionals, support persons, and clinicians) may be used to support student learning. Conversation sources are provided because the National Autism Indicators Report shows that the biggest predictor of independent living, having social relationships, and employment is being able to hold a conversation (Roux et al., 2015).

Talk With Me: A Step-by-Step Conversation Framework for Teaching Conversation Balance and Fluency (Mataya et al., 2017) breaks down the elements of a conversation that must be mastered to be proficient at conversing. The framework was developed and refined across many years based on a review of the research along with close observation of how people talk to each other—what conversations really sound like. The Conversation Framework provides a simple, easy-to-implement process specific enough to equip an autistic individual with the tools necessary to acquire conversation skills, and simple enough to be used at any age.

Conversation Club: Teaching Children with Autism Spectrum Disorder and Other Social Cognitive Challenges to Engage in Successful Conversations with Peers (Cannon et al., 2018) introduces conversation through a clubhouse filled with club members, including Friendly Freddy; the twins, Looking Louie, and Listening Lisa; Fix It Farrah; Good Memory Maria; New Words Nate; and the club mascot, Paco the Parrot. Students learn a variety of skills in club meetings that are designed to facilitate thinking about the social significance underlying each conversation skill (Muller et al., 2016).

Video-Based Instruction

The use of a customized video developed using a video camera, a digital camera, or even a cell phone is a powerful method of teaching new skills and/or reinforcing previously acquired skills. This strategy allows learning by observing and imitating behaviors in a dynamic format. Various people such as peers, siblings, parents, teachers, or students themselves may be videotaped as role models (Aldi et al., 2016; Radley et al., 2020).

Various forms of video-based instruction can support autistic individuals in learning and practicing skills: video modeling, technology tools, and commercially available videos.

Video Modeling

Video modeling provides autistics with a structure for acquiring new information that is compatible with their visual learning style. Examples include:

- Video-self modeling, where the individual views themself engaging in the behavior
- Video modeling, sometimes called traditional video modeling, features a peer who engages in the behavior
- Point-of-view modeling is used then the video is filmed at the individual's eye level and from their perspective
- Video prompting involves breaking the target behavior down into discrete steps in brief video clips (LaCava, 2021)

Video modeling can be effective as it allows the autistic individual to watch themselves or a peer appropriately perform a target behavior. Another benefit of video instruction is that the scene can be paused and replayed repeatedly for learners who require repeated viewing to learn new information.

In addition to teaching new skills, video modeling may be used to reduce anxiety. For example, a child who experiences anxiety related to visiting the school library may benefit from this strategy. The student's teacher can create a brief video showing what students do during library time as a way to prime the child. Video used as a priming strategy (Humphrey-Rush, 2020) can create predictability in the library visit and thereby reduce the student's anxiety. Step-by-Step Implementation Checklists on video modeling as well as modules to teach this EBP may be found at https://ncaep.fpg.unc.edu/).

Technology Tools—Apps, Software, and Virtual Reality

Today's technology has provided software programs, applications, simulations, augmented reality, and virtual environments as supplemental options for instruction. Accessing resources via technology provides independence and practice for the learner, as well as opportunities for using high-leverage practices such as direct and explicit instruction, prior to or after accessing the technology (McLeskey et al., 2017).

For those skills needing direct or small-group instruction, an iPad-based app or software can often create interest in the skill to be taught. As discussed in other chapters of this book, evidence suggests that autistic individuals can be better engaged using a visual medium. Technology tools available via apps and other digital media can be used as part of direct instruction or practice opportunities. This is a constantly growing and changing area of practice. Searching the Apple app store or working with the school-based technology team is recommended to remain current on software. In addition, feature-matching tools can assist teams when making decisions about specific types of technology that may benefit a particular student (see below).

- SIFTS (https://sifts.ocali.org/) focuses on assistive technology (AT); was developed to support decision making, matching student needs to available AT resources and tools.
- Understood Tech Finder (https://www.understood.org/en/tools/tech-finder) is a search engine to help identify both AT and instructional technologies that are rated by experts (Mosher & Carreon, 2021).

Mosher and Carreon (2021) identified apps that support direct instruction in social skills. These include:

- The Social Express. Designed for ages 6-18, the Social Express provides animated interactive lessons using social narratives and video modeling to assist in developing social skills, understanding perspectives, and creating strong relationships.
- Virtual Reality Opportunities to Implement Social Skills (VOISS). Virtual reality offers a more recent mechanism for teaching social skills, for example. VOISS uses social situations and scenarios to teach and support middle school students as they work to learn and practice appropriate social responses (https://projectvoiss.org/app/).

Commercially Available Videos

Again, capitalizing on the visual strength of autistic individuals (LaCava, 2021), many commercial videos can be effective in teaching and/or reinforcing skills, and are available online through platforms such as YouTube. This digital medium is constantly growing and changing with new options being developed regularly. We include a couple examples here.

- **Coulter Videos—Manners for the Real World: Basic Social Skills.** This video (https://www.youtube.com/watch?v=Nj7T728nWFc) demonstrates how to act during some of the most common interactions between people. Designed for upper-elementary students through adulthood, the video features clear descriptions and demonstrations of appropriate behavior in the areas of personal hygiene, conversations, introductions, telephone and Internet use, table manners, behavior for ladies and gentlemen, manners in public, serving as a host, and being a guest.

- **Social Skills Videos for Autistic Kids.** This series, available on YouTube (https://www.youtube.com/playlist?list=PLCB65E70D72CF7155), addresses the needs of younger students. A Muppet-type character named Buddy works to master activities of daily living. Tools such as behavior modeling, visual schedules, social stories, and direct instruction are used to help Buddy along the way.

- **Mind Reading: The Interactive Guide to Emotions** (Baron-Cohen et al., 2007). While emotion recognition challenges in autism have been widely recognized (APA, 2013; Loth et al., 2018), few materials have been developed to address this issue. One of the primary instructional supports used to develop emotion and mental state recognition is Mind Reading, a multimedia computer software program. The program provides a structured and systematic approach to learning emotion recognition in face and voice. Mind Reading is made up of three main components: (a) the Emotions Library, (b) the Learning Center, and the (c) Games Zone. The software also includes quizzes to assess progress. A home screen organizes the components and is the starting point for the program. There is also a log-in screen to use once users have chosen which area they wish to start with during a given session. Throughout the program, on the bottom of the screen is a navigation bar that allows the user to quickly see and move to various parts of the program. This multimedia technology has been used successfully to teach basic and complex emotion recognition to adults and children (Davidson et al., 2021; LaCava et al., 2007).

Stop, Observe, Deliberate, Act (SODA)

Created by Bock (2001) to serve as a social behavioral learning strategy, SODA helps autistic children and youth "attend to relevant social cues, process these cues, ponder their relevance and meaning, and select an appropriate response during novel social interactions." A visual strategy that has broad application, SODA utilizes the Think Aloud, Think Along model (Andrews & Mason, 1991). It contains the following steps:

- **Stop.** This step prompts the individual to develop an organizational schema in which an interaction is to occur. Specifically, the child attempts to define the activities and their order as well as identify a location near the activities from which he can observe to obtain additional information that will help him participate in the activity successfully.

- **Observe.** The point here is to observe the environment for clues to effective and successful intervention. Aspects of the environment targeted for observation may include length of conversations, number of individuals involved in conversations, tone of conversations (i.e., formal, casual), strategies utilized to begin and end conversations, nonverbal language, and any routines that may be in place.

- **Deliberate.** In this phase, the individual develops a plan for interacting in the new environment. This includes deciding on a topic of conversation, identifying strategies that may lead to successful interactions (i.e., appropriately beginning a conversation, using eye contact, maintaining appropriate social distance), and analyzing how the child thinks she will be perceived by others if she does or does not follow the routines he has identified.

- **Act.** At this point, the child becomes an active participant in the novel environment, carrying out the strategies she identified in the deliberation phase. This stage serves as a platform for generalizing skills that were learned in another environment.

Shown to be effective with autistic children and adolescents (Bock, 2001, 2007a, 2007b), SODA is not self-contained but relies on using social skills developed through direct instruction or coaching formats in group or individual settings. SODA's importance lies in the fact that it allows students to approach unique situations without impulse and use social skills in a context that is appropriate.

Figure 11.3. Overview of the SODA Strategy.

Acronym Letter	Question to Ask Self
Stop	Where should I go to observe?
	What is the room arrangement?
	What is the routine or schedule?
Observe	What is/are _____ doing?
	What is/are _____ saying?
	What happens when _____ say and do these things?
Deliberate	What would I like to do?
	What would I like to say?
	How will _____ feel when I do and say these things?
	How will _____ act when I do and say these things?
	Why will _____ act this way?
Act	When I go to _____ I plan to: (a) (b) (c) (d)

Interpretation Strategies

No matter how well developed their skills, situations will arise that the autistic person does not understand. In addition to confusion, this may result in extreme stress (Morrison et al., 2020). To help prevent this from happening, someone in the environment must serve as an interpreter. In the following, we look at a variety of ways to help explain—interpret—the social environment.

Cartooning

Cartooning promotes social understanding by using simple figures and other symbols in a comic strip format. Speech, thought bubble symbols, and, sometimes, color are used to help the individual see and analyze a situation. Adults can draw a social situation to facilitate understanding or assist the learner in creating their own illustrations.

Arwood et al. (2015) called the cartoon a "form of visual language" and "storytelling in picture form" (p. 1). According to these authors, cartooning is used to (a) explain and change behavior, (b) improve academic and social skills, and (c) help individuals better manage time. Cartoon figures play an integral role in several other intervention techniques, including pragmaticism (Arwood et al., 2015) and Comic Strip Conversations™ (Gray, 1994.)

Figure 11.4. Example of a Cartoon.

Created by Ronda Schelvan

Sensory Awareness

Approximately 85% of autistic people have difficulty identifying and understanding their emotions. They may not receive the signals necessary for this to occur or may confuse one emotion for another (i.e., mistake hunger for anger) and, therefore, need help "interpreting" (Mahler et al., 2024).

The little known but extremely important sensory system called interoception helps us to "feel" our internal state or conditions of our body (for more information, see Chapter 7: Sensory/ Regulation). The interoceptive system brings in information such as pain, body temperature, itch, sexual arousal, hunger, and thirst. It also helps bring in information regarding heart and breathing rates and when to use the bathroom. In addition, this system lets individuals know when they are irritated, overwhelmed, upset, or anxious—all of which are related to potential meltdowns.

The Interoception Curriculum: A Step-By-Step Framework for Developing Mindful Self-Regulation (Mahler, 2022) provides a systematic, guided process to develop and build interoceptive awareness. It contains 25 lessons to help individuals from preschool through adulthood understand the information they receive from their organs and inside their body. Research supports its use (cf. Mahler et al., 2024).

Rating Scales

Related to challenges understanding their emotions, many autistic individuals have difficulty self-calming (Myles, 2024). Therefore, it is important to provide strategies that will help them to understand their emotions and to respond appropriately. Two rating scales address this important topic.

Stress-Tracking Thermometer

Using McAfee's (2013) stress-tracking thermometer, autistics learn to:

- Identify and label their emotions using nonverbal and situational cues
- Assign appropriate values to different degrees of emotion, such as anger
- Redirect negative thoughts to positive thoughts
- Identify environmental stressors and common reactions to them
- Recognize the early signs of stress
- Select relaxation techniques that match their needs

Figure 11.5. Stress Thermometer.

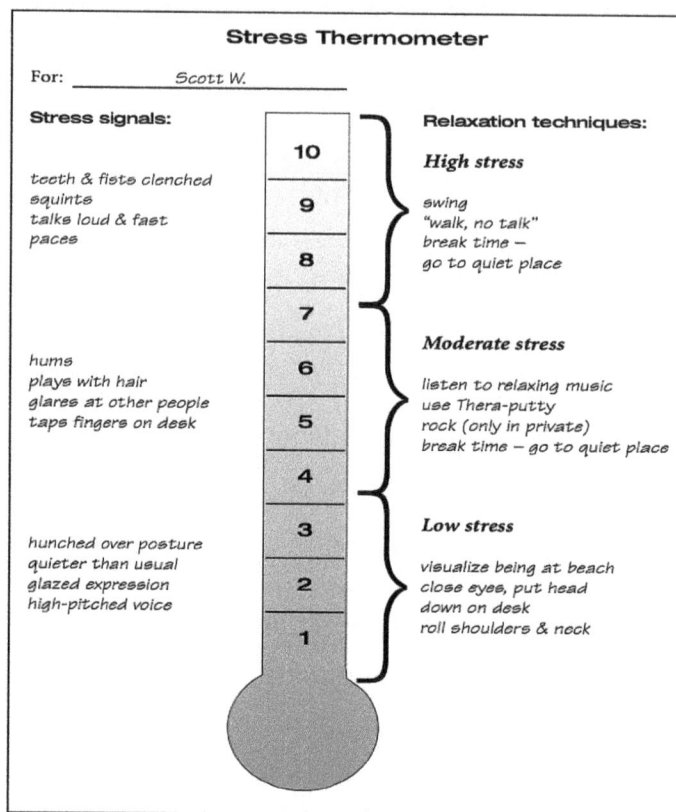

Stress Thermometer

For: _____ *Scott W.*

Stress signals:

teeth & fists clenched
squints
talks loud & fast
paces

hums
plays with hair
glares at other people
taps fingers on desk

hunched over posture
quieter than usual
glazed expression
high-pitched voice

10
9
8
7
6
5
4
3
2
1

Relaxation techniques:

High stress

swing
"walk, no talk"
break time –
go to quiet place

Moderate stress

listen to relaxing music
use Thera-putty
rock (only in private)
break time – go to quiet place

Low stress

visualize being at beach
close eyes, put head
down on desk
roll shoulders & neck

From McAfee, Jeanette. *Navigating the Social World: A Curriculum for Individuals with Asperger's Syndrome, High Functioning Autism and Related Disorders* (p. 47). Future Horizons (2013).

Incredible 5-Point Scale

The Incredible 5-Point Scale was developed to help autistic children as well as adolescents and adults (Buron & Curtis, 2021) to understand themselves and, therefore, to be able to better regulate their behavior. The scale is unique in that it has a wide range of applications. For example, it can be used as an obsessional index, a stress scale, a meltdown monitor, and so on. Individuals learn to recognize the stages of their specific behavioral challenges and methods to self-calm at each level.

The Incredible 5-Point Scale identifies, in the individual's own words, (a) a term to describe their behavior at 1, 2, etc.; (b) what the behavior feels like at each number; and (c) what they can do to address the behavior at each level.

Figure 11.6. Incredible 5-Point Scale.

5	I AM GOING TO EXPLODE!!!
4	I AM GETTING ANGRY
3	I AM A LITTLE NERVOUS
2	FEELING OK
1	CALM AND RELAXED

From www.5pointscale.com

Situation, Options, Consequences, Choices, Strategies, Simulation (SOCCSS)

The SOCCSS strategy (Roosa, 1995) is designed to help students understand social situations and develop problem-solving skills by putting behavioral and social issues into a sequential format. Through use of this adult-directed strategy, students come to understand cause and effect and realize that they can influence the outcome of many situations by the decisions they make. The strategy may be used one-on-one or as a group activity, depending on the situation and students' needs.

SOCCSS consists of the following six steps.

- **Situation.** After a social problem occurs, the adult helps the individual identify who, what, when, where, and why. The goal is to encourage the individual to share these variables independently. At first, however, the adult may assume a more active role by asking questions, reflecting, and prompting.

- **Options.** The adult and student brainstorm several options the student might have chosen in the given situation. Brainstorming means accepting and recording all responses without evaluating them. Initially, the adult usually must encourage the youth to identify more than one option for something that could have been done or said differently.

- **Consequences.** For each behavior option generated, a consequence is listed. The adult asks the student, "So what would happen if you ... (name the option)?" Some options may have more than one consequence. It is often difficult for students to generate consequences if they have difficulty determining cause-and-effect relationships. Role-play at this stage can serve as a prompt in identifying consequences.

- **Choices.** Options and consequences are prioritized using a numerical sequence or a yes/no response. Following prioritization, the student is prompted to select the option that (a) appears doable and (b) will most likely help the student obtain personal wants or needs.

- **Strategies.** A plan is developed to carry out the option if the situation occurs. Although the adult and student collaborate on the stages of the plan, the student should ultimately generate the plan to ensure a feeling of ownership and commitment to use the strategy.

- **Simulation.** Roosa has defined this practice in a variety of ways: (a) using imagery, (b) talking with another about the plan, (c) writing down the plan, or (d) role-playing. The student evaluates personal impressions of the simulation. Did the simulation activity provide the skills and confidence to carry out the plan? If the answer is "no," additional simulation must take place.

Although designed to be used following the occurrence of a social problem, the strategy can also be used as an instructional strategy. For example, teachers can identify problems students are likely to encounter and address them using SOCCSS so that students have a plan prior to a situation occurring.

Figure 11.7. Situation-Options-Consequences-Choices-Strategies-Simulation (SOCCSS) Worksheet.

SOCCSS Worksheet

Situation	
Who	When
What	Why

Options	Consequences	Choices

Strategy – Plan of Action

Simulation	Select One
1. Find a quiet place, sit back and imagine how your Situation would work (or not work) based on the various Options and Consequences.	
2. Talk with a peer, staff, or other person about your plan of action.	
3. Write down on paper what may happen in your Situation based on your Options and Consequences.	
4. Practice your Options with one or more people using behavior rehearsal. Start simple and easy for learning. Only make it difficult to test the learning.	
5. _____	

Simulation Outcomes

Followup

From *Asperger Syndrome and Adolescence – Practical Solutions for School Success* (pp. 112-113), by B. S. Myles and D. Adreon, 2001, Shawnee Mission, KS: AAPC Publishing. Reprinted with permission.

Attribution Retraining *by Sherry Moyer, LMSW*

While it is key to understand the thoughts and feelings of self and others to have successful social interactions, it is also helpful to understand one's role in events and the impact they have. Understanding these issues can also lead to success in academics, communication/social skills, and sensory/regulation.

Due to their neurology (Fernandes et al., 2022), autistic individuals typically need instruction and support in this area. One way to offer such support is through attribution retraining, which teaches learners to better understand their role in events using the following three parameters (Weiner, 1986):

1. **Is this situation internal or external to me?** The learner is taught that it is possible to control or change many internal factors, although it may be a challenge. Likewise, they learn about items—external factors—that may not be directly under the individual's control; some cannot be changed; others may be altered with effort and assistance from another. A student who does not understand these concepts may feel that they caused a situation over which they had no control. On the other hand, the student may blame others for an action over which they, the learner, had control (Moyer, 2009).

   - To understand what the student needs, it is important for them to understand themselves. If they understand their personal characteristics and skills, they can determine whether a match exists between these and the activity or context. In short, to get the most from an activity or environment, it is helpful to understand what characteristics/skills are needed and at what level.

   - A mismatch may be minimized if the learner is primed for the activity with a direct discussion of how specific characteristics and skills match or do not match the context. A lack of match may require (a) a home base before the activity to "shore up" personal resources and approach the situation more calmly; (b) a social narrative that describes what the individual can do to better enjoy the activity; (c) a video model of the activity viewed before it occurs; (d) a reinforcer; and (f) a home base after the activity to destress.

Figure 11.8. Internal and External Attribution.

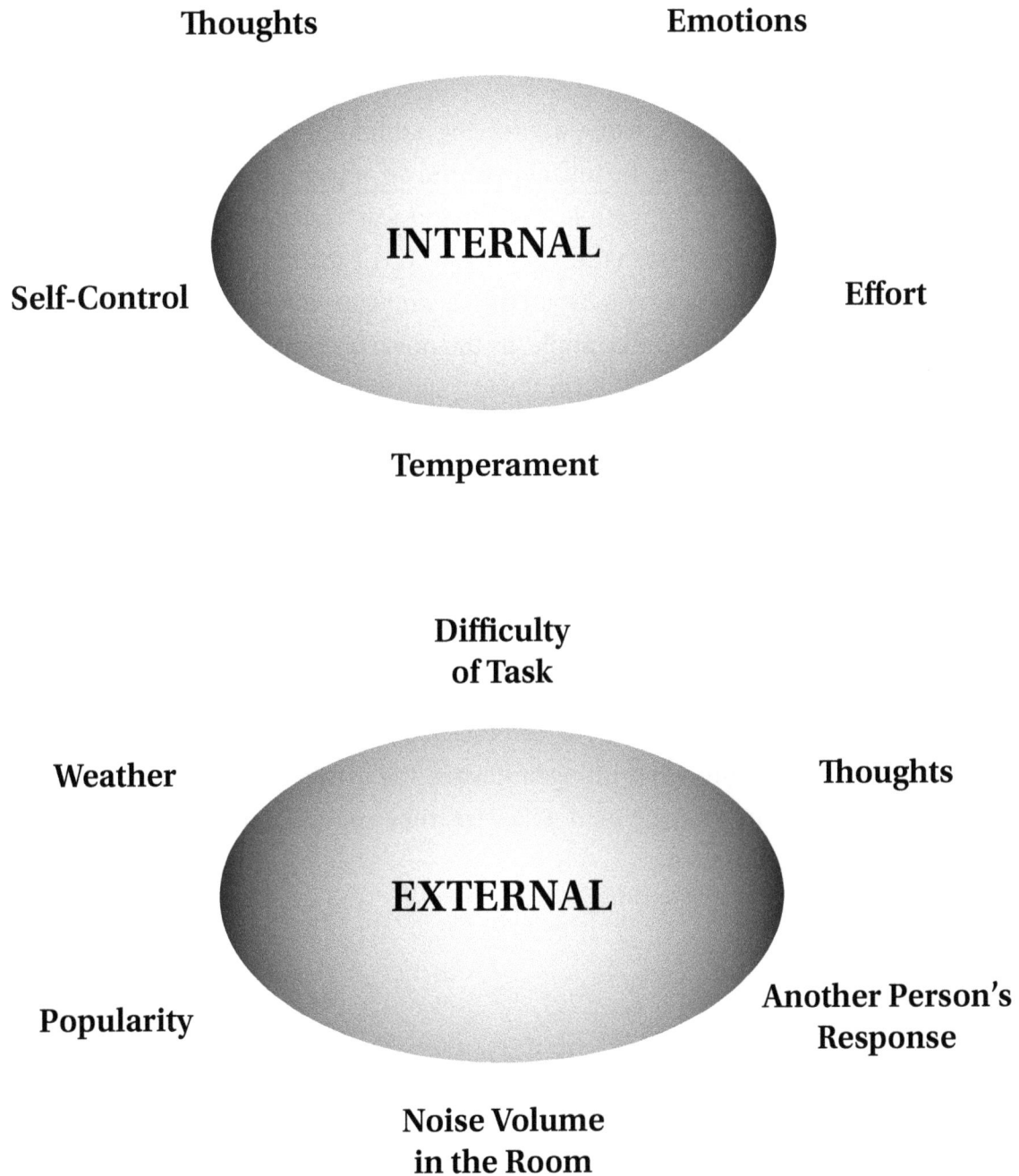

Thoughts　　　　　　Emotions

INTERNAL

Self-Control　　　　　　Effort

Temperament

Difficulty
of Task

Weather　　　　　　Thoughts

EXTERNAL

Popularity　　　　　Another Person's
Response

Noise Volume
in the Room

Conclusion: Some things are naturally part of us; some things are not.

2. **Is the situation stable or unstable?** Autistic students learn that events, contexts, and people are constantly changing, and it is often difficult to predict those changes. For example, just because you went to a movie theater once, does not mean that you will have the same type of experience in that same theater when you go a second time. Why? Many items within that movie theater would qualify as unstable or changing from one time to the next: (a) the temperature could be different, (b) the movie is certainly different, (c) perhaps they are serving a different kind of popcorn, and so forth. In addition, elements may be unstable within an activity. The first math problem was easy; the second was impossible. Your mood was cheery at first, but less so as the activity went on. The noise in the room when you began the first task was minimal, but increased dramatically as you began the second task. Emotions also contribute to an unstable environment. For example, as the noise becomes louder, tolerations lessen, and behavior may escalate (Moyer, 2009).

   - Students need to be taught that although they may understand generally what will happen in an activity, change will occur. To that end, it is essential that students learn to analyze an environment/activity and identify its many aspects. In that way, students, with support, can predict how these aspects can vary from time to time. This will allow the individual to develop a "toolkit" of items that might be needed in similar activities.

   - Instruction on how to predict if, when, and how one behavior or element may change within an activity is also essential. In this case, the student can prepare in advance through priming or destressing to meet the ever-changing behavior or environmental element. Likewise, they could be prepared with supports in case change occurs.

Figure 11.9. Stable and Unstable Attribution.

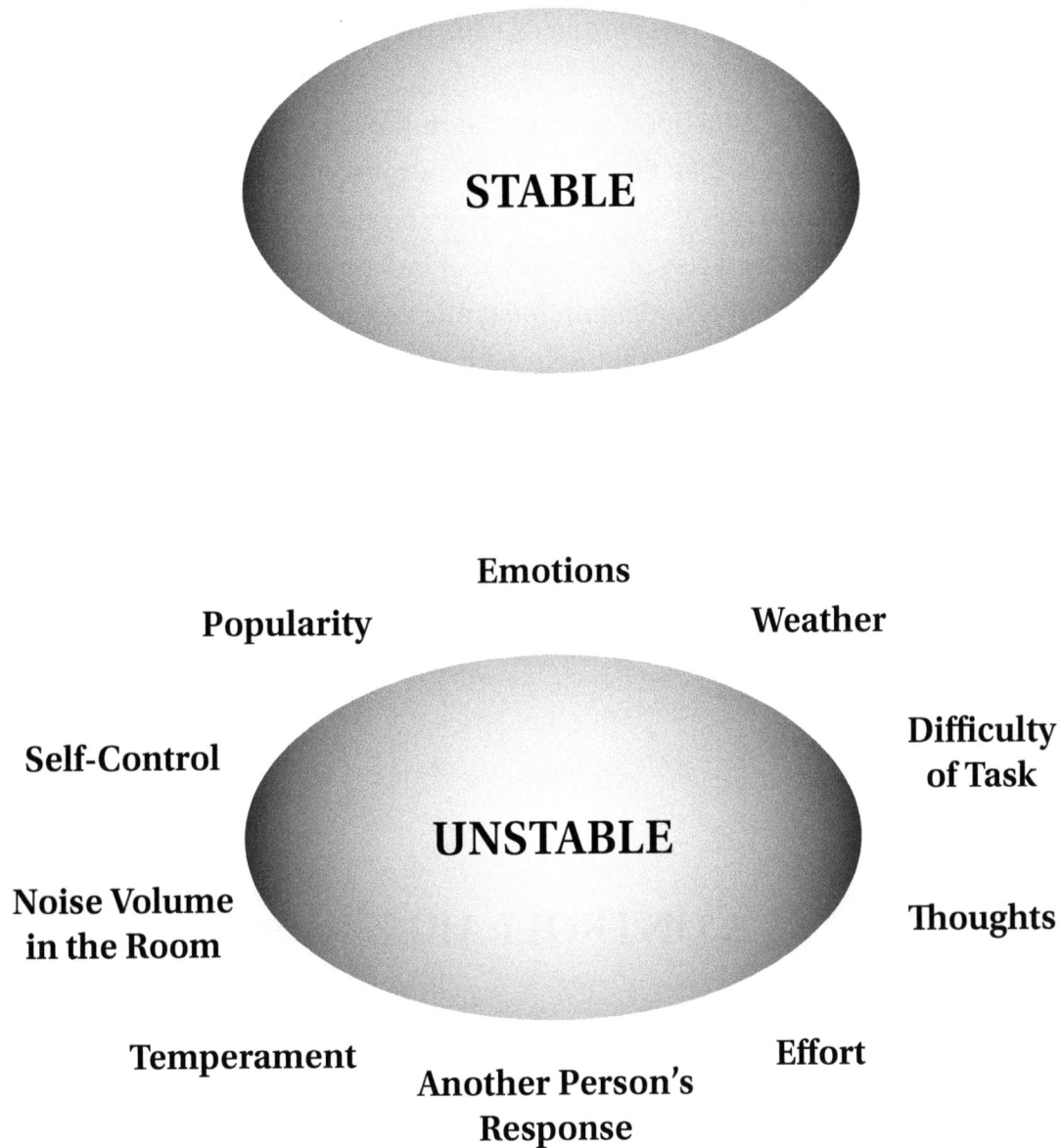

Conclusion: Not many things will ALWAYS stay the same.

3. **Is the situation controllable or uncontrollable?** Is there any way that I can have a positive influence or effect on the outcome of my circumstances? What things can I change in an activity or context? What do I have no control over? Once the learner can identify the type of situation they are faced with, they can structure for success (Moyer, 2009).

   - For controllable situations, students learn how to identify elements that may not be supportive. Then they can learn how to request or effect a change.
   - Identifying supports is more effective when the learner understands which uncontrollable aspects are compatible or incompatible with how they process and learn. When the student understands that a mismatch exists, they can be prepared with supports that help with potentially troublesome uncontrollable aspects.

Figure 11.10. Controllable and Uncontrollable Attribution.

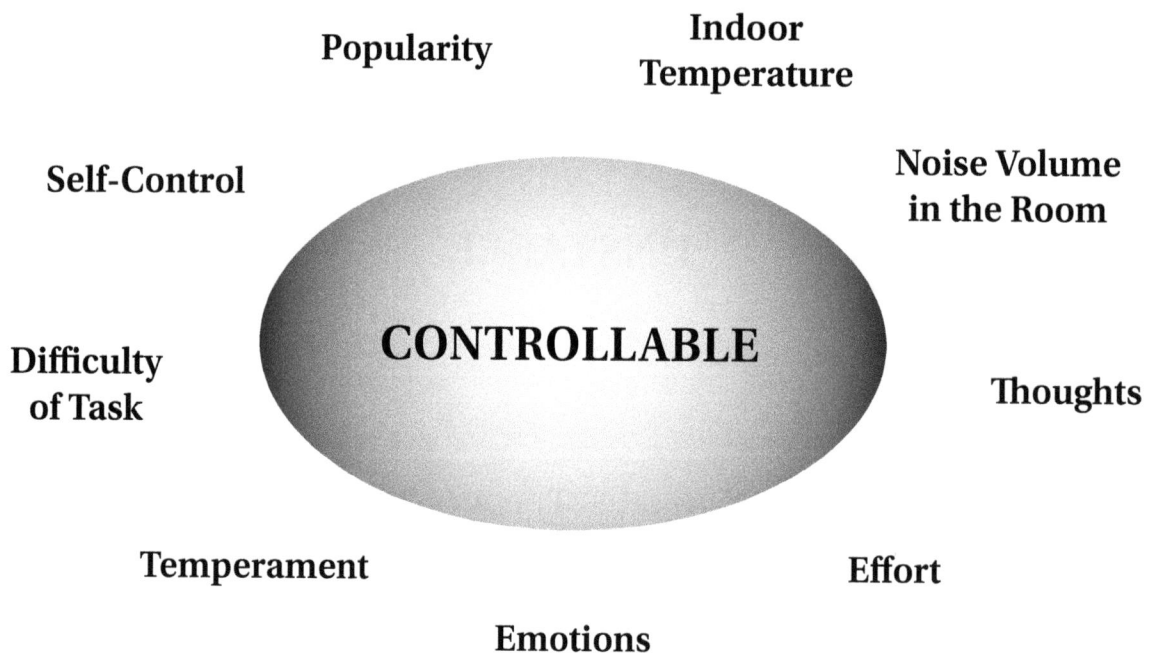

Popularity

Indoor
Temperature

Self-Control

Noise Volume
in the Room

CONTROLLABLE

Difficulty
of Task

Thoughts

Temperament

Effort

Emotions

Figure 11.10 (continued)

Weather   **UNCONTROLLABLE**   **Another Person's Response**

Conclusion: We may have more control over more things than we think.

In general, most students attribute their circumstances as being internal to them, stable, and uncontrollable. Such a pattern leaves the person with very little incentive or motivation to expend any effort to try to make things better. For instance, if you thought that every time you took a math test you would fail because you are not smart enough, or because you thought the teacher did not like you, you would very likely not be motivated or optimistic that you could positively influence your outcomes.

Because attribution retraining involves an individual's perceptions, the objective is not to arrive at a right or wrong answer but to conduct an evaluation of the circumstances that leads to positive behaviors. Attribution retraining teaches autistic individuals to better understand an environment/activity by (a) conducting an analysis of environments and tasks, creating an awareness of their component parts; (b) determine whether each of these component parts are internal/external, stable/unstable, controllable/uncontrollable; and (c) develop and implement a plan to ensure that supports are in place to address any mismatches between the individual and their environment.

Summary

Autistic students often require direct and extensive instruction, including how to interpret the environment. In many cases, such instruction is a prerequisite for academic, social, and behavior success. This can occur in an individualized or small-group setting. For example, for the many students who experience challenges with detecting anxiety in themselves, instruction in a one-on-one setting may precede successful social interactions (see Chapter 7: Sensory/Regulation).

Development of Supports

Many skills that are used in a general education setting require repeated teaching and significant time and practice to internalize by the student—time that is often not available to classroom teachers. Thus, special educators, related services personnel, and paraprofessionals often assume the responsibility for developing and/or identifying supports needed by autistic children and youth. They may also have to teach the student, and perhaps the general education teacher, how and when to use a given strategy or support with the student to build their independence. Visual schedules, task cards, sensory supports, and communication systems (i.e., language boards, Picture Exchange Communication System [Frost & Bondy, 2002]) are samples of supports that are often personally developed and/or selected for specific students. These are discussed further in Chapter 7: Sensory/Regulation and Chapter 8: Communication/Social Skills.

When completing a CAPS, it is important to designate not only what supports need to be developed and/or selected, but also (a) who will develop them, (b) who will teach use of the support, and (c) how and when its effectiveness will be evaluated. The CAPS Support Development Form can be helpful in this regard to keep everybody on track.

Figure 11.11. Sample CAPS Support Development Form.

Student Name: _____   Date: _____

Support	Who Will Develop Support	Date Support Needed	Who Will Teach Support Use	When to Evaluate Effectiveness	How to Evaluate Effectiveness

Summary

Not only is specially designed instruction required for autistic students, but they often need individualized materials to be successful across multiple environments. Although used in general education and community settings, many supports, such as those described in this chapter, are most likely developed by special education or related services personnel outside of the environment in which they will eventually be used. These supports are included on the CAPS and, thus, become a part of the student's instructional program.

Bibliography

Aldi, Catarina, Alexandra Crigler, Kelly Kates-McElrath, Brian Long, Hillary Smith, Kim Rehak, and Lisa Wilkinson. "Examining the Effects of Video Modeling and Prompts to Teach Activities of Daily Living Skills." *Behavior Analysis in Practice* 9 (2016): 384-388.

Anixt, Julia S., Jennifer Ehrhardt, and Amie Duncan. "Evidence-Based Interventions in Autism." *Pediatric Clinics* (2024).

American Psychiatric Association. (2013). *Diagnostic and Statistical Manual for Mental Disorders* (5th ed., text revision). Author (2013).

Andrews J. F., & J.M. Mason. (1991). "Strategy Usage Among deaf and Hard of Hearing Readers." *Exceptional Children* 57 (1991): 536-545.

Arwood, Ellen L., Mabel M. Brown, M.M., and Kaulitz, Carole. *Prosocial Language: A Way to Think About Behavior.* Apricot (2015).

Baron-Cohen S, Ofer Golan, Sally Wheelwright, and J.J. Hill. *Mind Reading: The Interactive Guide to Emotions.* Jessica Kingsley Limited (2007).

Bock, Marjorie A. "SODA strategy: Enhancing the Social Interaction Skills of Youngsters With Asperger Syndrome." *Intervention in School and Clinic* 36, no. 5 (2001): 272-278.

Bock, Marjorie A. "The Impact of Social-Behavioral Learning Strategy Training on the Social Interaction Skills of Four Students With Asperger Syndrome." *Focus on Autism and Other Developmental Disabilities* 22, no. 2 (2007a): 88-95.

Bock, Marjorie A. "A Social-Behavioral Learning Strategy Intervention for a Child With Asperger Syndrome: Brief Report." *Remedial and Special Education* 28, no. 5 (2007b): 258-265.

Buron, K. D., & Curtis, M. *The Incredible 5-Point Scale: Assisting Students in Understanding Social Interactions and Managing Their Emotional Responses* (2nd edition—revised). Five Point Publishing (2021).

Cannon, Lynn, Jonna Clark, Courtney, Kornblum, Eve Muller, and Michael Powers. *Conversation Club: Teaching Children With Autism Spectrum Disorder and Other Social Cognition Challenges to Engage in Successful Conversations With Peers.* AAPC Publishing (2018).

Davidson, Denise, Elizabeth Hilvert, Adrien M. Winning, and Michael Giordano. "Recognition of Emotions from Situational Contexts and the Impact of a Mind Reading Intervention in Children With Autism Spectrum Disorder." *Child Psychiatry & Human Development* (2022): 1-12.

Fernandes, João Miguel, Sara Soares, Ricardo Lopes, Rita Jerónimo, and J. Bernardo Barahona-Corrêa. "Attribution of Intentions in Autism Spectrum Disorder: A Study of Event-Related Potentials." *Autism Research* 15, no. 5 (2022): 847-860.

Frost, L., & Bondy, A. *The Picture Exchange Communication Systems Training Manual.* Pyramid Educational Products 2022.

Gagnon, Elisa. *Power Cards: Using Interests and Enthusiasms to Teach Social Problem Solving and Emotional Regulation Skills to Autistic Students.* 5 Point Publishing (2023).

Gray, Carol. *The New Social Story™ Book, Revised and Expanded 15th Anniversary Edition: Over 150 Social Stories That Teach Everyday Skills to Children and Adults With Autism and Their Peers.* Future Horizons (2016).

Gray, Carol. *Comic Strip Conversations.* Future Horizons (1994).

Gray, C.A., & Joy D. Garand. "Social Stories™: Improving Responses of Students with Autism with Accurate Social Information. *Focus on Autistic Behavior* 8 no. 1 (1993): 1-13.

Humphrey-Rush, Amanda Margaret. "Does Video Priming and Video Modeling Help to Reduce Anxiety and Increase Social Behaviors for Adults Who Have a Diagnosis Of Autism Spectrum Disorder or Intellectual Disability When Starting Paid Employment?." PhD diss., The University of Waikato, 2020.

LaCava, P. (2021). Video Modeling: An Online Training Module. (Providence: Rhode Island College, Special Education Department). In Ohio Center for Autism and Low Incidence (OCALI), *Autism Internet Modules*, www. autisminternetmodules.org. OCALI.

LaCava, Paul G., Ofer Golan, Simon Baron-Cohen, and Brenda Smith Myles. "Using Assistive Technology to Teach Emotion Recognition to Students With Asperger Syndrome: A Pilot Study." *Remedial And Special Education* 28, No. 3 (2007): 174-181.

Loth, Eva, Lúcia Garrido, Jumana Ahmad, Ekaterina Watson, Alexa Duff, and Bradley Duchaine. "Facial Expression Recognition as a Candidate Marker for Autism Spectrum Disorder: How Frequent and Severe are Deficits?" *Molecular Autism* 9, no. 1 (2018): 1-11.

Mahler, Kelly, Kerri Hample, Carly Ensor, Mary Ludwig, Laura Palanzo-Sholly, Adelaide Stang, Dominic Trevisan, and Claudia Hilton. "An Interoception-Based Intervention for Improving Emotional Regulation in Children in a Special Education Classroom: Feasibility Study." *Occupational Therapy In Health Care* (2024): 1-15.

Mataya, Kerry, Ruth Aspy, & Hollis Schaffer. *Talk With Me: A Step-by-Step Conversation Framework for Teaching Conversational Balance and Fluency for High-Functioning Individuals with Autism Spectrum Disorder*. Future Horizons (2017).

McAfee, Jeanette. *Navigating the Social World: A Curriculum for Individuals With Asperger's Syndrome, High Functioning Autism, and Related Disorders*. Future Horizons (2013).

McLeskey, James, *Council for Exceptional Children, and Collaboration for Effective Educator Development, Accountability and Reform. High-Leverage Practices in Special Education*. Council for Exceptional Children (2017).

Morrison, Kerrianne E., Kilee M. DeBrabander, Desiree R. Jones, Daniel J. Faso, Robert A. Ackerman, and Noah J. Sasson. "Outcomes of Real-World Social Interaction for Autistic Adults Paired With Autistic Compared to Typically Developing Partners." *Autism* 24, no. 5 (2020): 1067-1080.

Mosher, Maggie A., and Adam C. Carreon. "Teaching Social Skills to Students With Autism Spectrum Disorder Through Augmented, Virtual and Mixed Reality." *Research in Learning Technology* 29 (2021).

Moyer, S. *The ECLIPSE Model: Teaching Self-Regulation, Executive Function, Attribution, and Sensory Awareness to Young People With Asperger Syndrome, PDD-NOS, and Related Disorders*. AAPC Publishing (2009).

Müller, Eve, Lynn R. Cannon, Courtney Kornblum, Jonna Clark, and Michal Powers. "Description and Preliminary Evaluation of a Curriculum for Teaching Conversational Skills to Children With High-Functioning Autism and Other Social Cognition Challenges." *Language, Speech, and Hearing Services in Schools* 47, no. 3 (2016): 191-208.

Myles, Brenda Smith. *Autism and Difficult Moments: Practical Solutions for Meltdowns*. Future Horizons (2024).

Radley, Keith C., Evan H. Dart, Kayleigh J. Brennan, Kate A. Helbig, Erica L. Lehman, Magenta Silberman, and Kai Mendanhall. "Social Skills Teaching For Individuals With Autism Spectrum Disorder: A Systematic Review." *Advances in Neurodevelopmental Disorders* 4 (2020): 215-226.

Roosa, J. B. *Men on the Move: Competence and Cooperation: Conflict Resolution and Beyond*. Author (1995).

Roux, A. M., P. T. Shattuck, J. E. Rast, J. A. Rava, and K. Anderson. "National Autism Indicators Report: Transition Into Young Adulthood. Life Course Outcomes Research Program," AJ Drexel Autism Institute, Drexel University. (2015).

Steinbrenner, Jessica R., Kara Hume, Samuel L. Odom, Kristi L. Morin, Sallie W. Nowell, Brianne Tomaszewski, Susan Szendrey, Nancy S. McIntyre, Serife Yücesoy-Özkan, and Melissa N. Savage. "Evidence-Based Practices for Children, Youth, and Young Adults with Autism." FPG Child Development Institute (2020).

Weiner, Bernard. *An Attributional Theory of Motivation and Emotion.* Springer (1986).

Wilcox, Gabrielle, Laura M. Morett, Zachary Hawes, and Eleanor J. Dommett. "Why Educational Neuroscience Needs Educational And School Psychology to Effectively Translate Neuroscience to Educational Practice." *Frontiers in Psychology* 11 (2021): 618449.

Wolfberg, Pamela J. *Peer Play and the Autism Spectrum: The Art of Guiding Children's Socialization and Imagination: Integrated Play Groups Field Manual.* AAPC Publishing (2003).

Wong, Connie, Samuel L. Odom, Kara A. Hume, Ann W. Cox, Angel Fettig, Suzanne Kucharczyk, Matthew E. Brock, Joshua B. Plavnick, Veronica P. Fleury, and Tia R. Schultz. "Evidence-Based Practices for Children, Youth, and Young Adults With Autism Spectrum Disorder: A Comprehensive Review." *Journal of Autism and Developmental Disorders* 45 (2015): 1951-1966.

CHAPTER 12

The M-CAPS: Using CAPS in Secondary School, Postsecondary Settings, on the Job, and Beyond

The structure of middle/high school is different from the structure of the elementary grades. At the elementary level, students often remain in the same setting all day or infrequently move from class to class, except for some specials. But in middle and high school, the school day is structured by time and subject, and students often move from room to room each hour with brief stops at their lockers in between.

This chapter overviews how CAPS can be used in middle and high school but with some modifications compared to the elementary grades. That is, while the traditional CAPS works for some courses, it is not applicable to others. This is where the Modified Comprehensive Autism Planning System (M-CAPS) comes in. While basically the same structure, the M-CAPS differs somewhat from the form used during the elementary years.

The Comprehensive Autism Planning System (CAPS)

Some classes in middle and high school mirror in structure those that are taught in elementary school. For these classes, the traditional CAPS may be used. Physical education (PE) is an example of a class for which the CAPS by time and activity would be most appropriate.

Students who have work experiences, community-based opportunities, and extracurricular activities would also have a traditional CAPS completed for these classes.

The Modified Comprehensive Autism Planning System (M-CAPS)

When students enter middle and high school, most change rooms and teachers for each class. They may have as many as nine teachers in nine different classrooms during a typical school day. Despite their movement from classroom to classroom, the activities in which students participate in each academic class are similar. That is, in each class students are likely to be required to participate in a mixture of (a) independent work, (b) group work, (c) tests, (d) lectures, and (e) homework. From this standpoint, the activities in English class and geometry are the same.

The multidisciplinary team that plans the program for an autistic high school student who spends extensive time in general education classrooms develops the student's program using the M-CAPS, and each of the student's academic teachers shares the same document. That is, the M-CAPS used in biology is the same as the M-CAPS used in sociology. The supports are the same. As such, the M-CAPS is an effective means of communicating to educators who teach academic subjects the types of supports students need during each activity.

A blank copy of the M-CAPS form as well as a sample completed M-CAPS for middle/high school academic classes follow.

Figure 12.1. Blank M-CAPS.

The Modified Comprehensive Autism Planning System (M-CAPS)							
Child/Student: _____ Date: _____							
Activity	Skills to Teach	Structure/ Modifications	Reinforcement	Sensory/ Regulation	Communication/ Social Skills	Data Collection	Generalization to Community
Independent Work							
Group Work							
Tests							
Lectures							
Homework							

Figure 12.2. Sample CAPS for an Academic Class.

The Modified Comprehensive Autism Planning System (M-CAPS)			
Child/Student: Jonnah		Date: 8/17	
Activity	**Skills to Teach**	**Structure/ Modifications**	**Reinforcement**
Independent Work	• Task completion • Asking for help when stuck	• Task Organizer • Organization calendar *Prompt to use; systematically fade* • Peer buddies (trained by special educator)	• Completing home/class work *From reinforcer menu*
Group Work	Conversation Rules	• Task Organizer • Organization calendar *Prompt to use; systematically fade* • Peer buddies (trained by special educator)	• Completing home/class work *From reinforcer menu*
Tests	Task completion	• Task Organizer • Organization calendar *Prompt to use; systematically fade*	• Calming skills • Conversation • Test completion *From reinforcer menu*
Lectures	Attention to task	• Task Organizer • Organization calendar *Prompt to use; systematically fade*	• Calming skills • Conversation *From reinforcer menu*
Homework	• Task completion • Materials and supplies needed	• Homework Checklist 1. Prompt to use and systematically fade; 2. Double check with student)	Homework turned in *From reinforcer menu*

Figure 12.2 (continued)

Sensory/ Regulation	Communication/ Social Skills	Data Collection	Generalization to Community
• Relaxation techniques • Coping cards • Ear plugs • Stress thermometer	Help card *Prompt to use; systematically fade*	• Task Organizer • Organization Calendar (P/I, daily)	Ask for help when completing homework, as needed
• Relaxation techniques • Coping cards • Stress thermometer	• Conversation cues • Hidden curriculum notebook • Cues for commenting and asking questions • Social narrative about group work	• Task Organizer • Organization Calendar (P/I, daily)	Use cue cards for lunch conversation
• Relaxation techniques • Coping cards • Stress thermometer	• Cues for commenting and asking questions	• Task Organizer • Organization Calendar (P/I, daily)	Use Organization Calendar for turning in assignments working independently
• Relaxation techniques • Coping cards • Stress thermometer	• Conversation cues • Cartooning • Hidden curriculum notebook • Cues for commenting and asking questions	• Task Organizer • Organization Calendar (P/I, daily)	Use hidden curriculum notebook at home
• Relaxation techniques • Stress thermometer	N/A	Homework turned in complete (Y/N, daily)	Turning in classwork

The benefits of using the M-CAPS in middle and high school are many, and include the following:

- The student uses the same types of supports across classes, which allows them to see the flexibility of supports, which in turn facilitates their understanding of the concept of generalization (e.g., "Whenever I am stressed, I can use my coping cards. It doesn't have to be only in Mr. Miu's room.").

- Communication is fostered among academic teachers because these teachers share the same documents and have access to the same types of supports for a given student.

- The student's case manager and team can easily track successes and challenges across academic subjects. For example, if Aponi is experiencing problems during independent work in psychology, the team can consult the other academic teachers to identify whether problems also exist with independent work in their classes. Thus, the M-CAPS is an efficient way to determine and implement supports across academic subjects.

The M-CAPS can also be a valuable tool beyond high school. For example, autistic students who enter a two- or four-year college or university may find that the M-CAPS provides the type of structure they need to be successful in their classes. The M-CAPS easily communicates what the student needs to be successful across activities and may be shared with Office of Disabilities staff and college professors. In addition, it supports student self-advocacy. That is, autistic students can approach faculty members with the M-CAPS and use it as a starting point to discuss student strengths and needs.

Summary

The CAPS and M-CAPS are tools that can be used across a student's school years. They are just as applicable in first as in 12th grade. Further, they may be used in college settings as structured self-advocacy tools that allow the student to have supports in place to facilitate academic success.

CHAPTER 13

The CAPS Process

A s illustrated throughout the book, CAPS is designed to examine a student's program and build upon the supports and strategies that are already in place in the student's individualized education program (IEP) and elsewhere. In addition to understanding the CAPS system itself, it is important to know how to develop a CAPS.

For the best results, as many team members as possible should participate, including (a) student, (b) parents, (c) general education teacher, (d) special education teacher, (e) intervention specialist, (f) paraprofessional, (g) speech language pathologist, (h) occupational therapist (OT), (i) physical therapist (PT), (j) school psychologist, (k) guidance counselor, (l) school administrator, (m) regional education support personnel, and others as appropriate and relevant.

This chapter provides a structure to facilitate the development of a CAPS. Specifically, it defines the roles of those participating on a CAPS team and outlines what each member does as part of the overall effort to design an effective CAPS.

Team Member Roles

Team members assume one of three roles: facilitator, recorder, or team member.

Facilitator

1. **Who is the facilitator?** This person is usually a current team member with a general understanding of the student. It may be the school psychologist, general educator, special educator, SLP, OT, PT, parent, or anyone with a vested interest in the student's education.
2. **What is the role to the facilitator?** The facilitator explains the process, enlists team members, and ensures that all team members take ownership of the process and follow through with commitments

Recorder

1. **Who is the recorder?** The recorder may be any one of the team members present at a given meeting. The team should choose someone with strong clerical skills. The recorder will be key to making sure the team has good documentation of the student's CAPS and that it is disseminated in a timely manner to all involved.
2. **What is the role of the recorder?** The recorder uses the CAPS form to record the supports for the target student. It is recommended that the recording occur on a computer linked to a projection system. This allows all team members to view the process as it occurs and facilitates immediate distribution of the completed documents to all team members.

Team Members

1. **Who are the team members?** All individuals on the multidisciplinary team, including parents and student, as appropriate, serve as team members.
2. **What is the role of the team members?** All team members participate in providing information about the student, as well as identifying strategies and supports for each area outlined in the CAPS.

Starting to Plan the CAPS

Developing a CAPS is a two-step process. The first step consists of developing a Baseline CAPS; the second step involves developing the CAPS that will be used on a daily basis.

Step 1: **Baseline CAPS.** The Baseline CAPS represents the status quo for the student—the place at which the team can begin to look at what additional supports are needed. It is important that, when created, this document becomes a part of the student archives, since it allows for easy identification of student growth.

Step 2: **CAPS.** As detailed in this chapter, the CAPS is developed by the team based on the student's needs. The CAPS, which is used on a daily basis, includes supports in all areas, as needed, for all activities across the student's day. As such, it becomes the student's program. This CAPS is used to support the student on a daily basis.

Planning for a student is a dynamic and multifaceted process. Thus, a team approach is needed. Planning a CAPS can take up to a whole day, depending on the complexity of student needs and the number and type of supports to be identified. The following provides an overview of the development process by looking at each of the areas making up the CAPS.

Time and Activity

This reflects the student's daily schedule and includes all academic and nonacademic classes. If students need assistance during transitions between activities, transitions are also listed as an activity.

Time	Activity	Skills to Teach	Structure/ Modifications	Reinforcement	Sensory/ Regulation	Communication/ Social Skills	Data Collection	Generalization to Community
8:00	Breakfast							

- **Time.** This section indicates the clock time of each activity that the student engages in throughout the day.
- **Activity.** Activities include all tasks and activities throughout the day in which the student requires support: academic periods (e.g., reading, math) and nonacademic times (e.g., recess, lunch). It is possible that transitions may appear several times on the CAPS.

Facilitator: Lead the team in a "virtual" or actual walk through of the student's day. Start with the moment the student enters the school. Complete these two columns for the entire day before adding ANY supports and strategies.

> *Hint:* You may want to have someone play the role of the student and actually move to each activity to be sure you are reporting all activities and transitions.

Recorder: Record clock times and name of each activity. Be sure to ask for clarification if needed.

- **Team:** Consider each activity or expectation per each block of time. There may be more than one activity in a time block. For example, under circle time you may have the Pledge, announcement, singing, and so on.

Skills to Teach

Skills to Teach includes specific goals and benchmarks from the student's IEP, grade-level state standards, core curriculum competencies as well as skills identified by parent, teacher, and student.

Time	Activity	Skills to Teach	Structure/ Modifications	Reinforcement	Sensory/ Regulation	Communication/ Social Skills	Data Collection	Generalization to Community
8:00	Breakfast	• Choose breakfast using language board • Table manners						

Facilitator: Complete each row of the CAPS going across. For the Baseline CAPS, lead the team to identify the skills that the student is currently learning. For the CAPS, lead the team in:

- **Prioritizing skills from the aforementioned areas.** Which skills will be taught first? Are some skills prerequisite to others? Will learning a specific skill early on, perhaps one of interest, provide momentum for learning new skills?
- **Identifying where skills can be taught and practiced.** Students will require direct instruction or some type of evidence-based practice (EBP) to learn a skill. Multiple practice opportunities that match how the individual learns are essential to ensure

that the individual is as independent and motivated as possible. We generally recommend that only one or two skills be listed in this area for each topic. When the student masters the skill, it can be removed and replaced by the next prioritized skill.

Recorder: If completing the Baseline CAPS, bullet all skills that the student is currently working on. If writing the CAPS, add the skills to teach the student. Take note of all objectives, standards, and goals. It will be helpful to indicate the type of goal or standard. Create a list of prioritized skills.
- Individualized education program (IEP)
- State standard (SS)
- Grade-level curriculum (GLC)

Team: Identify the skills to teach for each activity. Remember that in addition to academic objectives, you most likely need to include objectives related to structure/modifications, reinforcement, communication/social, and sensory/regulation.

Structure/Modifications (see Chapter 5)

Structure/Modifications can encompass a wide variety of supports, including placement in the classroom, visual supports (e.g., choice boards, visual schedules), and instructional strategies (e.g., priming, self-monitoring). Autistic learners generally learn best when the environment and instruction are visual and structured.

Time	Activity	Skills to Teach	Structure/ Modifications	Reinforcement	Sensory/ Regulation	Communication/ Social Skills	Data Collection	Generalization to Community
8:00	Breakfast	• Choose breakfast using language board • Table manners	• Choice board of breakfast items • Visual schedule • Fade prompts					

Facilitator: For the Baseline CAPS, lead the team to identify supports in place. For the CAPS that will be used on a daily basis, support the team to consider all methodologies in place and additional visual, auditory, physical adaptations that need to be in place for the student to be successful.

   Hint: You may want to start with the questions provided by TEACCH. According to Mesibov et al. (2004), the student should be able to answer or know the answer to these questions:

- What activity are they completing?
- How much do they need to complete?
- When are they finished?
- What is next?

Identify who will create supports and other important details following the structure of the CAPS Support Development Form.

Recorder: If completing the Baseline CAPS, bullet all structure/modifications that are in place. If writing the CAPS, add all the structure/modifications the student needs. Complete the CAPS Support Development Form for the CAPS.

CAPS Support Development Form

Child/Student: _____   Date: _____

Support	Who Will Develop Support	Date Support Needed	Who Will Teach Support Use	When to Evaluate Effectiveness	How to Evaluate Effectiveness

Team: Consider additional strategies and methodologies that will provide greater access to the general education curriculum.

Reinforcement (see Chapter 6)

If completing the Baseline CAPS, bullet all reinforcers that are in place. If writing the CAPS, add the student's reinforcers. While other sections of the CAPS may be left blank if the student does not need specific supports, the Reinforcement section must always be completed. We all need reinforcement. A part of the brain, called the mesocorticolimbic system, reacts when we are reinforced. Simply speaking, our neurology is wired for reinforcement. Aspy and Grossman (2022) astutely say that without reinforcement there is no learning.

Time	Activity	Skills to Teach	Structure/ Modifications	Reinforcement	Sensory/ Regulation	Communication/ Social Skills	Data Collection	Generalization to Community
8:00	Breakfast	• Choose breakfast using language board • Table manners	• Choice board of breakfast items • Visual schedule • Fade prompts	• Choice of food				

Facilitator: For the Baseline CAPS, lead the team to identify reinforcers in place. For the Daily CAPS, lead the team in completing a reinforcer assessment and completing this section.

Recorder: Take note of all reinforcing items identified by the team. If completing the Baseline CAPS, bullet all reinforcers that are in place. For the CAPS, use information from the assessment and team input to list bulleted items under Reinforcement. Complete the CAPS Support Development Form for the CAPS.

Team: Review the Reinforcer assessment. What does the student like to do during free time? What are areas of interest? How often is reinforcement needed?

Sensory/Regulation (see Chapter 7)

Recall that approximately 96% of autistic students experience sensory challenges and at least 50% experience meltdowns. Sensory and regulation supports are intended to keep the individual feeling calm, focused, and safe. The emphasis is on preventing sensory challenges and meltdowns so the student is better able to learn. The OT should provide direction.

Time	Activity	Skills to Teach	Structure/ Modifications	Reinforcement	Sensory/ Regulation	Communication/ Social Skills	Data Collection	Generalization to Community
8:00	Breakfast	• Choose breakfast using language board • Table manners	• Choice board of breakfast items • Visual schedule • Fade prompts	• Choice of food	• Eating			

Facilitator: For the Baseline CAPS, lead the team to identify sensory/regulation supports in place. For the CAPS, support the OT to (a) review a completed sensory instrument with the team, and (b) lead a discussion about the student's sensory issues. Identify who will create supports and other important details following the structure of the CAPS Support Development Form.

Recorder: If completing the Baseline CAPS, bullet all sensory supports already in place. For the Daily CAPS, record what supports the student needs for each activity. Complete the CAPS Support Development Form for the CAPS.

Team: Ask the OT to share the student's sensory strengths and needs. During this explanation it is often helpful for team members to have access to the sensory assessment protocol. With greater understanding of the student's sensory systems, team members can better assist in ensuring that sensory supports are well embedded within each activity.

Communication/Social Skills (see Chapter 8)

Specific communication and social supports are delineated in this section. The SLP should provide direction during the CAPS process. It is important to remember that all activities have a communication and social skills component—even those that, at first glance, seem completely devoid of both. For example, if you are taking a test, (a) you may need to raise your hand to ask for help; (b) you may have to wait quietly for the teacher to approach; (c) you will need to explain the issue concisely using a tone of voice that does not disrupt others; and (d) you will (hopefully) thank the teacher.

Time	Activity	Skills to Teach	Structure/ Modifications	Reinforcement	Sensory/ Regulation	Communication/ Social Skills	Data Collection	Generalization to Community
8:00	Breakfast	• Choose breakfast using language board • Table manners	• Choice board of breakfast items • Visual schedule • Fade prompts	• Choice of food	• Eating	• Language board (ensure that greetings, questions, peer names are on board) • Checklist of manners (review prior to and after lunch)		

Facilitator: For the Baseline CAPS, lead the team to identify supports in place. For the CAPS that will be used on a daily basis, have the SLP review the student's social communication profile. Remind the team that each student needs to use both receptive and expressive communication during each time period. In addition, each activity has a social component. Social interactions should be as natural as possible and match the structure of the activity.

- How does the student express information or needs?
- Is an augmentative and alternative communication (AAC) device needed?
- How does the student receive information?
- Is that method effective?
- How do we know it is working?
- Does the student have opportunities to engage in social interactions with peers and the teacher in class?

Identify who will create supports and other important details following the structure of the CAPS Support Development Form.

Recorder: For the Baseline CAPS, record what is in place. For the CAPS, communication and social supports should be identified for each activity. Bullet items on the CAPS. Complete the CAPS Support Development Form for the CAPS.

Team: Ensure that the student has the supports, instruction, and practice opportunities to communicate and socialize in each activity. Opportunities should match those experienced by peers.

Data Collection (see Chapter 9)

Typically, the section on data collection relates directly to the student's IEP goals and benchmarks. The Skills to Teach and Data Collection sections must match. That is, each activity has a data collection component.

Consider what type of data collection method best matches the target behavior or skill and how much data are needed to see a pattern of change. For example, on one activity, the data collection method may be recorded as E/15/MW. This indicates that event recording will be used to measure the behavior/skill for 15 minutes on Mondays and Wednesdays.

Time	Activity	Skills to Teach	Structure/ Modifications	Reinforcement	Sensory/ Regulation	Communication Social Skills	Data Collection	Generalization to Community
8:00	Breakfast	• Choose breakfast using language board • Table manners	• Choice board of breakfast items • Visual schedule • Fade prompts	• Choice of food	• Eating	• Language board (ensure that greetings, questions, peer names are on board) • Checklist of manners (review prior to and after lunch)	• Choice: I/P*, M-F • Manners: I/P for each skill, TW	

* I = independent; P = prompt.

Facilitator: For the Baseline CAPS, lead the team to identify the data collection procedures in place. For the CAPS, lead the team in discussing what data will be collected during each time block. The following questions should be answered:

- How can we embed the data collection?
- Does the data collection method match the resources available in the classroom?
- Does the data collection method match the Skills to Teach?

Recorder: Note for each Skill to Teach (a) the type of data to be collected, (b) how many minutes the data will be collected daily, and (c) the days that data will be collected. Complete the CAPS Support Development Form for the CAPS. Data sheets must be developed to facilitate taking data.

Team: Be creative in selecting data collection methods that fit within a classroom routine. Data are often not collected because the data collection method chosen requires materials and personnel not available in the environment.

Generalization to Community (see Chapter 10)

Because autistic individuals often have problems generalizing information across settings, this section of the CAPS ensures that generalization of skills is built into the student's program.

Time	Activity	Skills to Teach	Structure/ Modifications	Reinforcement	Sensory/ Regulation	Communication/ Social Skills	Data Collec	Generalization to Community
8:00	Breakfast	• Choose breakfast using language board • Table manners	• Choice board of breakfast items • Visual schedule • Fade prompts	• Choice of food	• Eating	• Language board (ensure that greetings, questions, peer names are on board) • Checklist of manners (review prior to and after lunch)	• Choice: I/ M-F • Manners: for each s TW	• Use language board during lunch and dinner at home • Use table manners checklist during meals

* I = independent; P = prompt.

Facilitator: Guide the team in answering the following questions:
- How can any of the skills and supports be used at different times of the day and in different environments?

- How can the student be empowered to initiate the skill and use the supports without prompts? It is often best to begin with one generalization target per activity and gradually add to them over time.

Recorder: Ensure that information generated by the team is placed on the CAPS form.

Team: Remember that generalization is the true measure of skill use. This should be an ongoing process. Continue to build generalization into the student's CAPS.

Summary

In addition to understanding the CAPS system itself, it is important that team members know how to develop the CAPS. Team members assume one of three roles, facilitator, recorder, or team member, all of which are critical to a comprehensive and effective CAPS for the individual student.

Bibliography

Aspy, Ruth & Barry Grossman. *Designing Comprehensive Interventions for High-Functioning Individuals with Autism Spectrum Disorders: The Ziggurat Model* (Release 2.0). Ziggurat Group (2022).

Mesibov, Gary., Victoria Shea, & Eric Schopler. *The TEACCH Approach to Autism Spectrum Disorders*. Klewer (2004).

CHAPTER 14

Using CAPS for Technical Assistance/Consultation

Lee Stickle, MsEd

C APS has additional uses beyond program planning and facilitating successful transitions across years. It can also be used by those who provide technical assistance in classrooms, on the job, or in the home. This type of consulting can add value to education programming.

What do consultants do?

- Consultants are uniquely positioned to identify gaps in training and programming as well as collaboratively address the identified gaps.
- Consultants advise educational teams in developing comprehensive education programs.
- Consultants may also provide training and coaching on the interventions and skills necessary to carry out programs.

This chapter reviews how the Kansas Technical Assistance Network (TASN) Autism and Tertiary Behavior Supports uses the CAPS to provide technical assistance and training. The mission of TASN Autism and Tertiary Behavior Supports is to support Kansas school districts in building local capacity to serve students with diverse learning needs through results-based professional development training and technical assistance. As such, TASN is often requested to provide consultation, follow-up, and coaching in general and special education classrooms for autistic learners. CAPS is an important part of that technical assistance process.

Generally speaking, we are asked to consult when the student and team are faced with a problem. According to the National Association of School Psychologists (NASP), "Problem-solving consultation has two important goals: (a) to provide methods (prevention and intervention) for changing a system, classroom, or child's behavioral, academic, or social problem; and (b) to improve the system and/or consultee's skills so it, he or she can prevent or respond effectively to future problems or similar problems in other children" (Kratochwill et al., 2008).

Why Use the CAPS When Consulting?

The CAPS was initially developed as an implementation plan. It was designed to provide a structure to ensure that the student's program developed in the individualized education program (IEP) is delivered throughout the day. In addition, the CAPS helps teams identify when, throughout the school day, natural opportunities present themselves to work on a skill, provide an accommodation, or provide reinforcement.

From a consultant's point of view, CAPS provides both a structure and differentiated method to gather information. The gathered information can then be used to make recommendations, identify gaps, and, to a limited extent, help us to identify the fidelity with which the IEP is being implemented. The flexibility of the tool allows us to adapt it to the unique needs of each consultation.

As part of our process, once the referral is received and the parent or guardian signs a multi-agency release of information document, we gather information via interviews. While it may seem more efficient to have interviewees complete the tools independently, we prefer to have a conversation with them either in person, via telephone, or using a video conferencing platform. It has been our experience that we can begin to develop rapport during the interview process. We also have the opportunity to ask follow-up questions and develop a more thorough understanding of each partner's concerns.

The most accurate information is gathered from those who trust that you are working in the interest of the child and that your goal is to improve programming not only for the child, but for those who are engaged in delivering it.

The Process

TASN's technical assistance begins with a request for assistance from a school or school district. To receive technical assistance, the school/district must agree to (a) provide at least two referral questions to guide technical assistance and make accessible for review student records with permission from all concerned parties; (b) school-based observation(s) by TASN staff; and (c) participation by the team, including parent/guardian and student, when possible, in interviews, program development activities, training, and ongoing coaching.

Analysis of the student's program begins with a review of their IEP and related documents. A records review provides information about the student's academic and behavioral history. These frequently include the student's medical background and past experiences. Old behavioral support plans may show the progression of a student's problem behavior and identify interventions that were successful or unsuccessful in the past. Finally, a records review may identify environments where a student has experienced success and was less likely to engage in problem behavior (Freeman, nd).

The technical assistance provider inserts into a CAPS form the information contained in the IEP using black ink/type. It is important to gather all the necessary information; for example, some IEPs have a separate section where modifications and accommodations are recorded. It is important to tie that information to specific activities throughout the day. If the IEP does not specify this information, it is critical to gather it in an pre-observation interview with the educator and parent.

As consultants, we want the information that we collect to be as comprehensive as possible. Our work does not start when we enter the classroom; it begins with information gathering.

The following instruments are used to conduct interviews (see Appendix at the end of the chapter):

- **TASN Teacher Interview.** The case manager or primary teacher is asked questions about (a) school; (b) classroom environment; (c) teacher strengths and needs; (d) family; and (e) student, focusing on strengths, special interests, and motivators.

- **TASN Parent/Guardian Interview.** The parent/guardian is interviewed about (a) their child at home and school, (b) child history, (c) community outreach and community-based interventions, (d) child perceptions, and (e) additional information.

- **Self-Determination Checklist and Assessment (optional).** An elementary and secondary version, developed by the I'm Determined Project, asks students about their school's goals for them as well as their personal goals. In addition, students are asked to rate their self-determination skills.

- **Community Service Provider Interview.** Community service providers are asked about the student's (a) family, (b) interpersonal relationships, (c) school, (d) vocation, (e) optimism, (f) coping and savoring, (g) talents and savoring, (h) community life, (i) relationship permanence, (j) resilience, (k) sleep, (l) cultural stress, and (m) concerns. Even though most autistic students are supported through multiple systems, case managers often do not have the opportunity to gather information from all service providers. By gathering information from community providers, we can leverage the work of all partners to align interventions and identify which strategies that have been effective. Thus, the Community Service Providers Interview is essential and informative.

After the records have been reviewed and the interviews have been conducted, an observation occurs. TASN has customized the CAPS form for this type of technical assistance. Specifically, the following elements have been modified to create the Observation CAPS (O-CAPS):

- A row was added to identify the Reason(s) for Referral
- A row was added for Transition between each activity
- A Student-to-Teacher Ratio column was added
- The Activity Column was modified to also include setting (general education classroom, special education classroom, cafeteria, etc.)
- The Data Collection column was divided on a diagonal. The top section is used to collect data during the observation; the bottom section provides an area for noting the presence or absence of the target behaviors identified in the referral questions.

Figure 14.1. The O-CAPS

Observation Comprehensive Autism Planning System (O-CAPS)

Child/Student: ______________________ Date: ______________________

Time	Ratio	Activity	Skills to Teach	Structure/ Modifications	Reinforcement	Sensory/ Regulation	Communication/ Social Skills	Data Collection
Transition								
Transition								
Transition								

Referral Question 1: ______________________

Referral Question 2: ______________________

From *Kansas Technical Assistance and Support Network: Autism and Tertiary Support* by L. Stickle (n.d.). Used with permission.

CAPS

Prior to the classroom, employment, or community observation, the technical assistance provider lists in black (shown in regular font here) on the O-CAPS the Structure/Modification, Reinforcement, Sensory/Regulation, and Communication/Social supports obtained from the records, interviews, and IEP for at least two activities.

The observer then notes what supports are in place for each academic and nonacademic activity during the classroom observation. In addition, the observer notes the supports available during each transition between activities/classes; if the learner experiences transition difficulties, the observer indicates if one stage of the transition is particularly challenging (i.e., disengage, shift, reengage) and includes suggestions, as appropriate. The observer also collects data for each activity using the referral questions provided by the school or district and the targeted skills to teach. This information is presented in blue (bold here). Suggestions for additional supports are included in red (shown in italics here).

Following the observation, the observer meets with the team, including the parent/guardian, to review the O-CAPS and other information gathered during the consultation process. Once all the information has been shared, the team and the observer complete the student's CAPS. At this point, information is transferred from the O-CAPS and entered into the traditional CAPS form.

The final step in the process is completion of the Technical Assistance Action Plan. The plan includes the student's referral questions as well as the steps needed to implement the student's new program, including person(s) responsible, resources needed, date completed, and follow up.

The O-CAPS information noted in red (italics here) becomes part of a Technical Assistance Action Plan from which the team makes decisions on various issues, including:
- What supports are needed?
- Who will develop the supports and by when?
- What types of professional development are needed to implement the CAPS, who will provide it, and when will occur, if needed?
- How will communication occur among all team members, including parent/guardian, regarding the learner's program?

- What resources are needed by the school team to carry out the program identified on the CAPS?
- When and how will coaching occur to ensure fidelity of implementation?

The Technical Assistance Action Plan is printed on NCR paper with a copy for teacher, parent, technical assistance provider, and administrator (see Appendix). This type of form is used because many districts in Kansas, especially those located in rural and frontier regions, have limited resources, including photocopy machines and various forms of technology.

Mala: A Brief Illustration

Mala is an 13-year-old autistic middle school student. She struggles with peer relationships; organization, planning, and responsibility; following directions; transitioning; and regulation prompted the team to contact TASN for assistance.

Following the records review and completion of the interviews, Mala was observed during algebra, physical education and their associated transitions, and an O-CAPS was completed. Mala's team and TASN completed her CAPS for algebra and physical education and two transitions using information from the O-CAPS. Based on TASN's information, the team then decided which support to place on the CAPS.

Figure 14.2. Mala's O-CAPS

Observation Comprehensive Autism Planning System (O-CAPS)				
Child/Student: **Mala**			Date: **Today**	
Time	**Ratio**	**Activity**	**Skills to Teach**	**Structure/ Modifications**
8:15-9:01	23-2	Algebra	Algebraic computation 1. Basic computation 2. Solving a problem when given steps (Mala did not appear to understand what she should be doing) Use of strategy cards and checklists	1. Calculator (present, but Mala said using it was cheating). 2. Directions given 1-on-1. Directions given; so specific that they applied only to the problem she was working on. 3. Reteach previously taught skills (not part of the lesson). 4. Extended time for tests (Not observed). (Several problems were done incorrectly before feedback was provided.) Did not bring math book; supplied by teacher. Query: Was book in backpack? Yes. 1. *Provide/teach Mala how to use a problem-solving checklist to determine what questions she needs to ask to identify which type of problem she is to solve.* 2. *Teach Mala to use a formula chart that will guide her application of the rules.* 3. *Prime Mala the day for before about upcoming assignments.* 4. *Provide frequent feedback to prevent faulty reasoning.*

Figure 14.2 (continued)

Reinforcement	Sensory/ Regulation	Communication/ Social Skills	Data Collection
None Verbal praise? *Verbal praise* *Provide area on self-monitoring sheet where Mala can assess "good reasoning."*	Mala can choose seat: She sits at a table with her back to her classmates. She is allowed to use a whiteboard for computation. **Mala appeared anxious: hand wringing, quick glances around room, increased anxiety when people were near. She checked to make sure her bag was zipped and under her chair. She measured the tabletop with her hands to determine the space that was "hers."** **She covered her ears while trying to do assignment. Whiteboard was next to her, but she preferred to write.** 1. *OT consult needed.* 2. *Calming strategies: calming cards, self-calming curriculum.* 3. *Place a desk in the front of the classroom to help Mala filter out over-stimulation.* 4. *Provide a separate space for independent work.* 5. *Provide headphones to block out noise.*	None **Mala was not called on during class. Peers greeted her; she did not respond.** 1. *Include the requirement to greet or return the greeting of at least one peer on Mala's self-monitoring form.* 2. *Prepare and present a math problem in advance of lesson. Tell Mala that she will be asked to answer the specific question.* *Have a friend accompany during passing period.*	Data <hr>Referral ?s +

Figure 14.2 (continued)

Time	Ratio	Activity	Skills to Teach	Structure/ Modifications
Transition		Move to 2nd period	3. Organization 4. Planning 5. Responsibility	None. **Bell rang. Mala packed her book bag, walked quickly to the next class avoiding physical contact in the halls. Verbal reminders to transition.** 1. Checklist *(luggage tag on the outside of her bag indicates to check the checklist in her locker).* 2. *Checklist in her locker of materials needed for each class.* 3. *Organize materials for each class so that everything is in one binder; color-code binder and books for each class.* 4. *Write expectations on whiteboard at the front of the room:* *a. Check homework.* *b. Math book, page 37, problems 1-18 (even)* 5. *Make planner entry.*
9:05-9:51	56:3	PE Scooter Hockey	None from IEP **Teamwork Communication** Fitness Greeting others Complimenting	None **Mala was allowed to sit at the back of her squad with space between herself and others. She was allowed to push herself on a scooter without a partner. Rules were explained to Mala by the teacher.** *Post rules for the entire class. Consider posting (a) rules and (b) reminder to greet and make at least one comment to a peer in the PE locker.*
Transition		Move to 3rd	Same as above	

Figure 14.2 (continued)

Reinforcement	Sensory/ Regulation	Communication/ Social Skills	Data Collection
	Release 1 minute early to relieve anxiety in the hallways.	*Have a friend accompany during passing period.*	
None **None** **Self-monitoring?** *Self-monitoring sheet*	None **Allowed to avoid others and to wear long sweatpants; dressed out in bathroom stall.** *Allow Mala to be the person pushing the partner instead of vice versa.*	None **Mala did not speak with peers or teachers. They did not speak with her either. She followed directions given to the group.** *Self-monitoring sheet inside locker with rules; goal to initiate and respond to at least one peer.*	 +

Figure 14.2 (continued)

Time	Ratio	Activity	Skills to Teach	Structure/ Modifications
9:55-10:41	14:2	English	Write a 3-to-5 line paragraph using MLA format. **Scored 3.0 on rubric on final draft.**	Tests to be read aloud. Extra time for tests. **Not a test day; no modifications.** **Did not remove pencil from backpack; did not ask for one.** **Query: Was pencil in backpack? Yes.** *Provide scoring rubric as a guide for writing.* *Provide an MLA format checklist.*

Figure 14.2 (continued)

Reinforcement	Sensory/ Regulation	Communication/ Social Skills	Data Collection

None in IEP
 	
Verbal praise from teacher (1)
 	
Verbal praise
	None in IEP.
	
	Arrived in class sighing and pounded on desk 7 times before sitting down. Anxiety?
	
	No interactions with peers.
	
	Sat at a table with her back to the class.
	
	1. *To minimize anxiety:*
	  a. *Consider brief break before class.*
	  b. *Consider early release from PE to allow for cool-down time.*
	2. *OT consult needed.*
	3. *Calming strategies: calming cards, self-calming curriculum.*
	4. *Perhaps add a couple of student desks to the classroom for those who prefer to sit apart.*
	5. *Place Mala's desk in front of the classroom to help filter overstimulation.*
	6. *Provide a separate space for independent work.*
	7. *Provide headphones to block out noise.*
		None in IEP
		
		Minimal interaction.
		
		Script some interactions; practice during social skills time and perhaps with entire class.
		
		Have students read to each other in small groups and score each other using the rubric as a conversation starter.	

Figure 14.2 (continued)

Time	Ratio	Activity	Skills to Teach	Structure/ Modifications
Transition		Stayed in same classroom	1. *Organization* 2. *Planning* 3. *Responsibility*	None **When the bell rang, Mala stood up, grabbed her backpack, pushed in her chair, unzipped her backpack, got out her notebook, sat down, and put the backpack under her chair.** **She used the routine to transition to another class although she remained in the same room at the same table.** **The packing of the backpack seemed to signal the end of one class; opening the backpack indicates the beginning of the next class. Mala is successful in transitions that have a specific beginning and end. If they lack either, she adds them.** **Mala does not always have the correct materials even if they are in her backpack. In addition, the transitions seem challenging. Perhaps because of movement: Shift? Sensory?** *See above for transition supports.*

Figure 14.2 (continued)

Reinforcement	Sensory/ Regulation	Communication/ Social Skills	Data Collection
None Self-monitoring sheet	None *Early release*	*Have a friend accompany during passing period.*	

Referral Question 1: *Following directions*

Referral Question 2: *Peer interactions*

From *Kansas Technical Assistance and Support Network: Autism and Tertiary Support* by L. Stickle (n.d.). Used with permission.

As illustrated on the following pages, when Mala's CAPS was completed, it contained:

- Target skills to teach, identified and/or developed based on the IEP, interviews, observation, and TASN suggestions for at least two activities and two transitions
- Supports that addressed Mala's structure/modification, reinforcement, sensory, and communication/social strengths and needs for the activities and transitions
- Data collection procedures
- Supports that can be generalized throughout Mala's day at school, home, and during community activities.

Figure 14.3. Mala's CAPS

Comprehensive Autism Planning System (CAPS)				
Child/Student: *Mala*			Date: *Today*	
Time	**Ratio**	**Activity**	**Skills to Teach**	**Structure/ Modifications**
8:15 – 9:01	23-2	Algebra	Algebraic computation Basic computation	1. Calculator with directions; point out that using a calculator is not cheating. 2. Problem solving checklist; follow up with 1-on-1 directions, if needed. 3. Reteach previously taught skills (entire class). 4. Extended time for tests. 5. Checklist that prompts Mala to check work with teacher after completing 2 problems. 6. Before providing book, prompt with "check your backpack." 7. Travel Card (categories: materials to class, interaction with peers, used supports (i.e., calming strategy), homework turned in, participate in class, reasoning). Extras points for sitting with class. Attach math question that Mala will be asked the following day on Travel Card.
Transition		Move to 2nd period	Materials to class Ready to work (organization, planning, responsibility)	1. Checklist (luggage tag) on the outside of her backpack indicating to check the checklist in her locker. 2. Checklist in her locker indicating materials needed for each class. 3. Organize materials for each class so that everything is in a single binder and books for each class. Color-code binder and books for each class. 4. Review expectations and class activities on whiteboard at the front of the room. 5. Make planner entry.

Figure 14.3 (continued)

Reinforcement	Sensory/ Regulation	Communication/ Social Skills	Data Collection	Generalization to Community
Target 1: *Following Directions*			Target 2: *Interacting in Groups*	
1. Verbal praise. 2. Reinforcement tied to Travel Card goals.	1. Labeled area for backpack. 2. Headphones to clock noise. 3. Separate space for independent work. 4. Student desks at back of classroom for all. 5. Mala's desk in front of the classroom away from stimulation (5 min early). 6. Calming cards. *Note: Mala's case manager will introduce these changes with a walk through the day's schedule before they are implemented.*	1. Conversation starter cards (reviewed during Social Living class). 2. Prompt from teacher to greet a peer, as needed.	Grade book Travel Card	Travel Card throughout the day
	See above; early release with peer.	1. Conversation starter card (reviewed during Social Living class). 2. Luggage tag also contains prompt for Mala to greet and make one comment to at least peer.	Travel Card	Conversation starter cards for Scouts and horseback riding

Figure 14.3 (continued)

Time	Ratio	Activity	Skills to Teach	Structure/ Modifications
9:05-9:51	56:3	PE Scooter Hockey	Teamwork Communication Fitness Greeting others	1. Allow her to sit at the back of her squad with space between herself and others, as needed. 2. Allow Mala to be the person pushing the scooter. 3. Post in locker rules and reminder to greet and make one comment to at least one peer. 4. Travel Card.
Transition		Move to 3nd period	Same as above	
9:55-10:41	14:2	English	Write a 3- to 5-line paragraph using MLA format. Score at least 3.0 on rubric for final draft.	1. Tests to be read aloud. 2. Extra time for tests. 3. Provide and *teach* a scoring rubric as a guide for writing. 4. Provide MLA format checklist. 5. Travel Card.

Figure 14.3 (continued)

Reinforcement	Sensory/ Regulation	Communication/ Social Skills	Data Collection	Generalization to Community

1. Verbal
2. Reinforcement with Travel Card
	1. Allow Mala to wear long sweat-pants.
	2. Allow Mala to dress out in bath-room stall.
	3. Early release with peer to destress.
	4. Calming cards posted in locker.
		1. Post in locker:
		  a. Rules.
		  b. Reminder to greet and make at one com-ment at least one peer.
			PE Standards
			
			Travel Card
				Calming cards at home

Verbal praise	1. Labeled area for backpack. 2. Headphones to block noise. 3. Separate space for independent work. 4. Student desks at back of classroom for all. 5. Mala's desk in front of classroom away from stimu-lation. 6. Early release with peer (5 min early) 7. Calming cards. *Note: Mala's case manager will introduce these changes with a walk through the day's schedule before they are implemented.*	1. Conversation starter cards (reviewed during Social Living class) 2. Have student score and discuss in small groups each other's work using rubric. Start with one peer for Mala.	Rubric Travel Card	Label areas in all classrooms

Figure 14.3 (continued)

Time	Ratio	Activity	Skills to Teach	Structure/ Modifications
Transition		Stay in the same class	Materials to class Ready to work (organization, planning, responsibility)	1. Checklist (luggage tag) on the outside of her backpack indicating to check the checklist in her locker. 2. Organize materials for each class so that everything is in a single binder and books for each class. Color-code binder and books for each class. 3. Review expectations and class activities on whiteboard at the front of the room. 4. Make planner entry. 5. Provide special interest materials for Mala to review during this transition (Amelia Earhart or *National Geographic* website on computer) or prompt Mala to run an errand.

Specifically, in Mala's completed Technical Assistance Action Plan, her team identified (a) supports that had to be created, by whom, and by when; (b) instruction that Mala required in order to use supports; and (c) peer mentors who could support Mala's early release between classes. As illustrated on the next pages, the resource column of the Action Plan identified both resources Mala needed and any resources/training the staff needed in order to implement the plan.

Summary

The CAPS has many uses—it can serve as a program planning and professional development plan, a fidelity of implementation document, a transition support guide, as well as a technical assistance form. As such, it is an adaptable tool that allows service providers and other support staff to methodically collect information on all aspects of the student's program. Using the CAPS as an observation tool and pre-populating it with information gathered prior to the observation supports teams in considering many of the factors that influence student success.

Figure 14.3 (continued)

Reinforcement	Sensory/ Regulation	Communication/ Social Skills	Data Collection	Generalization to Community
Verbal praise		Luggage tag also contains prompt for Mala to greet one peer and make at least one comment	Travel Card	

When consulting, it is critical to gather the voices of those involved in planning the educational program. A consultation is more than a single observation. It is critical to have a comprehensive understanding of the barriers to success that the student is facing. It is incumbent upon the team to ensure that autistic children, youth, and adults have the supports and instruction that allows them to reach their limitless potential. CAPS contributes significantly to this process.

Bibliography

Freeman, Rachel. Functional Behavior Assessment. Accessed October 10, 2023 from https://specialconnections.ku.edu/behavior_plans (nd).

I'm Determined (2008). Accessed October 19, 2023 from https://www.imdetermined.org/tool/self-determination-checklist-student/.

Kratochwill, T. R., Margaret R. Altschaefl, and Brittany Bice-Urbach. "Best Practices in School-Based Problem-Solving Consultation: Applications in Prevention and Intervention Systems." *Best Practices in School Psychology* V (2008): 1673-1688.

Figure 14.4. Mala's Technical Assistance Plan

Action Plan For Technical Assistance Request # XXX–XX				
Child/Student: Mala	School: ABC School, 100 Main St., Small Town, KS 77777 555.555.5555			Date: 10/17
Team Members Involved in Action Plan: Mary Johnson, PE; Fred Sams, Algebra; Jon Swieski, English; Maria Tia, Resource; Fern Smith, parent				
Contact Person: Maria Tia				
Referral Question 1: How can we help Mala follow directions more independently?				
Referral Question 2: How can we support Mala to have more appropriate interactions with peers, especially in groups?				
Referral Question 3:				
Referral Question 4:				
Action Step: Task To Be Completed/Strategy Implemented	**Person(s) Responsible**	**Resources**	**Date Completed**	**Person Responsible for Follow-Up**
Create Supports 1. Problem solving checklist with math strategy prompts. 2. Travel Card (categories: material to class, interaction with peers, used supports (i.e., calming strategy), homework turned in, participate in class, reasoning). Extra points for sitting with class. Attach math question that Mala will be asked the following day on Travel Card.	Sams, Tia Tia with para support	Training for all staff who work with Mala on all supports. Principal to support. Consider curriculum to teach sensory awareness, general problem solving, and self-calming. Tia will identify resources.		Tia will follow up to schedule a brief meeting with Mala's teachers. 1 month after implementation, the team will meet by phone/in person to discuss Mala's progress. Parent will be asked how these changes have made an impact on Mala.

Figure 14.4 (continued)

Action Step: Task To Be Completed/Strategy Implemented	Person(s) Responsible	Resources	Date Completed	Person Responsible for Follow-Up
3. Checklist (luggage tag) on the outside of her bag indicating to check the checklist in her locker.		Tia		
4. Checklist in her locker indicating materials needed for each class.		Tia		
5. Organize materials for each class so that everything is in a single binder; color-code binder and books for each class.		Sams, Swieski		
6. Labeled area for backpack.		Sams, Swieski		
7. Headphones to block noise.		Sams, Swieski		
8. Separate space for independent work.		Tia with para support		
9. Student desks at back of classroom for all.		Swieski		
10. Mala's desk in front of the classroom away from stimulation.		Swieski		
11. Conversation cards.		Tia will work with Mala to identify Swieski		
12. Calming cards.				

CAPS

Figure 14.4 (continued)

Action Step: Task To Be Completed/Strategy Implemented	Person(s) Responsible	Resources	Date Completed	Person Responsible for Follow-Up
13. Rule and reminders to greet and make one comment to at least one peer (posted in PE locker).	Sams, Johnson			
14. Provide a scoring rubric as a guide for writing.	Swieski			
15. Provide an MLA format checklist.	Swieski			
16. Special interest materials.	Tia will work with Mala to identify			
Teach				
1. Using a calculator is not cheating.	Tia			
2. How to use all supports.	Tia			
Mentor Peers Who Can Support Mala's Early Release				
PE: MJ Cho, Sheila Jones				
Algebra: Helen Jeb, Carly Owens				
English: Margi Michaels, Sue Kernshaw				

Page _____ of _____   Date of Review: _____   White: Teacher   Yellow: Parent   Pink: TA Provider   Gold: Administrator

The Kansas Instructional Support Network is partially funded through Part B funds administered by the Kansas State Department of Education's Special Education Services. KISN does not discriminate on the basis of race, color, national origin, sec, disability, or age in its programs and activities. The following person has been designated to handle inquiries regarding the non-discrimination policies: Deputy Director, Keystone Learning Services, 500 E. Sunflower, Ozawkie, KS 66070, 785-876-2214.

From *Kansas Technical Assistance and Support Network and Tertiary Support* by L. Stickle (n.d.). Used with permission.

Chapter 14 Appendix

TASN Teacher Interview:
Questions to Be Answered Prior to Onsite Consultation

Directions:	Interview the teacher using the following questions. Use a conversational tone, rewordings questions as needed to enhance understanding.

Section 1: School

1. What school-wide systems of supports are in place (PBIS, MTSS, Tiers, other classroom teacher support)? Provide examples on how supports are used with this student.

2. Is there a team working with the student? IEP? Support Team? District Support Team (Autism Team, Behavior Team, SIT Team, outside community providers)?

3. If yes:
   a. Who are the people involved and what are their roles?

   b. What interventions have been recommended by the team?

   c. Which interventions have been implemented? How long was the intervention implemented? What did the data show?

Section 2: Classroom Environment

4. In which environments/settings does the student participate? Please be specific.

5. Who provides instruction in those environments?

6. What classroom strategies have been implemented by the teacher(s)?

7. How long was the intervention implemented?

8. What did the data show?

9. In which environments is the student most successful (general education, lunch, specials, speech, etc.)?

10. What strategies or interventions do the teacher(s) use with this student?

Section 3: Teacher

11. What are your strengths that help support the student?

12. Who do you seek out for guidance when you need support?

13. In thinking about the current needs of the student, are there any trainings and/or resources that would be helpful to you?

14. What do you hope to achieve as a result of our visit?

Section 4: Family

15. Do you communicate consistently with the family?

16. How often and in what form?

17. Are you aware of any significant events in the student's life that could be impacting him/her (e.g., family history, natural disasters, illness, death, move, deployments, home/school environments, relationships, homelessness, etc.)

Section 5: Student

1. What factors contribute to this student's success?

2. What are the student's strengths in the following areas?:
   a. Social:

   b. Emotional:

   c. Behavioral:

   d. Academic:

3. What are the student's special interests?

4. How have you gathered this information?

5. What motivates or reinforces the student?

6. How have you gathered this information?

TASN PARENT/GUARDIAN INTERVIEW

Directions:	Ask parent/guardian(s) the following questions. During the interview use a conversational tone and reword questions to enhance understanding, as needed.

Date completed and returned: _____

Child's name: _____

Parent/guardian name: _____

━━━━━━━━━━━━━━━━━━━━━━━━━━━━━━━━━━━━━━━

Your Child at School and Home

1. What are your child's strengths?

    a.

    b.

    c.

    d.

2. What does your child seem to struggle with the most?

    a.

    b.

    c.

    d.

3. If there could only be one goal for the school to work on with your child, which goal would be your priority? Ask the parent to elaborate.

4. What specific strategies would you like for the school to try in order to help your child improve in the areas in which they struggle the most?

5. Describe a positive aspect of working with your child's school and/or teacher.

6. Describe an area in which you would like more support from the school and/or your child's teacher.

7. Which of the following supports do you have in place for your student at home? Ask "tell me more" for each support, as necessary.

   ☐ Minimal distractions:

   ☐ Homework supplies:

   ☐ Proper diet:

   ☐ Adequate sleep:

   ☐ Check and sign student planner:

   ☐ Help with getting to school on time:

   ☐ Other: _____

   ☐ Other: _____

   ☐ Other: _____

8. How does your child prefer to spend their spare time?

9. Describe how your child's gets along with kids their age.

10. Describe your child's relationship with family members.

Child History

11. What is the student's current living situation?

12. Describe your child's development:

   a. Did your child reach average developmental milestones?

   b. How did your child approach the transition to school?

   c. Has there been any history of physical illness or injury?

   d. Has your child experienced any trauma, crisis, or loss?

Community Outreach and Community-Based Interventions

13. Is there ongoing communication and collaboration between the school and community service providers? If yes, please describe.

14. Are there specific gaps in services that you would like to see addressed?

Child Perceptions

1. What level of awareness/understanding does your child have of their needs/concerns?

2. How do they react to this?

3. What kind of coping mechanisms do they use?

Additional Information

1. How would you describe your family-school relationship?

2. What degree of trust would you say you experience with the other members of your child's team?

   - School:

   - Community supports:

   - Other:

Finish the following sentence: I will feel good about this next team meeting if:

Do you think it would be appropriate for your child to participate in the team meeting to discuss their goals and support plan?

Is there anything else you think is important for us to know before we come on site?

Child Interview (if appropriate)

- The student interview is tailored to the student's age and developmental level. Specifically, we are attempting to gather information from the student about their:

    o Strengths

    o Interests

    o Goals

    o Connections to people in various environments

    o Supports that they find helpful

    o Supports that they don't find helpful

    o Supports they would like to have added

Self-Determination Checklist
Elementary Student Self-Assessment

Student Name:_____   Date:_____

Self-Determination skills help you to know
- ❏ *yourself*
- ❏ *your goals*
- ❏ *supports you need to reach your goals*

Use the following scale to rate the statements below:
- **3 = almost always/most of the time**
- **2 = sometimes**
- **1 = rarely or never**

Rating			
3	2	1	I attend my IEP Meetings.
3	2	1	At school, my teachers listen to me when I talk about what I want or need.
3	2	1	At home, my parents listen to me when I talk about what I want or need.
3	2	1	I ask for help when I need it.
3	2	1	I know what I need, what I like and what I enjoy doing.
3	2	1	I tell others what I need, what I like and what I enjoy doing.
3	2	1	I take care of my things (pets, clothes, toys).
3	2	1	I make friends with others my age.
3	2	1	I make good choices.
3	2	1	I believe that working hard at school will help me to get good grades.

1. How can people around you (teachers, family, friends, etc.) help you to know yourself, know what you want and know what kind of help you need to reach your goals?

2008 Commonwealth of Virginia Department of Education
Training and Technical Assistance Centers - I'm Determined Project
Self-Determination Checklist ~ Elementary Student Self Assessment

Self-Determination Checklist
Student Self-Assessment

Student Name:_____   Date:_____

Self-Determination skills help you to know
- ❑ *yourself*
- ❑ *your goals*
- ❑ *supports you need to reach your goals*

Use the following scale to rate the statements below:
- 3 = almost always/most of the time
- 2 = sometimes
- 1 = rarely or never

Rating			
3	2	1	I set goals to get what I want or need.
3	2	1	I make plans for reaching my goals.
3	2	1	I check my progress on how I am doing toward my goals.
3	2	1	I attend my IEP Meetings.
3	2	1	I participate in my IEP Meetings.
3	2	1	I know the goals listed in my IEP.
3	2	1	At school, educators listen to me when I talk about what I want or need.
3	2	1	At home, my parents listen to me when I talk about what I want or need.
3	2	1	I have others in my life who help me to accomplish my goals.
3	2	1	I ask for help when I need it.
3	2	1	I know what I need, what I like and what I enjoy doing.
3	2	1	I tell others what I need, what I like and what I enjoy doing.
3	2	1	I help to make choices about the supports (educational services) and accommodations that I need in school.
3	2	1	I can describe my learning difficulties to others.
3	2	1	I believe I have control to direct my life.
3	2	1	I take care of my personal needs (clothes, chores, meals, grooming).
3	2	1	I make friends with others my age.
3	2	1	I make good choices.
3	2	1	I believe that working hard in school will help me to get a good job.

2008 Commonwealth of Virginia Department of Education
Training and Technical Assistance Centers - I'm Determined Project
Self-Determination Checklist ~ Student Self-Assessment   1

309

Self-Determination Checklist
Student Self-Assessment

1. What is one (1) goal that you have for yourself?

2. List three (3) things you can do to reach this goal.

3. How can people around you (teachers, family, friends, etc.) help you to build your self-determination skills?

4. List three (3) of your rights under the Individuals with Disabilities Education Act (IDEA) and the Americans with Disabilities Act (ADA).

2008 Commonwealth of Virginia Department of Education
Training and Technical Assistance Centers - I'm Determined Project
Self-Determination Checklist ~ Student Self-Assessment

2

310

Community Service Provider Interview

Directions: Interview the teacher using the following questions. Use a conversational tone, rewording questions as needed to enhance understanding.

FAMILY

	Tell me about the youth's family …
Seek to understand the nature of the relationships among the family and how family members communicate with one another.	• Who lives in the youth's home?
	• What has the youth shared about their family?
	• Who does the youth report getting along with best in their family?

INTERPERSONAL RELATIONSHIPS

	Tell me about the youth's relationships …
Seek to understand if the youth has the skills necessary to make friendships and maintain relationships with both peers and adults.	• Does the youth have a best friend?
	• Have they always had <u>lots of</u>/<u>not</u> many friends?
	• Why do you think that is?
	• Does the youth play with others at recess/during free time or sit with others in the cafeteria?
	• Do they seem satisfied with their relationships?

SCHOOL

	How does the youth feel about school …
	• Does the student like school?
Seek to understand if the youth likes or has ever liked school and if can they identify at least one adult who they trust at school.	• Who does the youth identify as a trusted adult at school?
	• Is the family's relationship with the school positive or negative? Tell me why.

VOCATION (for ages 14 and up)

	• Does the youth have a job or wish to be employed after high school?
Seek to understand if the youth knows what they want to be when they grow up, has been employed, is actively developing prevocational skills, or has post-graduation plans.	• Does the youth exhibit a particular aptitude for a particular vocational skill?

OPTIMISM

	Tell me how the youth perceives their future …
Seek to understand if the youth has a generally positive outlook, looks forward to things, and has a positive image of self in the future.	• How would you rate the youth's self-esteem on a scale of 1 to 10 (10 is very high)?
	• Does the youth have an overall positive or negative outlook on life?

COPING AND SAVORING

Seek to understand how the youth handles disappointment and responds to positive experiences.	• How does the youth respond to receiving feedback? • When faced with a setback or disappointment, what does the youth do to cope? • What do you wish they would do to cope with a setback or disappointment? • What does the youth consistently enjoy?

TALENTS AND INTERESTS

Seek to understand how the youth spends their free time and what they do particularly well.	Tell me what the youth is good at…
	   • What does the youth enjoy doing during free time?
	
	   • What's something the youth is particularly good at?
	
	   • What does the youth want to learn more about?

SPIRITUAL/RELIGIOUS

Seek to understand if religion/ spirituality provides the youth comfort and if the family is involved in a religious community.	• Does the youth's family spend time doing spiritual or religious activities like church or a youth group? • If yes, are the spiritual/religious activities a focal point of support for the youth and their family?

COMMUNITY LIFE

Seek to understand if the youth feels connected to their community or participates in any community activities like boys and girls club girl/boy scouts parks and rec sports, etc.	• Is the youth involved in any clubs, sports, or activities outside of school? • Are there community activities you wish the youth could participate in? • If yes, what are the barriers?

RELATIONSHIP PERMANENCE

Seek to understand if the youth has relationships with adults that have lasted a lifetime, is in contact with both parents, has long-standing relationships with relatives.	Tell me about the significant relationships in the youth's life … • Has the youth always lived with their parents? • If a biological parent is not in the home, what is the extent of the youth's relationship with that parent? • Does the youth have positive adult relationships outside the family?

RESILIENCE

Seek to understand what the youth knows about their strengths and how they use those strengths in times of difficulty or when trying to accomplish something.	• Think of a time when the youth was faced with a challenge and was able to push through to have a positive outcome? • If not, tell me more about that answer. **Coping** is taking a break from a challenging situation. **Resilience** is using problem solving to return to a task or activity.

SLEEP

Seek to understand if the youth often feels sleepy during the day or has a hard time falling/staying asleep at night.	• What time does the youth go to bed on school nights? • Is there a nighttime routine? • Does it take the youth a long time to fall asleep? • Does the youth wake up often during the night? • Is the youth often tired and difficult to wake in the morning?

CULTURAL STRESS

Seek to understand if the youth experiences distress/discomfort as a result of their own culture vs. the predominant culture in which they live.	• How long has the youth lived in this community? • If moved recently, what has that transition been like for the youth? • Does the youth feel comfortable and safe in the community? • Does the youth have other students in their class(es) that have the same cultural identity? (race, ethnicity, sexual orientation, gender identify, etc.) • Has this led to distress/discomfort for the youth? • Does the youth feel comfortable and safe at school or other places in the community? • Do you feel the people around the youth treat them with kindness and respect?

CONCERNS

Seek to understand the youth's perception of what they're struggling with the most.	<ul><li>What do you feel is the youth's greatest source of difficulty/distress?</li><li>When and how often does the youth experience this difficulty/distress? (prompt for time/date/location/ individuals present/etc.)</li><li>How does this difficulty/distress impact the youth's wellbeing and how they feel?</li><li>Has the youth received support for this in the past? Was it helpful?</li><li>If there could be only one goal for supporting your youth, what would you want that to be?</li><li>If there could only be <u>one</u> thing that the youth could learn, what would you want that to be?</li><li>Finish the following sentence: I will feel good about the team meeting if …</li></ul>

Action Plan For Technical Assistance Request #_____

Student _____ School_____ Date_____

Team Members Involved in Action Plan _____

_____

Contact Person _____

Referral Question 1		Referral Question 2	
Referral Question 3		Referral Question 4	

Action Step: Task to Be Completed/Strategy Implemented	Person(s) Responsible	Resources	Date Completed	Person Responsible for Follow-Up

Page ____ of ____   Date of Review: _____
White: Teacher   Yellow: Parent   Pink: TA Provider   Gold: Administrator

The Kansas Instructional Support Network is partially funded through Part B funds administered by the Kansas State Department of Education's Special Education Services. KISN does not discriminate on the basis of race, color, national origin, sec, disability, or age in its programs and activities. The following person has been designated to handle inquiries regarding the non-discrimination policies: Deputy Director, Keystone Learning Services, 500 E. Sunflower, Ozawkie, KS 66070, 785-876-2214.

From *Kansas Technical Assistance and Support Network and Tertiary Support* by L. Stickle (n.d.). Used with permission.

CHAPTER 15

Case Studies

As a culmination of the presentation and discussion of the CAPS system throughout this book, this chapter presents four case studies to illustrate CAPS in action: three for school and one for home. The first CAPS describes a program for Keolol, a preschool student. In the second case study, we meet Samantha, who is in an elementary school setting. The third case study introduces Julio, whose CAPS was developed for the home setting. Specifically, this CAPS established an evening routine for his family and him. Finally, Michael's CAPS addresses his needs in high school.

Each of the CAPS provides some pictorial representations of supports incorporated in the student's program. In the interest of space, only some are included here. In the actual CAPS plan, pictures of all supports would be included.

Preschool—Keolol[1]

Yu-Chi Chou, PhD

Keolol is a 5-year-old boy who attends preschool where he participates primarily in a special education classroom. He was diagnosed with autism at age 3. There are five students in Keolol's class, served by one teacher and one educational assistant. In addition to his special education classes, Keolol participates in group activities with same-age peers in an inclusive

---

1. Thanks to Judy Halvorson for developing this CAPS.

setting. He also receives services from a speech-language pathologist (SLP) and an occupational therapist (OT) within his special education classroom setting.

Cognitively, Keolol matches pictures to items and identifies basic pictures by name and function. He can also identify familiar items by pointing to objects. In addition, Keolol can complete academic tasks with verbal and visual prompts. Keolol is functionally nonverbal; he uses gestures and visual cues to communicate. He vocalizes primarily by making vowel sounds. Some vocal patterns are easily recognized as well. For example, he makes an "umm" sound to request food. Receptively, he uses gestures to respond to simple questions, such as "Where is your blue jacket?" and can share toys and objects on verbal request.

The Picture Exchange Communication System (PECS) is used to improve Keolol's communication skills. For example, when requesting a desired item, he assembles a phrase (I want + item) with a picture icon strip to request an item from a communication partner.

Keolol does not play socially interactive games, such as patty-cake, and does not engage in turn taking during play. In addition, he does not play creatively with toys.

From a sensory standpoint, Keolol does not like his head/hair or the back of his neck touched. Deep pressure is calming for Keolol as are textured balls and other fidgets. Motorically, Keolol can chew food and use an adapted spoon and fork. He can also pull the zipper on his pants up and down. He needs assistance with motor movements, such as climbing on/off a rocking horse.

Keolol's CAPS was designed to target several group activities that require social interaction. Specifically, the purpose of his CAPS was to improve his interactions with peers and build on his communication and social skills.

Strengths

Keolol can follow short auditory directions with visual prompts. He is also responsive to simple questions. His favorite type of reinforcement is social praise. Keolol can use gestures to point to objects and express needs. He excels at following routine activities.

Needs

Keolol needs systematic prompts to complete activities, such as following (a) a visual schedule to transition between activities, (b) visual prompts to initiate tasks, and (c) visual organizers to complete academic work. He needs to increase participation in interactive games and imitative play skills with peers. Moreover, he needs to improve communicative skills by continuing his use of PECS.

Comprehensive Autism Planning System

The team developed a CAPS for Keolol's half-day preschool program. The CAPS addresses the four activities that he participates in daily: recess, Hawaii cultural instruction, lunch, and group play. See the next page for Keolol's CAPS (figure 15.4).

The following are examples of the visual supports that are used throughout Keolol's program.

Figure 15.1. Keolol's
Daily Schedule

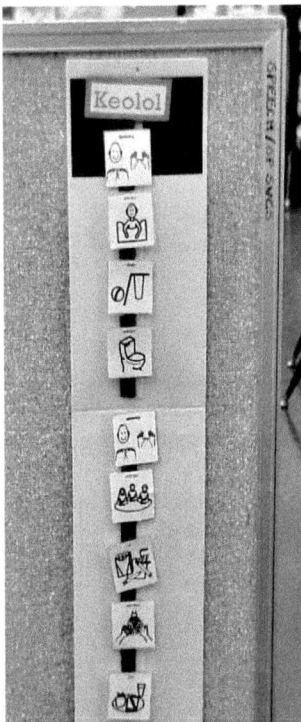

Figure 15.2. Keolol's Recess Visual Schedule.

Figure 15.3. Keolol's Visual Routine for Hawaiiana.

Figure 15.4. Keolol's CAPS.

Comprehensive Autism Planning System (CAPS)			
Child/Student: *Keolol*			
Time	**Activity**	**Skills to Teach**	**Structure/ Modifications**
10:00-10:20	Recess • Sit on rug with peers • Wait to be dismissed • Line up at door • Walk to recess area • Play with peers	• Use hands appropriately • Greet • Imitate a sequence of 2 actions w/peers (e.g., playing tag, playing catch) • Stand in line • Walk nicely • Wait turn • Follow simple verbal directions • Imitate a novel act in familiar activity	• Trained peers • Prompting • Social narrative • Visual mini-schedule • Gradually increase the length of time for an activity and/or # of activities
10:20-11:00	Hawaiiana • Discuss lessons and songs with Kupuna. Tape songs and/or videotape class singing song • Teach hand routines/ dance before Hawaiian class	• Use hands appropriately • Imitate peers and adults (one of the current songs is the Hokey Pokey in Hawaiian, so Mitchell needs to learn to imitate that dance) • Follow verbal directions	• Systematic prompting for independence • Visual supports for the sequence of hand, foot, and body
11:00-11:40	Lunch	• Bite, chew, then swallow food in mouth before taking next bite • Take one bite of a finger food at a time • Wait between bites • Calm hands while waiting	• Visual sequence of activity • Systematic prompting for independence • Self-monitoring chart
12:40-13:20	Group play • Have class peers come to Mitchell's room to practice Hawaiiana songs • Teach to play with toys and games • Teach games to play at recess	• Use hands appropriately • Imitate peers • Follow verbal directions • Imitate a sequence of 3 + actions • Imitate a novel act during a familiar activity	• Systematic prompting for independence • Train peers • Use play stations to teach how to play with more than one item during an activity period • Visuals of play routines

Figure 15.4 (continued)

Reinforcement	Sensory/ Regulation	Communication/ Social Skills	Data Collection	Generalization to Community
Choice of preferred activities	• Keep Keolol engaged so he does not put dirt, rocks, and other nonedible items in his mouth • Fidget items • Pica box	Prompting to engage with peers and imitate	Observation	• Playing with peers at recess • Participation in class with peers
Verbal praise	Fidget items	Prompting, as needed	Observation	Inclusion in general education class
Verbal praise	Prompting, as needed	Prompting to engage with peers and imitate	• Observation • Frequency counts of target behaviors	• Eating lunch in cafeteria at school • Eating at home with family • Eating in restaurants
• Choice of preferred games • Social reinforcement from peers	Calming toys: textured balls or other fidget toys	Prompting, as needed	Observation	• Playing with peers at recess • Joining group play in community

Figure 15.5. Keolol's Box With Sensory Fidgets.

Figure 15.6. Keolol's Lunch Visual Schedule.

Elementary School—Samantha

Christina R. Carnahan, PhD

Samantha or Sam is a 9-year-old girl in the second grade. She lives at home with her mother and sister. Sam is autistic and has a seizure disorder. She currently takes medication for seizures and hyperactivity. At home, Sam engages in solitary play or large-motor activities with her sister. Her mother reports that it is becoming increasingly difficult to take Sam into the community because of safety issues, such as running. Her primary concerns include Sam's participation in her community and development of skills that will lead to increased independence as she gets older.

Sam attends a large suburban elementary school where she receives all instruction in a special education classroom. Her schedule includes one-on-one academic instruction, small-group literacy and language activities, and a variety of gross-motor and sensory breaks embedded in the school day. Sam is functioning at a pre-academic level. Target skills include choice making, increasing verbal skills, and developing self-help skills, such as dressing, following directions, and moving independently through her environment.

Examples of specific academic tasks include matching pictures, sorting by category, and a variety of activities designed to increase her fine-motor skills. Issues related to lack of attention and focus make instruction difficult. It is often unclear if Sam lacks a skill or is simply not focused enough to demonstrate it. For these reasons, Sam often receives instruction in a small room connected to the special education classroom. Finally, Sam's school day includes individual and small-group sessions with the SLP, the OT, and the physical therapist (PT). She does not receive any additional therapies outside of the school day.

In the past year, Sam began vocalizing sounds that approximate words. She can verbalize five words, including "bye" and "play." However, she often needs verbal prompts such as, "Tell your friends bye" to use these words. She does not yet use these words spontaneously to make requests or interact with others. Sam knows where most items are located in the classroom. She frequently interrupts activities to run to a closet or shelf to obtain the items she wants or needs.

Increased socialization, independence, and community participation continue to be goals for Sam. At the start of the school year, she engaged in behavior deemed unsafe by the principal. For example, on the playground, Sam wrapped her legs around a little girl while playing on the jungle gym, causing her to fall and hit her head.

Sam also ran from her teachers on several occasions, attempting to engage them in games of chase. Because of these incidents, Sam now has limited access to the rest of the school building and peers. She eats lunch in the classroom and has indoor recess with a small group of peers. These behaviors also influence Sam's participation in the special education classroom. For example, during small-group activities, an adult always sits behind Sam to help her focus and keep her hands to herself, and when she transitions from one area of the classroom to another, an adult provides a physical prompt by touching Sam on the back or shoulder.

The team feels that Sam has made substantial progress during the last school year but still has significant concerns about behavior, independence, and socialization.

The team completed a Baseline CAPS to determine the interventions already in place. The team had a difficult time articulating target skills for activities, such as arrival, recess, and lunch. For other activities, the target skills were primarily pre-academic and included verbally approximating words related to the calendar and weather, sorting, and matching.

The primary teaching interventions included modeling paired with verbal directions and hand-over-hand prompting. The team also used hand holding as a strategy for managing Sam's behaviors. But despite the hand-holding intervention, Sam continued to wrap her legs around adults and students in the classroom. Sam received one-on-one therapy outside of the classroom from a SLP, OT, and PT for 40 minutes each per week. The team verbally praised Sam when she demonstrated the desired academic skills, such as correctly sorting or matching pictures. They also provided breaks every 5–10 minutes during the one-on-one work sessions.

Figure 15.7. Sam's Baseline CAPS.

Baseline: Comprehensive Autism Planning System (CAPS)			
Child/Student: Sam			
Time	**Activity**	**Skills to Teach**	**Structure/ Modifications**
8:50	Arrival		Hold Sam's hand as she walks from the bus to the classroom, and as you walk around the track
9:15	Literacy/Language Group	• Put days of the week in order on the calendar	Match pictures of days of the week to pictures on the calendar
9:30	Gross Motor/Sensory Group	• Jumping, hopping • Stand on one foot	"Cut-out" feet on the floor in the classroom
10:00	One-on-One Instruction	• Sorting • Matching	Model how to complete tasks while providing verbal instructions
11:30	Lunch (in room with teacher)		
12:00	Individual Recess		Hold S's hand as she walks around the track
12:30	Literacy/Language Activity Group	• Greet one peer when she comes to group • Identify the weather when presented with two pictures	• Match weather pictures to identical pictures on the weather board • Prompt to say hello, if needed

The team recognized that Sam had many sensory needs that influence her participation in school. Though the team was unsure about the type of sensory supports that would best meet her needs, they decided to use the outdoor running track and weighted vest. Sam used the track to take sensory breaks two times during the school day. The paraprofessional took Sam to the track when she arrived at school and during recess. They held hands as they walked slowly around the track, two times in the morning and five times at recess. Sam wore the weighted vest during the first 20 minutes of each one-on-one instructional session.

Figure 15.7 (continued)

Reinforcement	Sensory/ Regulation	Communication/ Social Skills	Data Collection	Generalization to Community
	• Walk two times around the track after hanging up backpack			
Verbal praise		• Verbalize beginning sound for each day of the week	Checklist indicating prompting level for each day	SLP 20 minutes, two times per week
• Drink of water and snack at the end of the activity • Verbal praise				
• Verbal praise • Break every 5-10 minutes	• Weighted vest for 20 minutes • Take breaks in the sensory area			
Verbal praise				
	Walk five times around the track			
Verbal praise		Verbally approximate the words hi, bye, sunny, windy, cloudy, and raining		SLP 20 minutes, two times per week to target sounds for greetings

Strengths

Sam has an exuberance for life that she often exhibits in school by darting to and from activities. She wants to have friends and, despite having a limited repertoire of play skills, she continues to initiate interactions with others. Sam's natural curiosity is also evident in the classroom. She is very interested in the materials that are available in the classroom. Her language skills are emerging, and she appears to want to use these skills with increasing frequency.

Needs

The team identified three primary areas of concern for Sam—transitioning, social interactions with others, and increasing attention and focus for learning. The first two areas, transitioning and social interactions, are closely related. Both involve her ability to independently move through the classroom and school environment.

Indeed, all Sam's school and community experiences are colored by her difficulty transitioning from one area to another. During transitions, Sam may run from the teacher. She may also attempt to wrap her legs or arms around her peers or the teachers. It seems that these rough-and-tumble play behaviors serve as Sam's primary strategy for interacting with others. Not only does such play provide much-needed sensory input, it also allows her to gain the attention of and interact with peers and adults.

Because Sam demonstrates physical behaviors such as those described above, she is rarely in the same learning space as others and has few social interactions or relationships with others. Sam does not appear to understand how her actions (e.g., running away or intruding on others' space) affect others. She also appears to lack the skills to engage others appropriately in games, turn-taking activities, or greetings.

During breaks and lunch, she interacts with adults or plays on her own. Staff members watch Sam closely when she is around other children. She needs physical and verbal prompts to maintain her own space or participate in turn-taking activities. For example, during a gross-motor group, each child had the opportunity to swing for 3 minutes. While one child swung, the others sat in their chairs waiting. Sam needed one-on-one adult support to sit in her chair and wait. When asked to transition back to her chair, she needed assistance from two adults to move from the swing to wait.

In addition to the needs described above, the team wants to help Sam increase her ability to focus and attend to learning materials. She currently participates in highly structured one-on-one teaching settings for 2-3 minutes. Even in these situations, she demonstrates sporadic attention to the learning materials. That is, she looks at the materials sometimes but not at other times. It is difficult to determine if Sam lacks a skill in a certain area or if her lack of focus keeps her from demonstrating a specific skill. The team feels that increasing Sam's focus and attention during instructional tasks will significantly improve her skill acquisition.

As mentioned, Sam needs support and instruction in transitioning, social interactions, and attention to academic learning materials. Specific skills to teach include (a) moving from one area to another without adult support, (b) interacting with others using socially appropriate behaviors, and the (c) focusing on (look at, respond to directions, etc.) a variety of academic learning material. The team identified these three target areas because they believe that improvements in these areas are pivotal to developing many other important life skills.

CAPS

The team collaborated to complete a new CAPS. They began by identifying important target skills related to each of Sam's identified needs and embedded them in each activity during the school day. Even activities, such as lunch and recess, were assigned target skills. Examples of specific skills include:

- Appropriately greeting peers
- Waiting for an extended period with decreasing adult support
- Turn taking
- Self-help skills, such as hanging up a jacket or backpack
- Appropriate use of playground equipment
- Academic-related targets, including communication, working to completion, and attending to learning materials for at least 5 minutes

Figure 15.8. Sam's CAPS.

	Comprehensive Autism Planning System (CAPS)		
	Child/Student: Sam		
Time	**Activity**	**Skills to Teach**	**Structure/ Modifications**
9:00	Arrival	• Enters the school building • Walks independently, Manages own materials and belongings • Greets 2 peers	• Visual supports: color-coding cubby, tape on the floor from school building door to classroom, picture checklist of steps to follow to unpack backpack, video model of a child leaving the bus and walking to the classroom • Backward chaining to increase independence
9:15	Literacy/Language Group	• Greet • Turn-taking • Chooses from a field of three pictures to comment on a book. For example, comment "I see __" using a voice output device. • Begins concept of print	• Visual timer to indicate the amount of time left in group • Tape on the floor indicating where chair, hands, and feet go • Video model to teach greeting skills (shown at start of group to support all group members) • Token board for number of turns Sam must take before he leaves the group.

Figure 15.8 (continued)

Reinforcement	Sensory/ Regulation	Communication/ Social Skills	Data Collection	Generalization to Community
Tangible (e.g., edibles) reinforcers provided throughout the process; move to the sensory/ play area after completing all steps in the process	• Weighted back-pack (place a few large books in his bag to provide heavy work during this time) • Embed OT services to support development of self-care skills	• Identify the 2 peers individuals prior to • Teach peers to approach Sam each morning • Use video modeling to teach greeting • Role play and practice • AAC device/language board	Enters building; walks independently, manages materials, greets, M-F, Y/N & prompts 9:00-9:10 (see data sheets)	Visual supports of bedtime routines
Tangible reinforcers paired with verbal praise for desired behaviors	• Weighted lap pad used as needed • Chewy candy or sucker provided while waiting for his turn to respond	• Modeling and repeated practice to teach greeting sand turn-taking • Errorless learning to teach commenting; fade prompts as matching pictures from books to those on the voice output device increases • Embed SLP services in group activities	• Choice: M,#, 15m • Turn-taking: T, #, 15m • Greets: W, #, 15m (see data sheets)	Greeting, turn-taking and commenting at Sunday dinner with extended family

CAPS

Figure 15.8 (continued)

Time	Activity	Skills to Teach	Structure/Modifications

9:30	Gross Motor/Sensory Group	• Turn-taking (indicate on AAC or verbally)
		• Attends to and follows group directions
		• Greets peers
		• Waits for at least two minutes with decreasing adult prompts
			• Visual timer
			• Tape on the floor to indicate where he should be
			• Visual directions
			• Use 1-on-1 sessions to teach:
			  • Waiting in a space. Increase waiting time/distance between him and the teacher.
			  • Following group directions: stand up, come here, etc.
			• Transition from play to work with decreased prompts

10:00	One-on-One Instruction	• Attends to work materials for at least five minutes • Follows directions • Works to completion • Academic goals and objectives: specific communication, self-help, and other objectives • Behavioral goals: waiting, walking independently from one area to another, following directions.	• First/then board: "first work, then play" • Tokens to indicate the number of tasks to complete before a break • Place his desk near the break area
11:30	Lunch (in room with teacher)	• Follow directions • Self-help skills including eats, opens containers, and washes hands • Communication skills including requests help and indicate finished using pictures	• Choice board to request items • Color-coded placemats, utensils, bowls, etc., to indicate personal items • "Finished" and "help" picture • Introduce cafeteria through walks etc.

332

Figure 15.8 (continued)

Reinforcement	Sensory/ Regulation	Communication/ Social Skills	Data Collection	Generalization to Community
• Highly motivating activities such as swinging, bouncing, and jumping • Pair tangible reinforcers with verbal praise for desired behavior such as transitioning back to his chair	• Weighted lap pad while waiting • Fidgets while waiting • Heavy work activities for calming before session begins • Embed PT services in group activities	• Video model of waiting • AAC device/language board	• Turn-taking: M/T, prompts, 15m • Attends: M/T, duration & prompts, 15m • Greets peers: W/TR, Y/N & prompts, all period (see data sheets)	Visual timer to indicate bedtime
• Choice board to choose reinforcer • High levels of reinforcement: small tangibles (e.g., edibles) as he works on a task, larger reinforcer provided upon task completion • Verbal praise for work completion and other desired behaviors	• Embed frequent sensory/play breaks throughout the work session (e.g., 3m work, 3m break). Breaks w/ sensory activities (e.g., deep pressure, heavy work) and free choice segments • Weighted lap pad while working • Water bottle with a resistant strew to drink from while working	AAC device/ language board	• Attends: T/W, duration, 15m • Follows directions: TR/F, # & prompts, 10m • Work completion: daily, gradebook • Academic goals: M?F, # & prompts, 10m • Behavioral goals: T?W, # & prompts, 10m (see data sheets)	First/then board for trips to grocery store
Highly motivating food items throughout the lunch bell	• Bounce and swing before lunch begins • Water bottle with a resistant straw Weighted utensils • Noise filtering headphones for cafeteria	• AAC device/language board • Gradually include 1-2 peers in lunch in the classroom • Prime for lunch with small group using video model	• Follows directions: TR/F, # & prompts, 10m • Requests help: M/T, Y/N & prompts, 30m • Indicates all done: W/TR, # & prompts, 30m (see data sheets)	• Use "finished" and "help" pictures at dinner • Use color-coded placements at dinner

Figure 15.8 (continued)

Time	Activity	Skills to Teach	Structure/Modifications
12:00	Individual Recess	• Uses playground equipment including w/peers • Turn-taking on equipment • Stays within a space	• Video model, modeling, prompting during individual recess • Gradually include 1-2 peers in his recess. • Gradually create group recess by walking around playground when other children are present
12:30	Literacy/Language Activity Group	• Greets 2 peers • Turn-taking • Chooses from a field of three pictures to comment on a book. For example, comment "I see __" using a voice output device. • Begins concept of print	• Visual timer to indicate time left in group • Tape on the floor indicating where he should keep his chair, hands, and feet • Video model to teach greeting skills (video model shown at start of group to support all group members) • Token board indicating number of turns to take before leaving group. • Errorless learning to teach commenting • Modeling/repeated practice to teach greeting and turn-taking

Many of these skills corresponded to several activities during the school day. For example, skills such as greetings, turn taking, and waiting were embedded in literacy and gross-motor groups. The team decided that these were so important that they would provide intense, systematic instruction for each of these skills during Sam's one-on-one sessions.

The following figure depicts the classroom area designed for individual instruction. Once Sam mastered a skill in the one-on-one sessions, the team planned for generalization to group activities. Generalization strategies included prompting the skills during each group activity and gradually fading the amount of support provided.

Figure 15.8 (continued)

Reinforcement	Sensory/ Regulation	Communication/ Social Skills	Data Collection	Generalization to Community
• Natural reinforces such as swinging, jumping, etc. • Embed tangible reinforcers during transitions		AAC device/ language board	• Playground equipment: M-F, # & prompts, 15m • Stays in space: M-F, % of time, 30m • Independence for 5 consecutive days before introducing 1 peer (see data sheets)	Use a video modeling to illustrate sitting at dinner
Tangible reinforcers paired with verbal praise for desired behaviors	• Weighted lap pad as needed • Chewy candy or sucker while waiting for turn to respond	• Embed SLP services in group activities • AAC device/language board	• Greets: T/W, # & prompts, 15m • Turn taking: TR/F, # & prompts, 10m • Comments: M?F, # & prompts, 10m (see data sheets)	Use reinforcers for following bedtime routine

Figure 15.9. Area Designed for Individual Work.

In addition to systematically teaching the target skills, the team provided intense visual, sensory, and reinforcement supports. Visual/structural supports included the use of a visual timer, token board, visual directions, and video models. During literacy group, the team began by showing Sam a token board with five tokens.

On the end of the board was a picture of the sensory area. After each of her turns, she removed a token from the board. When she had completed five turns, Sam was allowed to go to the break area where the OT had placed calming items.

Figure 15.10. Sample Visual Support.

Figure 15.11. Structure for Sam's Materials.

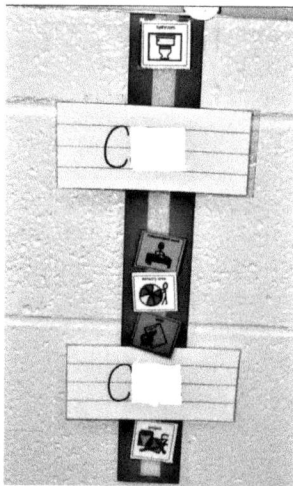

The teacher supplemented her verbal directions with visual directions. When indicating to Sam that it was time to take her turn, for example, she held up an orange card with a picture indicating "Your Turn." Once Sam completed her turn, the teacher handed her a picture card indicating "Wait."

The team also created video models to teach Sam the target skills. This intervention was especially helpful in teaching use of playground equipment. The teacher videotaped two students playing on the jungle gym and the swings. Sam viewed the video each day before going to recess.

Sensory supports also played an important part in increasing Sam's success at school. Instead of taking Sam to the track as they had done previously, the team worked to embed a variety of sensory activities throughout the school day. During group activities, she had access to items such as water bottles with resistant straws, weighted lap pads, and chewy candy. During breaks, Sam engaged in a variety of activities, including carrying a weighted backpack, swinging, and lying under heavy blankets. The team reinforced Sam's choice-making skills by allowing her to choose her own sensory activities several times during the school day.

Figure 15.12. Sam's Sensory Area.

The team realized that verbal praise alone was not reinforcing enough to promote learning and work completion for Sam. After talking with her mother, the teacher identified a variety of tangible reinforcers, such as small candy items, hot chocolate, and visually stimulating toys, that were effective for her. Sam was also highly motivated to work for movement-oriented breaks. As a result, the team embedded all of these items throughout the school day.

In addition to a movement-oriented break, the teacher gave Sam a small piece of chewy candy after she completed turn taking. She also used tangible reinforcers when Sam waited while others took their turns. Each tangible reinforcer was paired with verbal praise that clearly indicated the desired behavior. For example, when Sam sat and waited as a peer took a turn, the teacher handed her the piece of candy saying, "I like the way you are waiting quietly in your chair." Pairing the verbal praise with tangible reinforcers and breaks proved highly motivating for Sam.

In addition, the team also used a variety of specific teaching strategies, including systematic instruction and data collection. When teaching Sam to independently wait in a chair, for example, the team began by standing next to Sam as he sat in a chair for 15 seconds. At the end of the 15 seconds, the teacher provided reinforcement and directed Sam to the next task. They gradually increased the amount of time she waited in the chair and the distance between her and the teacher.

Data collection involved a variety of task analyses and use of checklists and anecdotal records. The teacher created a data collection schedule that allowed her to take data without feeling overwhelmed. She collected data on each academic skill at least once a week and data on

Sam's behavior on a daily basis. These records supported the team in making decisions about the effectiveness of specific interventions and strategies and regarding Sam's behavior during the school day.

The interventions helped increase Sam's success during the school day, at home, and in the community. She developed skills to support continual growth and a positive transition. At the end of the school year, Sam will transition to a new teacher in a new school. Using CAPS, the new team will have insight into Sam's strengths and needs, and a solid base of interventions to start the school year.

Home Setting—Julio

Jill Hudson, MS

Julio is a 12-year-old boy who lives at home with mom and dad, two younger sisters, Stephanie and Michelle, and a dog and cat. He is in the sixth grade and participates in the general education classroom with curriculum modifications. He has been nonverbal since he was 3, but his functional verbal communication is increasing with the aid of the Picture Exchange Communication System (PECS).

Julio's skills in discriminating letters are emerging, and, as a result, he is learning to recognize words in sentences. He can match sight words to pictures when provided limited choices and can independently write his first name. In addition, Julio can sequence numbers up to 20 and use one-to-one correspondence up to 10. He responds well to physical and verbal prompting. Julio has good navigation skills and can independently move around the school. Each day, he delivers newspapers to specific rooms throughout the school.

Julio enjoys playing UNO, playing with beads, or drawing patterns on his whiteboard. These pastimes are frequently used as reinforcers at school.

Transitions are the greatest challenge for Julio. If a situation involves a new or unknown adult, he often becomes dysregulated and throws items off his desk or kicks his chair to communicate what he cannot verbally express. To regulate himself, Julio often spins or talks in a loud voice. He can respond to redirection when given verbal or physical prompts.

Julio enjoys being active, especially engaging in physical interactions with his peers and siblings. He typically exhibits a friendly, playful demeanor and has a sense of humor. He is comfortable participating in his community and is frequently found greeting people with whom he comes into contact. Julio's typical routine at home after school includes down time and a quick snack before changing into more comfortable clothing. He prefers loose-fitting clothing that might not be appropriate for a school setting.

There are continual attempts to communicate verbally with Julio at home. For example, asking, "What do you want to drink, Julio?" and prompting him to respond by starting his sentence "I want _____." Approximately one half of the time he will answer with one word: "juice," "soda," or "drink." If he is not given a drink, he independently goes to the refrigerator and gets what he wants. During an independent event like this, there is no communication or interaction with family members.

Once a snack and drink are secured, Julio proceeds to the TV room to watch a favorite television show. If asked, "What do you want to watch, Julio?" he answers *Sesame Street* or *Sponge Bob*. If he is not asked about a program, he uses the remote control to find it himself. During this time Julio may also independently go to his room to retrieve his beads or music. If he selects music, he will bring it to a parent and pull on an arm or try to gain attention by saying "Mommy" or "Daddy" while handing his parent the player. Julio joins the family for dinner and makes one-word requests for desired items. Afterwards, he helps clean the dishes. Julio enjoys being near his family in the evening and initiates play interactions with his siblings. Occasionally, he prefers to be alone, but typically not for more than two hours. After some leisure time with his family, Julio begins his evening routine. This consists of completing any assigned schoolwork, taking a bath, reviewing his calendar, and going to bed.

Strengths

Julio has many strengths, including his sense of humor. He often initiates playful behavior with his family members and enjoys wrestling and being tickled. He initiates verbal greetings with parents and siblings, including hugs. He can follow simple commands such as, "Put your dishes in the sink" or "Get your cup." He is friendly and comfortable and enjoys his time off from school by watching videos or listening to music, going into the community, and performing some life skills tasks.

Needs

Julio's verbalization skills are emerging. Strengthening these skills will allow him to ask for his needs, wants, and desires to be met. He currently grabs at items and people to initiate. His parents agree that Julio's three biggest needs are (a) more verbalization, (b) more physical activity, and (c) increased social interaction with siblings.

CAPS

Julio's CAPS (figure 15.16 on the following pages) was designed by his father to be used at home. Julio's father attended a series of autism-related workshops where he learned about CAPS and thought this system would help Julio interact more with his family. It builds in supports and structure for Julio as he enters an environment that should be relaxing, safe, and comfortable. By providing structure, CAPS provides opportunities to encourage skill development with his family and trusted community members.

The following shows (a) Julio's social script that he can use to tell his sisters and dad that he wants to exercise, (b) the communication script that his sisters use to respond to Julio, and (c) Julio's communication board.

Figure 15.13. Julio's Social Script to Request That His Family Exercise With Him.

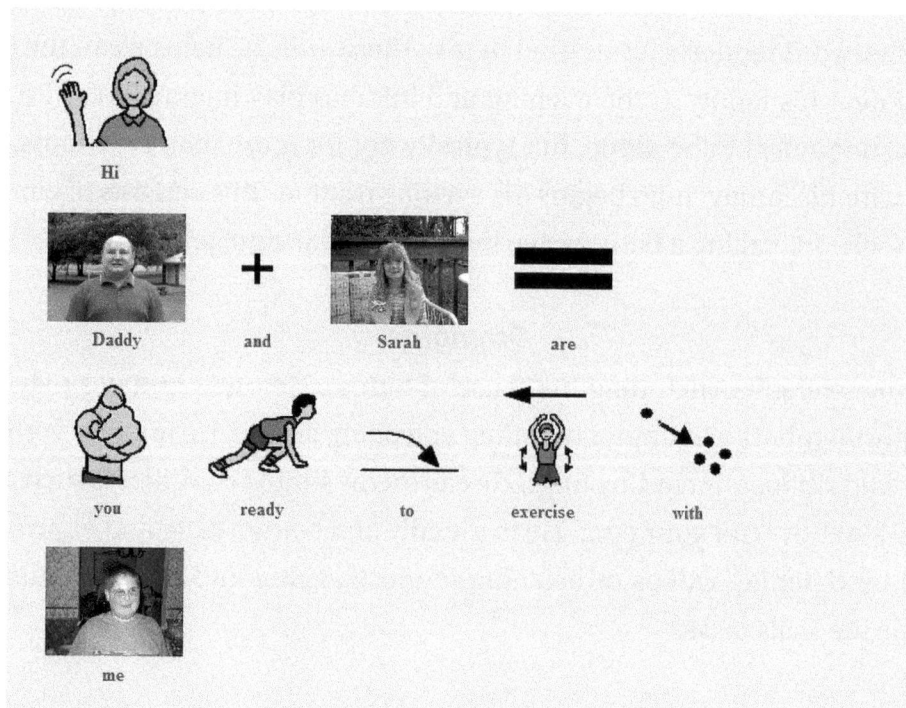

Figure 15.14. Julio's Sisters' Response.

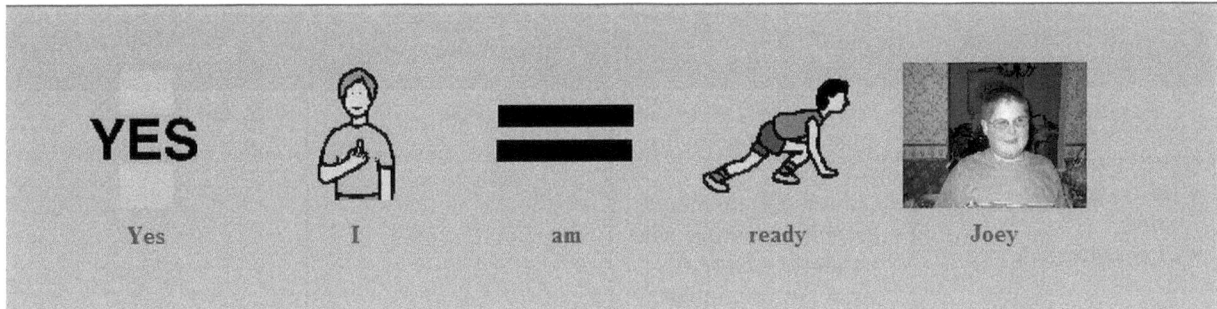

Figure 15.15. Julio's Communication Board.

Figure 15.16. Julio's CAPS.

Comprehensive Autism Planning System (CAPS)			
Child/Student: *Julio*			
Activity	**Skills to Teach**	**Structure/ Modifications**	**Reinforcement**
<u>Home from school</u> • Greet family members • Have a quick snack and drink • Change clothing	• Follow a daily schedule after coming home from school • Greet family members • Parents encourage Julio to talk about day at school by prompting	Visual schedule	Hugs and greetings
<u>Free time</u> • Watch TV • Listen to music w/ headphones • Play with beads • Play game with family	• Parents encourage communication by oral prompting • Do you want your music or beads and What show do you want to watch on TV?	Visual schedule	Watching television programs and family interactions
<u>Dinner with family</u> • Chore: put away clean dishes • Chore: put dirty dishes in dishwasher	Eat meal with family members	Visual schedule	Interaction is the reinforcer
• Complete assigned homework	• Homework assignment completion • Attending to task for 5 min.	• Timer set for 5 minutes • Visual schedule	Cutting and gluing activities
<u>Bedtime routine:</u> • Bath • Calendar • Prayers	Parents encourage communication by oral prompting calendar routine and scripted prayers	• Calendar • Scripted routine	Bath is reinforcing as is playing with beads in bed

Figure 15.16 (continued)

Sensory/ Regulation	Communication/ Social Skills	Data Collection	Generalization to Community
Hugs from family members Greetings from family members	• Smiles and laughs when he sees family members; hugs and says hi • Greets sisters with hi and first names • Communication board • Prompt, as needed	Observation	• Communication board used throughout evening activities. • Greeting in community
Beads	• Julio will respond when asked what show he wants to watch on TV by saying either "Sesame Street or Sponge Bob • Communication board • Scripts for game playing	Observation	Choice making at grocery store
Family members eat and encourage Julio to talk about meal	• Parents ask Julio what he wants for dinner • Family members eat and encourage Julio to talk about meal • Communication board • Prompt, as needed	Observation	• Ordering food at a restaurant and participate in conversation while there. • Cleaning up room
Working with different textures and products like children's project glue	• Parents review homework with Julio with lots of encouragement • Softly and slowly verbalizing to Julio. Sometimes he requires hand-over-hand on written material. Julio is interested in anything that involves making something. He really likes cutting and working to glue paper symbols "pictures" in place.	Observation	Independence work at school
Bath activities and beads	Julio will remain close to family members during this time.	Observation	Following routines on family outings

Middle/High School—Michael

Amy Bixler Coffin, MS

Michael is a 16-year-old autistic teen. He lives with his mother and two younger brothers, one of whom is diagnosed with attention deficit-hyperactivity disorder and obsessive compulsive disorder; the other has learning disabilities. Michael's mother and father divorced when Michael was 10 years old. Michael and his brothers spend every other Saturday with their father, who lives approximately 45 miles away. His mother is an LPN who works second shift from 3 to 11 PM, four days a week. Her parents, who live in the same neighborhood as she and the boys, take turns caring for the boys while their mother is at work. Michael takes medication for anxiety as well as medication to assist with sleeping.

Until recently, Michael had never slept through the night without waking up every 2-3 hours. When he was approximately 3 years old, his mother noticed that he was developing differently from his same-age peers. Michael did not socialize and preferred to play alone. He would spend hours looking at books and magazines. He was very verbal in an "exacting manner." His expressive language skills far exceeded those of his peers.

Michael often reacted strongly to sensory stimuli. Loud noises bothered him, and he did not like being touched lightly. After a visit to his pediatrician where she expressed her concerns, Michael's mother was assured that she was overreacting. It was not until Michael turned 6 that he was diagnosed with autism.

Throughout elementary school Michael received special education services, including speech and language therapy focusing on pragmatic language and social skills as well as OT. After transitioning to middle school, Michael no longer received direct therapy services. At the end of eighth grade, he was dismissed from both therapies.

Michael is currently in the second quarter of his sophomore year of high school, attending all general education classes. He is enrolled in biology, history, English literature, algebra, composition, and physical education. His schedule also includes a daily support period where he receives assistance with organizational skills and social skills.

Baseline CAPS

Due to a high number of discipline referrals and a decline in his grades, Michael's teachers decided to meet to complete a Baseline CAPS (figure 15.17) for him. After discussing the requirements of each class, all his teachers agreed that Michael was struggling in the following areas: (a) completing independent work, (b) working in groups, (c) taking tests, (d) participating in lectures, and (e) completing homework assignments.

The staff then determined the specific skills that they believed to be the most important for him to learn, including task completion, attention to task, and conversational rules. Interventions currently being used were recorded; all were deemed appropriate to address the target skills. Documentation of the various ways in which data were collected was also recorded.

Strengths

Michael is a bright young man with above-average intelligence. He exhibits excellent rote memory skills, can quickly memorize the most recent statistics of any Major League baseball player, and can easily recall those stats in conversation. He enjoys talking about stats with his peers and visiting with his mother's friends.

Needs

Although he excels in math and history, Michael receives mostly C's on his report card as 25% of grades for all academic classes is based on homework assignments. Michael tends to forget to write his assignments down in his school planner and often forgets materials needed to complete assignments. As a result, he repeatedly does not do his homework and frequently does not remember to turn in assignments that he has completed.

Michael has few friends at school. He tends to keep to himself in social situations. When time allows, he prefers looking at sports magazines and memorizing baseball players' batting statistics rather than socializing with his peers. When he does participate in conversation with peers, he stands very close and often attempts to dominate the conversations around topics of his special interests, such as sports. When peers become disinterested in what he is saying, he does not recognize their nonverbal gestures or lack of interest. Although the topic of this

Figure 15.17. Michael's Baseline CAPS.

Baseline: Comprehensive Autism Planning System (CAPS)			
Child/Student: Michael Thomas			
Activity	Skills to Teach	Structure/ Modifications	Reinforcement
Independent Work	Task completion	• School planner • Verbal reminders by all teachers	• Completed in-class and homework assignments • Good grades
Group Work	Conversational rules	• Teacher reminders with facial expressions of approval/disapproval • Assigned peer • Weekly verbal reminders of group activities	Peer interaction
Tests	Task completion	• School planner • Verbal reminders of upcoming tests • Test dates announced by teachers	Test completion
Lectures	Attention to task	Sitting in front of room	Appropriate conversation
Homework	• Task completion • Materials and supplies needed	• School planner • Binder • Book bag	• Homework turned in • Higher grades on report card

interest is similar to peers his age, he has become extremely focused with baseball statistics and incessantly studies magazines the Internet and magazines, often at inappropriate times during classes. Michael's mother reports that he does not have friends that he sees on the weekends or in the evenings. Instead, he prefers socializing with her and her friends.

Figure 15.17 (continued)

Sensory/ Regulation	Communication/ Social Skills	Data Collection	Generalization to Community
	Asking for help when stuck	Teacher grade book	• Hand in homework in other classes
	Verbal reminders from teachers on what/how to interact in group after interaction occurs	Referrals to office or after school detentions	
	Asking for help when stuck	• Test completion • Test scores	Use planner across classes
	Teacher cues on appropriate topics/times to speak	Referrals to office or after school detentions	
		Homework turned in complete	

Michael's M-CAPS

Michael's team began generating ideas for Michael's CAPS that would focus on strengthening existing skills, building new skills, and preventing challenging behaviors. Team members agreed that Michael needed information to be presented visually as much as possible and, therefore, began modifying the interventions listed on his Baseline CAPS, as it became evident that most interventions were presented orally. The following depicts Michael's M-CAPS (figure 15.18) and his CAPS developed for his PE class.

Figure 15.18. Michael's M-CAPS.

Modified Comprehensive Planning Systems (M-CAPS)			
Child/Student: *Michael Thomas*			
Activity	**Skills to Teach**	**Structure/ Modifications**	**Reinforcement**
Independent Work	• Task completion • Asking for help	• Task organizer (prompt) • Organization calendar • (prompt) • Systematic fading to independence • Peer buddies	• Reinforcer menu: in-class work and home-work • Verbal
Group Work	• Conversation rules • Task completion	• Task organizer (prompt) • Organization calendar (prompt) • Systematic fading to independence • Trained peer buddies	• Reinforcer menu: in-class work and home-work • Verbal
Tests	Test completion	• Task organizer (prompt to use) • Organization Calendar (prompt to use) • Academic progress • Systematic fading procedures for independent use	• Conversation • Test completion • Verbal
Lectures	Attention to task	• Task organizer (prompt to use) • Organization Calendar (prompt to use) • Systematic fading procedures for independent use • Plot flow chart	• Conversation • Verbal
Homework	• Task completion • Materials and supplies needed	• Homework checklist • Supply checklist (prompt to use and double check with student)	• Reinforcer menu (turning in completed homework and bringing supplies) • Verbal

Figure 15.18 (continued)

Sensory/ Regulation	Communication/ Social Skills	Data Collection	Generalization to Community
• Relaxation techniques • Coping card • Stress Thermometer	Help card on desk	• Task organizer (I/P, daily) • Organization calendar (I/P, daily) • Gradebook • Asking for help: (TR/F, #/#number needed, 15 m)	Use task Organizer and organization calendar across day
• Relaxation techniques • Coping cards • Earplugs • Stress Thermometer • Take a break card	• Topic, comment, story, question card (direct instruction) • Cartooning • Hidden curriculum notebook • Social narrative	• Task organizer (I/P, daily) • Organization calendar (I/P, daily) • Gradebook • Conversation (compare to peer) (M/T, #, 15m)	• Use hidden curriculum information during Scout meetings • Introduce conversation to Independent Work time
• Relaxation techniques • Coping cards • Earplugs • Stress Thermometer • Take a break card	Cues for commenting and asking question	• Task organizer (I/P, daily) • Organization calendar (I/P, daily) • Gradebook	Use task organizer for home chores
• Coping cards • Stress Thermometer • Take a break card	• Conversation cues • Cartooning • Hidden curriculum notebook • Cues for commenting and asking questions	• Task organizer (I/P, daily) • Organization calendar (I/P, daily) • On-task (M, duration, 15m)	Use conversation skills at dinner
N/A	N/A	• Homework turned in complete • Gradebook • Materials to class (T/W, N/Y)	• Use supply checklist for Scouts • Help make grocery list

Figure 15.19. Michael's CAPS for PE.

Comprehensive Planning System (CAPS)			
Child/Student: Michael Thomas			
Activity	Skills to Teach	Structure/Modifications	Reinforcement
PE	• Participation in group sports • Accepting loss	• Calendar of competitive sports • Run errands, as needed (behavior: space invasion, loud voice; when game ends) • Review sportsmanship guidelines cue cards (with entire class) • Present 5-minute warning card	• Participation • Accepting loss (reinforcer menu for both) • Verbal reinforcer

One of the biggest areas of focus was Michael's need to learn how to interact with peers and adults. To help develop this skill, visual supports were created, which included commenting cue cards. Sensory supports such as coping cards and a stress thermometer (see Chapter 11: Instruction Often Occurring in Specialized Settings) were also designed to assist Michael in self-monitoring his behavior when with peers and adults.

Figure 15.20. Coping Cards.

Take 2 deep breaths with eyes closed.	Press hands together and count to 10 slowly.	Repeat to myself 3 times "Breathe in; hold; breathe out."

Figure 15.19 (continued)

Sensory/ Regulation	Communication/ Social Skills	Data Collection	Generalization to Community
• Ear plugs • Calming cards • Sensory breaks • Stress Thermometer	• Game statistician • Peer buddy • Social narrative	• Time in PE (M/W, duration) • Meltdowns (M-F, #) for the entire period	Accept loss during games in Scouts

Figure 15.21. Stress Thermometer.

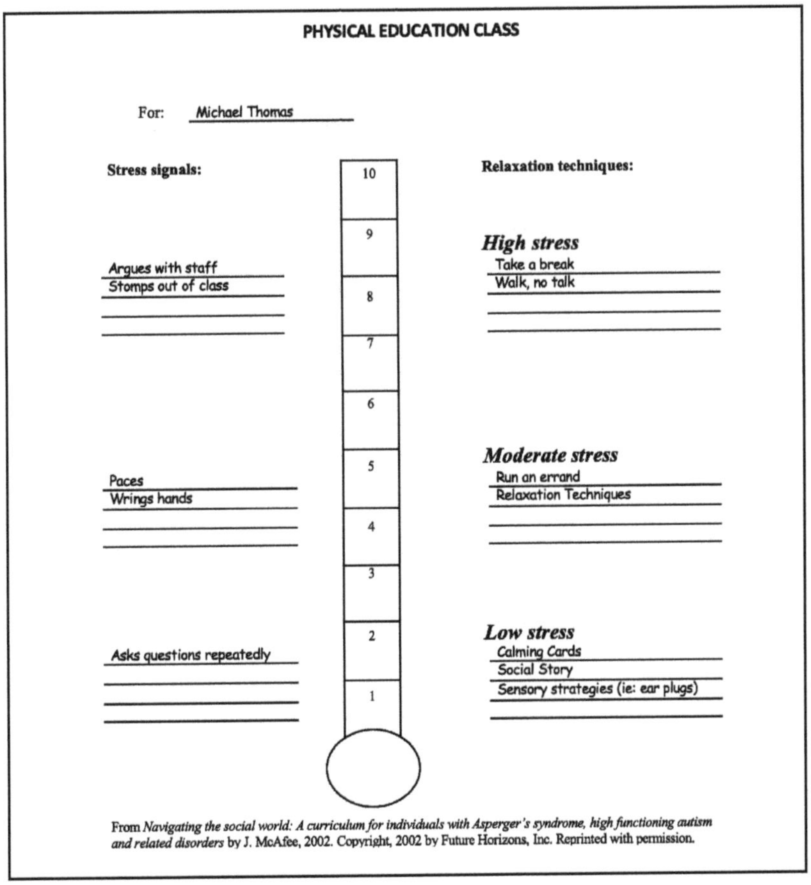
PHYSICAL EDUCATION CLASS
For: Michael Thomas
Stress signals:
Argues with staff
Stomps out of class
Paces
Wrings hands
Asks questions repeatedly
10
9
8
7
6
5
4
3
2
1
Relaxation techniques:
High stress
Take a break
Walk, no talk
Moderate stress
Run an errand
Relaxation Techniques
Low stress
Calming Cards
Social Story
Sensory strategies (ie: ear plugs)
From Navigating the social world: A curriculum for individuals with Asperger's syndrome, high functioning autism and related disorders by J. McAfee, 2002. Copyright, 2002 by Future Horizons, Inc. Reprinted with permission.

Taking into consideration Michael's special interest, the team crafted reinforcers around sports-related activities to help motivate him to complete tasks and follow classroom rules. Similarly, Michael's mother created a reinforcer menu for home to encourage him to complete homework assignments.

Figure 15.22. Reinforcer Menus for Home.

School Reinforcer Menu for Michael

MY REWARDS
▪ 10 minutes of reviewing baseball statistics in personal magazines/books
▪ 15 minutes to do research on the Internet on baseball/ sports statistics/events
▪ Time to browse books in the school library

Home Reinforcer Menu for Michael

MY REWARDS
▪ 30 minutes of time to browse the web
▪ Trip to local baseball cards store
▪ 30 minutes of video games

Recognizing that Michael struggled with organizational skills, supports were put into place to provide him with the structure necessary to organize himself and his school materials, such as activity calendars, including one for a long-term writing assignment.

Figure 15.23. Activity Calendar.

Composition: Writing Assignment

Sunday	Monday	Tuesday	Wednesday	Thursday	Friday	Saturday
			1	2 Have topic chosen for composition	3	4
5	6	7	8 Have outline completed for composition	9 Begin research for composition	10 Continue research	11
12	13 Continue research	14 Continue research	15 Continue research	16 Continue research	17 Continue research	18
19	20 Turn in graphic organizer for composition	21 Begin writing rough draft	22 Continue writing rough draft	23 Continue writing rough draft	24 Continue writing rough draft	25
26	27 Continue writing rough draft	28 Finish writing rough draft	29 Turn in first rough draft of composition	30		

Michael's PE class was modified to address his sensory needs. For example, supports, such as ear plugs, were provided to assist him in participating in group sports activities.

Michael's teachers met approximately once a month for the remainder of the school year to revisit his CAPS, giving them the opportunity to review data collected on the various supports being used. As a result, minor adjustments were made to his CAPS, as needed.

Summary

As illustrated in the case studies in this chapter, CAPS, including the Baseline CAPS and M-CAPS (Modified Comprehensive Autism Planning System), is adaptable across ages, settings, educational levels, activities, and instructional methodologies.

As such, it is a valuable tool to help teams, including parents, tie all the pieces together to create and implement a successful program for autistic students. This "practical IEP" guides program implementation across the school day and fosters communication among the educational team, including family members. In addition, CAPS facilitates transitions from school year to school year by showing receiving teachers exactly what supports the student needed (and when) the previous year to support student success.

About the Authors

SHAWN A. HENRY

Executive director at the Ohio Center for Autism and Low Incidence (OCALI), where he concentrates on developing statewide change efforts in promoting advances in the training of professionals serving students with autism and providing supports for families. He was previously the program director of training and evaluation at the Kentucky Autism Training Center, University of Louisville (KATC), where he coordinated targeted professional development throughout the state. These experiences, as well as serving as an elementary special education teacher, primarily teaching students with autism, led Shawn to develop the Comprehensive Autism Planning System (CAPS).

BRENDA SMITH MYLES, PhD

Formerly a professor in the Department of Special Education at the University of Kansas, she is the recipient of the Autism Society of America's Outstanding Professional Award, the Princeton Fellowship Award, American Academy of Pediatrics Autism Champion, and two-time recipient of the Council for Exceptional Children Burton Blatt Humanitarian Award. Brenda has made over 3,000 presentations all over the world and written more than 300 articles and books on autism. In addition, she collaborated with the three organizations who identified evidenced-based practices in autism. In a survey conducted by the University of Texas, she was acknowledged as the second most productive applied researcher in ASD in the world.

Milton Keynes UK
Ingram Content Group UK Ltd.
UKHW050855050924
447771UK00014B/98

9 781957 9849